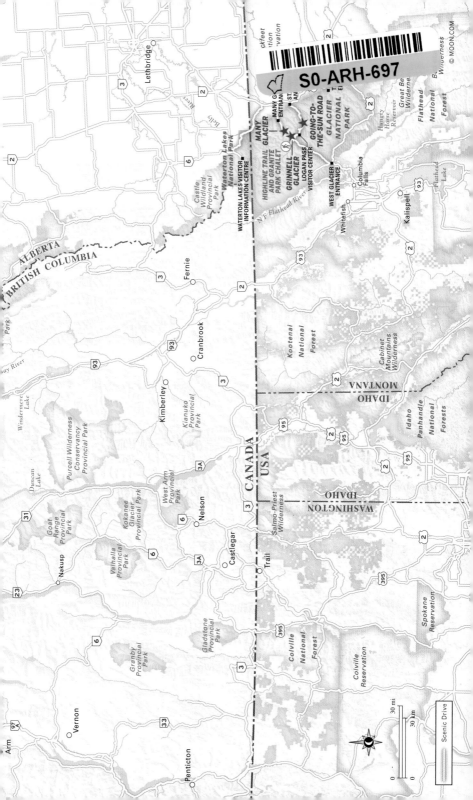

S0-ARH-697

CONTENTS

34

75

84

90

129

234

Although every effort was made to make sure the information in this book was accurate when going to press, research was impacted by the COVID-19 pandemic and things may have changed since the time of writing. Be sure to confirm specific details, like opening hours, closures, and travel guidelines and restrictions, when making your travel plans. For more detailed information, see page 264.

Grinnell Glacier basin, Glacier

WELCOME TO GLACIER, BANFF & JASPER

SNOWCAPPED PEAKS, GLACIERS AND ICE FIELDS, MULTIHUED lakes, rushing rivers, alpine meadows, and abundant wildlife make Glacier, Banff, and Jasper a trio of national parks that are rivaled by few places in the world.

Located in Montana just south of the U.S.-Canada border, Glacier preserves some of the wildest country in the United States. Captivating scenery, epic trails, and huge lakes fill this park's one million acres. While Glacier National Park is known as the Crown of the Continent, Banff National Park, located to the north in Alberta, Canada, is the crown jewel among all of Canada's national parks. Stunning lakes are backdropped by towering mountains that are enjoyed by skiers in the winter and hikers the rest of the year. Directly to the north, Jasper National Park is Banff's quieter, but still mountainous and beautiful, sibling. Connecting the two is one of the most scenic of scenic drives, the Icefields Parkway, which passes rushing rivers, breathtaking overlooks, and the largest and most accessible glacier field in the three parks, the Columbia Icefield.

Lac Beauvert, Jasper

BEST DAYS IN GLACIER, BANFF & JASPER

Day 1

1 Start with a day in Glacier National Park. Hit the road early for a drive along **Lake McDonald,** stopping at pullouts between 6-8 miles (9.7-13 km) up to drop to the shoreline for photos (page 59).

2 Climb the west side of Going-to-the-Sun Road through the west-side tunnel, navigate the hairpin curve at The Loop, and stop at **Haystack Falls Overlook** for photos. Other photogenic overlooks include Big Bend and Oberlin Bend (page 61).

3 Stop for a good while at **Logan Pass,** the highlight of the drive, and tour the paved interpretive trail (page 61).

4 From Logan Pass, hike the **Hidden Lake Overlook** trail, where you can see glacial features, wildflowers, and wildlife. If you have energy, continue on to Hidden Lake before returning (page 75).

5 Descend the west side of Going-to-the-Sun Road through the East Side Tunnel and spot a glacier through binoculars from **Jackson Glacier Overlook** (page 64).

6 Pull into Rising Sun and hop on the tour boat for a scenic narrated spin around the turquoise **St. Mary Lake.** Spend the night in St. Mary or another spot on the east side of the park (page 65).

Day 2

7 It's a 260-mi (420-km) drive from Glacier National Park to Banff. Plan for about 4.5 hours to make the trip. If you want to stretch your legs upon arrival, take a walk along the **Bow River** (page 141).

8 Afterward, ride the **Banff Gondola** to the top of Sulphur Mountain for sweeping views across the town and beyond. Plan on dining at the mountaintop restaurant, or at a local favorite in town like Park. Stay overnight in the town of Banff (page 122).

Day 3

9 This morning's itinerary includes two lakes, and you'll need to rise early as crowds gather before sunrise at both places. Go first to **Moraine Lake,** which is nestled among towering mountains. Be sure to arrive before 6am to get a parking spot (page 134).

10 **Lake Louise,** with its much-photographed turquoise water, is the next stop, and with that, you will have reached two world-famous lakes by 9am. Stroll along the lakeshore and take lots of photos (page 129).

11 Drive north along the Icefields Parkway. For stunning views and abundant wildflowers, stop near Bow Lake and make the trek to **Helen Lake,** one of the best hikes in Banff. Overnight at historic Num-ti-jah Lodge (page 144).

Day 4

12 In the morning, continue north to Jasper National Park and the **Columbia Icefield** to see a glacier field up close (page 182).

13 Hike the trail to **Wilcox Pass,** taking in views of Mount Athabasca and Athabasca Glacier along the way (page 200).

14 Drive past the town of Jasper to **Maligne Canyon,** where the fast-flowing Maligne River has cut a deep canyon in the limestone bedrock. At the top end of the canyon, the Wilderness Kitchen is an ideal lunch stop (page 187).

15 Continue along Maligne Lake Road, which ends at **Maligne Lake.** Jump aboard a tour boat for a cruise to Spirit Island (page 190).

16 You could begin your return trip to Glacier or Banff, or better still spend the evening in the town of Jasper, dining at the **Fairmont Jasper Park Lodge** and enjoying an evening stroll around Lac Beauvert (page 217).

ITINERARY DETAILS

- This itinerary works best **June–August,** when most or all roads are usually open. This is also peak travel season.

- This itinerary starts in Glacier National Park and ends in Jasper. Allow **8 hours** for the 430-mi (700-km) drive back to your starting point.

- Plan to reach Glacier's Going-to-the-Sun Road **early in the morning** and make minimal stops to be able to get a parking spot at Logan Pass.

- **No RVs, trailers, or vehicles longer than 21 feet (6.4 m)** are permitted on Glacier's Going-to-the-Sun Road from Avalanche over Logan Pass to Rising Sun. You can take a guided bus tour or free shuttle to see Going-to-the-Sun Road instead.

- Make accommodation and camping **reservations** as far in advance as possible.

spring biking on Going-to-the-Sun Road, Glacier

SEASONS OF GLACIER, BANFF & JASPER

SPRING
(APR.-JUNE)

Although saddled with unpredictable weather, off-season in Glacier National Park offers less-hectic visits. Low-elevation trails are usually snow-free in May, but **minimal commercial services are open.** When **Going-to-the-Sun Road is closed to vehicles** until about mid-June, bikers and hikers tour it without cars. May-June rains intersperse with cobalt-blue skies.

Late spring is a good time to visit Banff and Jasper: You'll **avoid the crowds,** and you'll **save money.** Spring is notable for **long days** of sunlight (in late June it stays light until after 10pm) and a sense of optimism for the upcoming warm months.

Temperatures

Glacier: 38 to 72°F (3 to 22°C)
Banff and Jasper: 59 to 68°F (15 to 20°C)

SUMMER
(JULY-MID-SEPT., HIGH SEASON)

Summer attracts crowds in Glacier National Park, when **lodges, campgrounds, and trails are open.** It's peak visitation season, with the best weather crammed into July and August. **Going-to-the-Sun Road opens usually mid-June to mid-October.** Mosquitoes descend in early summer, and snow buries some trails into July before wildflowers peak in late July and huckleberries ripen in August. Wildfire season is late July through September.

In Banff and Jasper, the **weather is unbeatable** during the summer. The season is dominated by long, warm—and sometimes hot—days, everything is open, and there's plenty to do and see. **Crowded parks, higher prices,** and difficulty securing **reservations** are the downside of summer travel.

Temperatures

Glacier: 47 to 84°F (8 to 29°C)
Banff and Jasper: 72 to 86°F (22 to 30°C)

FALL
(MID-SEPT.-NOV.)

Fall in Glacier brings unpredictable weather, but also less-hectic visits. Low-elevation trails are usually snow-free in October, but **minimal commercial services are open.** Warm bug-free days and cool nights usher in the larch and aspen turning gold, while peaktop snow descends in September. **Going-to-the-Sun Road closes to vehicles** in mid-October.

Like spring, fall is an excellent time to visit Banff and Jasper; you'll **avoid crowds** and **save money.** Fall can be delightful, especially September, with lingering **warm temperatures** and a noticeable decrease in crowds immediately after the early part of the month. There's also a chance to see **fall colors:** Larch turn a brilliant yellow throughout subalpine areas of Banff in mid- to late September.

Temperatures

Glacier: 33 to 72°F (1 to 22°C)
Banff and Jasper: 59 to 77°F (15 to 25°C)

WINTER
(DEC.-MAR.)

Minimal commercial services are open in winter in Glacier National Park. Snow closes most park roads, which become quiet **snowshoeing and cross-country ski trails.** Winters are cold, with Arctic fronts sometimes plunging temperatures below 0°F (-18°C).

In Banff and Jasper, **ski resorts** begin opening for the winter in late November. The best **powder snow** conditions are **January-February,** although for enthusiasts looking for a combination of good snow and warmer weather, March is an excellent time of year to visit.

Temperatures

- **Glacier:** 14 to 32°F (-10 to 0°C)
- **Banff and Jasper:** 14 to 32°F (-10 to 0°C)

Lake McDonald in fall

Winter brings skiers to Sunshine Village and other Banff resorts.

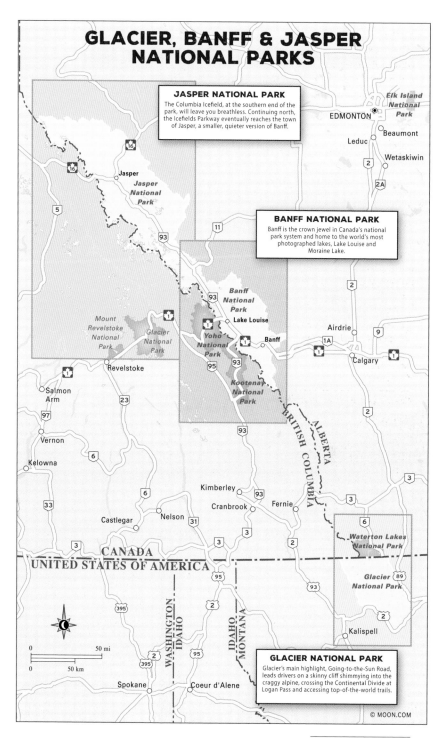

GLACIER, BANFF & JASPER NATIONAL PARKS

JASPER NATIONAL PARK
The Columbia Icefield, at the southern end of the park, will leave you breathless. Continuing north, the Icefields Parkway eventually reaches the town of Jasper, a smaller, quieter version of Banff.

BANFF NATIONAL PARK
Banff is the crown jewel in Canada's national park system and home to the world's most photographed lakes, Lake Louise and Moraine Lake.

GLACIER NATIONAL PARK
Glacier's main highlight, Going-to-the-Sun Road, leads drivers on a skinny cliff shimmying into the craggy alpine, crossing the Continental Divide at Logan Pass and accessing top-of-the-world trails.

EDMONTON
Elk Island National Park
Beaumont
Leduc
Wetaskiwin
Jasper
Jasper National Park
Mount Revelstoke National Park
Glacier National Park
Revelstoke
Salmon Arm
Vernon
Kelowna
Castlegar
Nelson
Banff National Park
Lake Louise
Yoho National Park
Banff
Airdrie
Calgary
Kootenay National Park
BRITISH COLUMBIA
ALBERTA
Kimberley
Cranbrook
Fernie
Waterton Lakes National Park
Glacier National Park
Kalispell
CANADA
UNITED STATES OF AMERICA
WASHINGTON
IDAHO
MONTANA
Spokane
Coeur d'Alene

0 — 50 mi
0 — 50 km

© MOON.COM

NEED TO KNOW: GLACIER

- **Park website:** www.nps.gov/glac
- **Entrance fee:** $35 per vehicle ($25 winter)
- **Main entrance: West Glacier Entrance** (year-round)
- **Main visitor centers: Apgar Visitor Center** (year-round, weekends only in winter), **St. Mary Visitor Center** (late May-early Oct.), **Logan Pass Visitor Center** (mid-June-mid-Sept.)
- **In-park hotel and activity reservations:** www.glaciernationalparklodges.com
- **Campsite reservations:** www.recreation.gov
- **Gas in the park:** None; closest in West Glacier, East Glacier, and St. Mary
- **Travel times:** 4.5 hours to Banff; 7.5 hours to Jasper

NEED TO KNOW: BANFF

- **Park website:** www.pc.gc.ca/banff
- **Entrance fees:** C$10 adult, C$8.40 senior, children free, up to a maximum of C$20 per vehicle
- **Main entrance: Banff East Gate** (Trans-Canada Highway; year-round)
- **Main visitor center: Banff Visitor Centre** (town of Banff; year-round)
- **In-park hotel and activity reservations:** www.banfflakelouise.com, www.bestofbanff.com
- **Campsite reservations:** www.reservation.pc.gc.ca
- **Gas in the park:** town of Banff, Lake Louise, Saskatchewan River Crossing
- **Travel times:** 4.5 hours to Glacier; 3.5 hours to Jasper

NEED TO KNOW: JASPER

- **Park Website:** www.pc.gc.ca/jasper
- **Entrance fees:** C$10 adult, C$8.40 senior, children free, up to a maximum of $C20 per vehicle
- **Main entrance: Jasper East Gate** (Highway 16; year-round)
- **Main visitor center: Jasper Visitor Centre** (town of Jasper; year-round)
- **In-park hotel and activity reservations:** www.jasper.travel
- **Campsite reservations:** www.reservation.pc.gc.ca
- **Gas in the park:** town of Jasper
- **Travel times:** 7.5 hours to Glacier; 3.5 hours to Banff

Larch Valley

Wilcox Pass

BEST OF THE BEST
GLACIER, BANFF & JASPER

BEST HIKES

HIGHLINE TRAIL AND GRANITE PARK CHALET
Glacier National Park
STRENUOUS
Beginning at Logan Pass, this stunning point-to-point walk tiptoes along the Continental Divide to historic Granite Park Chalet before dropping to The Loop. Hikers often see mountain goats, bighorn sheep, bears, or wolverines.

GRINNELL GLACIER
Glacier National Park
MODERATE-STRENUOUS
A boat ride clips mileage off the route to Grinnell Glacier. It's the shortest route to see a glacier up close.

LAKE AGNES
Banff National Park
MODERATE
This walk is a good introduction to hiking in the Canadian Rockies, especially in fall when the larch trees have turned a brilliant gold.

GRIZZLY-LARIX LAKES LOOP
Banff National Park
EASY-MODERATE
Accessible by gondola from the valley floor, this hike in the flower-filled Sunshine Meadows high above the tree line leads to some of the most photogenic viewpoints in the region.

WILCOX PASS
Jasper National Park
MODERATE
Views of the Columbia Icefield are unmatched along this trail. It climbs through a stunted forest of Engelmann spruce and subalpine fir to a ridge with panoramic views of Mount Athabasca and the Athabasca Glacier.

BALD HILLS
Jasper National Park
MODERATE-STRENUOUS
The sweeping views from this hike take in the jade-green waters of Maligne Lake, the Queen Elizabeth Ranges, and the twin peaks of Mount Unwin and Mount Charlton.

Grinnell Glacier Trail, Glacier

Bald Hills, Jasper

Sunshine Meadows and Rock Isle Lake, Banff

BEST VIEWS

HIDDEN LAKE OVERLOOK
Glacier National Park

Stand atop the Continental Divide at Hidden Lake Overlook on a 2.6-mi (4.2-km) round-trip adventure from Logan Pass, where you might spot baby mountain goats.

MANY GLACIER HOTEL DECK
Glacier National Park

Lounge on the large deck of this historic hotel, which overlooks Swiftcurrent Lake and a mountainous panorama. Bring a pair of binoculars so you can spot bears, mountain goats, and bighorn sheep.

SULPHUR MOUNTAIN
Banff National Park

Take the Banff Gondola 2,300 vertical feet (700 vertical m) to the summit of Sulphur Mountain. From the observation deck at the upper terminal, a boardwalk leads to a breathtaking 360-degree view that includes the town, the Bow Valley, Cascade Mountain, Lake Minnewanka, and the Fairholme Range.

LAKE LOUISE SKI RESORT
Banff National Park

During summer, the main ski lift at the Lake Louise resort whisks visitors up the face of Mount Whitehorn to Whitehorn Lodge. The view from the top—across the Bow Valley to Lake Louise and the Continental Divide—is among the most spectacular in the Canadian Rockies.

ATHABASCA GLACIER
Jasper National Park

The Athabasca Glacier, an arm of the massive Columbia Icefield, fills a valley right beside the Icefields Parkway, making access easy—the best views are from the Icefield Centre and Toe of the Glacier trail.

MALIGNE LAKE
Jasper National Park

Maligne Lake is the second largest glacier-fed lake in the world. Take a tour boat to Spirit Island or stroll along the lake's shoreline to take in the stunning vistas.

town of Banff from Sulphur Mountain (top);
view from Hidden Lake Overlook, Glacier
(bottom left); Athabasca Glacier, Jasper
(bottom right)

BEST GLACIAL FEATURES

GLACIERS

Glaciers are slow-moving ice. Aided by gravity, the ice presses down, forming a thin elastic barrier that carries the mass toward the glacier's toe, where it may calve off in chunks. For a glacier to move, a certain amount of ice is needed—usually a surface of at least 25 acres (10 hectares) and a minimum depth of 100 feet (30 m). Glacier, Banff, and Jasper National Parks hold some must-see glaciers.

Grinnell Glacier
Glacier National Park

The shortest trail to an active glacier in Glacier National Park climbs to Grinnell Glacier, a small, thinning glacier melting into Upper Grinnell Lake. You can walk the entire trail round-trip or hop on the Many Glacier tour boat shuttle to chop the distance.

Saskatchewan Glacier
Banff National Park

The short, steep hike up Parker's Ridge ends with sweeping views down to Saskatchewan Glacier, one of the largest glaciers connected to the Columbia Icefield.

Athabasca Glacier
Jasper National Park

Nowhere in Banff or Jasper does a glacier come as close to a road as the Athabasca, with an interpretive center, bus tours, and hiking in the vicinity.

GLACIAL LAKES

Glacier, Banff, and Jasper National Parks are renowned for the turquoise color of many lakes. Finely ground particles of debris from melting glaciers is washed downstream, and are suspended in the water of local lakes. It is this "rock flour" reflecting the blue-green sector of the light spectrum that gives lakes the unique color.

Lake Louise
Banff National Park

Lake Louise is Banff's best-known glacial lake, and with good reason—its turquoise color is mesmerizing, it is easily accessible by everyone, and the lakefront hotel is one of the world's grandest mountain resorts.

Lower Waterfowl Lake
Banff National Park

Beside the Icefields Parkway, the intense turquoise color of Lower Waterfowl Lake is in stark contrast to the sheer cliffs of surrounding mountains.

Maligne Lake
Jasper National Park

Maligne Lake is the world's second largest glacial-fed lake. Hike along the shoreline, go canoeing, or take a boat tour to Spirit Island.

CIRQUES

Glacier-carved hollows in the slopes of mountains are known as cirques.

Iceberg Lake
Glacier National Park

A trail ascends up to a lake tucked in

a cirque below two peaks connected by two arêtes of serrated peaks. You may even see icebergs in late summer floating here below the tall surrounding walls.

Helen Lake
Banff National Park
Helen Lake lies in a glacial cirque and is reached by a trail that boasts spectacular views and passes through extensive wildflower meadows.

Maligne Lake, Jasper

INDIGENOUS PEOPLES OF GLACIER, BANFF & JASPER

Glacier, Banff, and Jasper National Parks and the surrounding lands are on the traditional land of the Blackfeet, Blood (or Kainai), Piegan (or Piikani), Salish, Kootenai (Kootenay in Canada), Shuswap, Stoney, and Gros Ventre People.

Spanning what became the U.S.-Canadian border, the **Blackfeet,** or Niitsitapi ("original people"), include several nomadic groups who based much of their livelihood on hunting bison in the vast prairies on the Continental Divide's east side. In Canada, the Siksika, or Blackfoot, were the first to meet European traders. (To refer to the group, *Blackfoot* is used in Canada, and *Blackfeet* is used in the United States.) Other groups include the Blood (or Kainai) and Piegan (or Piikani). For thousands of years, according to legend, their lands ranged from the Saskatchewan to Yellowstone Rivers.

The land of the **Salish** and **Kootenai** are on the Continental Divide's west side, where they hunted, trapped, and fished. They ventured east over the mountains on annual bison hunts. Known as the Ktunaxa, the Kootenai (in Canada *Kootenay*) were the first human beings to enter the Canadian Rockies and comprise seven bands spanning the western Rockies from southern Alberta to Missoula, Montana. For the Kootenai, the Lake McDonald area was a place for sacred dances, hence its original name of Sacred Dancing Waters.

The Canadian Rockies are also the land of the **Shuswap,** who traveled into the mountains on and off for many thousands of years, hunting caribou and sheep. The descendants of the Shuswap people live on the Kinbasket Shuswap Reserve, just south of Radium Hot Springs, to the west of Kootenay National Park.

Around 1650, the mighty Sioux nation began splintering, with many thousands moving north into present-day Canada. Although these immigrants called themselves **Nakoda** (people), other tribes called them **Assiniboine** (people who cook with stones) because of their traditional cooking methods. The white people translated *Assiniboine* as Stone People, or **Stoney** for short. Today, the Stoney people live on a sprawling reserve just outside Banff's eastern boundary.

NAMES

In Glacier, many of the Blackfeet names used for land features were given other names, but some remain: Going-to-the-Sun Mountain, Two Medicine Lake, Pitamakin Pass, and Running Eagle Falls.

Although Europeans introduced their own names to natural features throughout Banff and Jasper, Indigenous names such as Saskatchewan River and Lake Minnewanka remain, and other traditional names are slowly being restored.

LEARNING MORE

North American Indian Days

The Blackfeet celebrate their culture during North American Indian Days in Browning, Montana. Dressed in regalia, the community dances and drums together. Traditional horse skills are part of the rodeo.

Sun Tours

406/732-9220 or 800/786-9220; http://glaciersuntours.com

Blackfeet-owned Sun Tours goes to Logan Pass and back in coaches with big windows for sightseeing. Blackfeet guides give insight into the park's rich Indigenous heritage from the days of the buffalo to modern spirituality.

Native America Speaks

For more than three decades, Glacier's naturalist programs have included the acclaimed Native America Speaks program in summer. Look for shows in park lodges, St. Mary Visitor Center, and at campground amphitheaters, including Chewing Blackbones outside Babb. Free 45-minute evening campground amphitheater shows feature members of the Blackfeet, Salish, and Kootenai people who use storytelling, humor, and music to share their culture and heritage. Check the park newspaper for the current schedules and location of presentations.

At the St. Mary Visitor Center's auditorium, the **Two Medicine Lake Singers and Dancers** draw standing-room-only crowds for demonstrating Blackfeet dances in full traditional regalia. Appearing at park lodges and campground amphitheaters, Jack Gladstone, a Grammy-nominated Blackfeet musician, blends storytelling and music in *Triple Divide: Heritage and Legacy*, a one-hour multimedia walk through Glacier's history from the Blackfeet perspective.

Buffalo Nations Luxton Museum

1 Birch Ave.; 403/762-2388; www.buffalonationsmuseum.com

This museum is dedicated to the heritage of the First Nations of Banff, Jasper, and adjacent lands. The collections contain memorabilia from local resident Norman Luxton, who had a lifelong relationship with the Stoney people.

Lake Minnewanka in Banff National Park

BEST SCENIC DRIVE

ICEFIELDS PARKWAY

DRIVING DISTANCE: 143 mi (230 km)
DRIVING TIME: 4 hours
START: Lake Louise
END: Jasper

The Icefields Parkway, between Lake Louise and Jasper, is one of the most scenic, exciting, and inspiring mountain roads ever built. From Lake Louise this paved route parallels the Continental Divide, following in the shadow of the highest, most rugged mountains in the Canadian Rockies. Although the entire parkway can be driven in four hours, it's likely you'll want to spend at least a day, probably more, stopping at each of the viewpoints, hiking the trails, watching the abundant wildlife, and just generally enjoying one of the world's most magnificent landscapes.

The parkway remains open year-round, although winter brings with it some special considerations. The road is often closed for short periods for avalanche control. Check road conditions in Banff or Lake Louise before setting out. And be sure to fill up with gas; no services are available between November and April.

In Banff, highlights along the way include **Crowfoot Glacier,** with its glacial claws clinging to the mountain's steep slopes, sparkling **Bow Lake,** and impossibly green **Peyto Lake.** Across the park boundary in Jasper, the **Columbia Icefield** and **Athabasca Glacier** should not be missed. Other highlights on the Jasper side include **Sunwapta Falls** and **Horseshoe Lake,** which is popular with cliff-divers. The town of Jasper is the northern terminus of the parkway.

Icefields Parkway

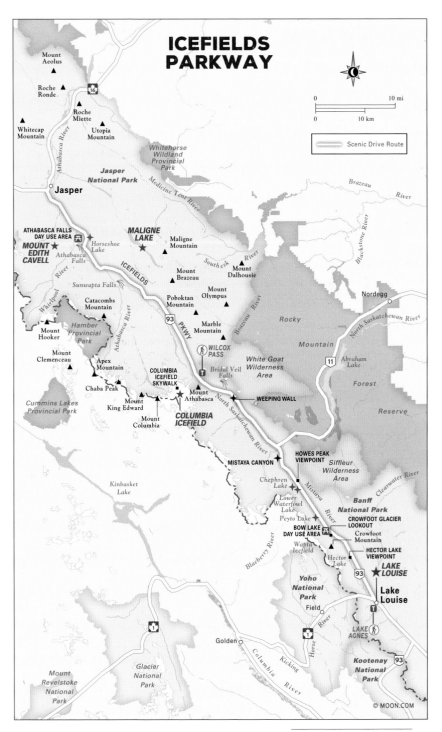

ICEFIELDS PARKWAY

Mount Aeolus ▲

Roche Ronde ▲

Roche Miette ▲

Whitecap Mountain ▲

Utopia Mountain ▲

[16]

Athabasca River

Whitehorse Wildland Provincial Park

Jasper National Park

Medicine Tent River

Brazeau River

Jasper ●

MALIGNE LAKE

Maligne Mountain ▲

ATHABASCA FALLS DAY USE AREA

MOUNT EDITH CAVELL

Horseshoe Lake

Athabasca Falls

Sunwapta Falls

Whirlpool River

ICEFIELDS

Mount Brazeau ▲

Southesk River

Mount Dalhousie ▲

Blackstone River

Nordegg ●

Mount Olympus ▲

Poboktan Mountain ▲

Athabasca River

[93]

PKWY

Marble Mountain ▲

WILCOX PASS 🚶

Bridal Veil Falls

White Goat Wilderness Area

Rocky

Brazeau River

North Saskatchewan River

Mountain

[11]

Abraham Lake

Catacombs Mountain ▲

Mount Hooker ▲

Hamber Provincial Park

Mount Clemenceau ▲

Apex Mountain ▲

Chaba Peak ▲

Cummins Lakes Provincial Park

COLUMBIA ICEFIELD SKYWALK

Mount King Edward ▲

Mount Athabasca ▲

Mount Columbia ▲

COLUMBIA ICEFIELD

Forest

Reserve

◀ **WEEPING WALL**

North Saskatchewan River

MISTAYA CANYON ▶

HOWES PEAK VIEWPOINT

Siffleur Wilderness Area

Clearwater River

Kinbasket Lake

Chephren Lake

Mistaya River

Lower Waterfowl Lake

Peyto Lake

BOW LAKE DAY USE AREA

Banff National Park

CROWFOOT GLACIER LOOKOUT

Crowfoot Mountain ▲

HECTOR LAKE VIEWPOINT

Wapta Icefield

Hector Lake

LAKE LOUISE ★

[93]

Blaeberry River

Lake Louise ●

Yoho National Park

Horse River

Field ●

LAKE AGNES

Golden ●

Columbia River

Kicking Horse River

Kootenay National Park

[93]

Mount Revelstoke National Park

Glacier National Park

© MOON.COM

0 ―――― 10 mi

0 ―――― 10 km

▭▭▭ Scenic Drive Route

PRACTICE SUSTAINABLE TRAVEL IN GLACIER, BANFF & JASPER

- Bring a refillable **water bottle** instead of disposable plastic bottles.
- Buy locally made products.
- Go with local park-approved guide companies.
- Bring **binoculars** to watch wildlife while maintaining a safe distance between you and the animals. **Drones** are prohibited in all U.S. and Canadian national parks so as not to disturb wildlife.
- Minimize driving by hiking, biking, paddling, and skiing to experience the parks, and ride shuttles where available.
- Turn off the car engine rather than idling when you use pullouts to watch wildlife.
- Use established paved or gravel pullouts for wildlife-watching and photography. Park in trailhead parking lots rather than on the roadside.
- Be a conscientious park visitor by following **Leave No Trace** at all times.
- Adjust your schedule to visit crowded sites at less popular times or seasons.
- Always have a Plan B in case crowds and full parking lots preclude your Plan A.

Horseshoe Lake

Grinnell Glacier, Grinnell Lake, and the Continental Divide

GLACIER NATIONAL PARK

THE UNDISPUTED "CROWN OF THE CONTINENT," GLACIER NATional Park preserves some of the nation's wildest country, where terrestrial forces have carved jagged mountain ridges, red pinnacles, and glacier-carved basins into the landscape. Waterfalls roar, ice cracks, and rockfalls echo in scenery still under the paintbrush of change. The park boasts a tremendous geological heritage, plus a cultural history as sacred Native American land.

Glacier also hosts a rich diversity of wildlife. Grizzly bears and wolves top the food chain. Mountain goats prance on precarious ledges. Wolverines romp in high glacial cirques. Bighorn sheep graze in alpine meadows while pikas shriek nearby.

Slicing through the center of the park, historic Going-to-the-Sun Road is an unforgettable experience, climbing up a narrow cliff through tight twists and hairpin turns. Tunnels, arches, and bridges lead sightseers over precipices where seemingly no road could go. Along the way, visitors can feast their eyes on ice-abraded valleys, thundering cascades, mammoth lakes, and serrated peaks.

Glacier National Park holds not only the imprints of glaciers past, but also those that are still present. The park's glaciers fuel North America's major rivers, with crystal-clear water tumbling to Hudson Bay, the Gulf of Mexico, and the Pacific. But those glaciers will soon meet their demise. That change will repaint the scenery once again.

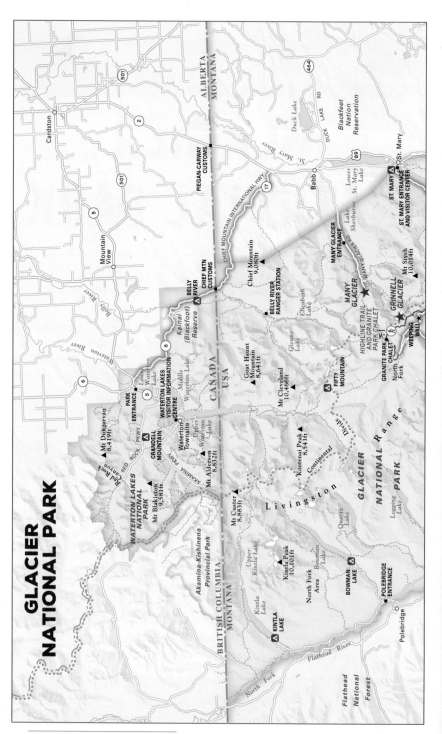

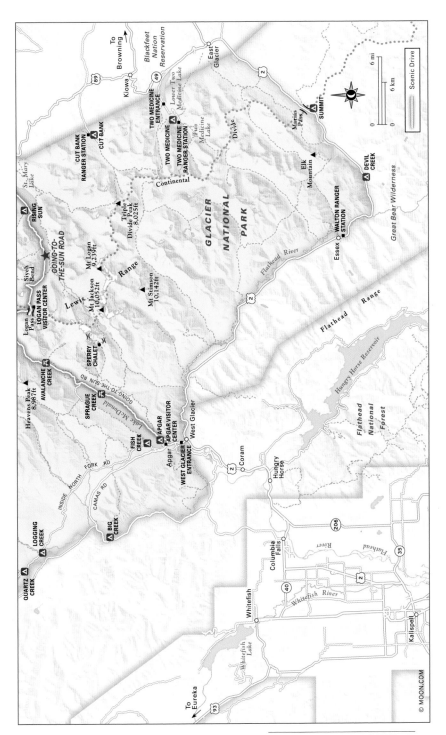

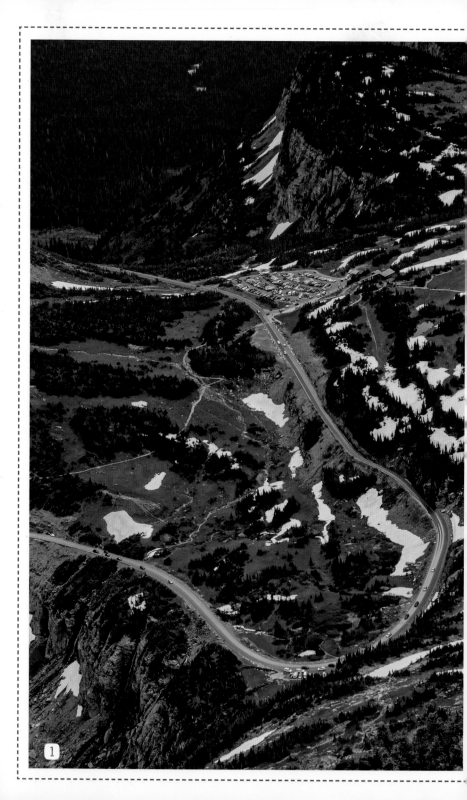

TOP 3

★ **1. GOING-TO-THE-SUN ROAD:** The 50-mi (81-km) road is a testament to human ingenuity and nature's wonders, with scenic surprises around each corner (page 60).

★ **2. MANY GLACIER:** Many Glacier is a setting of dreams: chiseled peaks, idyllic lakes, pastoral meadows (page 66).

★ **3. GRINNELL GLACIER:** See Grinnell Glacier before it melts completely. Hikers on the trail to the glacier often spot grizzly bears (page 81).

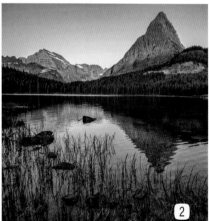

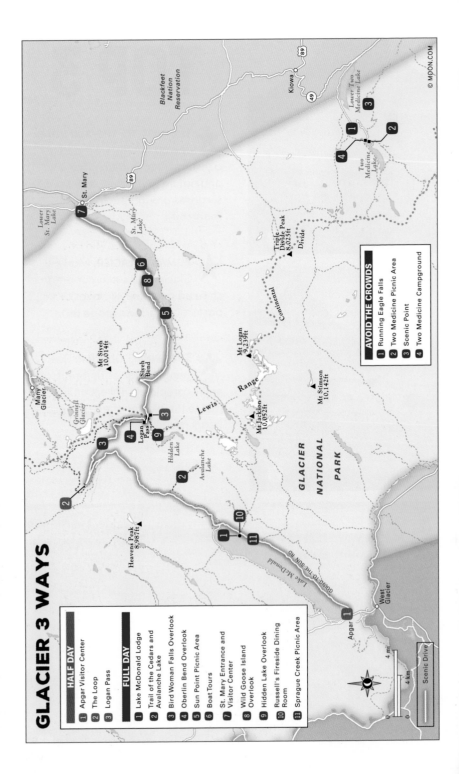

GLACIER 3 WAYS

HALF DAY
1. Apgar Visitor Center
2. The Loop
3. Logan Pass

FULL DAY
1. Lake McDonald Lodge
2. Trail of the Cedars and Avalanche Lake
3. Bird Woman Falls Overlook
4. Oberlin Bend Overlook
5. Sun Point Picnic Area
6. Boat Tours
7. St. Mary Entrance and Visitor Center
8. Wild Goose Island Overlook
9. Hidden Lake Overlook
10. Russell's Fireside Dining Room
11. Sprague Creek Picnic Area

AVOID THE CROWDS
1. Running Eagle Falls
2. Two Medicine Picnic Area
3. Scenic Point
4. Two Medicine Campground

© MOON.COM

Blackfeet Nation Reservation

Lower Two Medicine Lake

Kiowa

Two Medicine Lake

St. Mary

Lower St. Mary Lake

St. Mary Lake

Triple Divide Peak 8,025ft

Continental Divide

Mt Siyeh 10,014ft

Siyeh Bend

Mt Logan 9,239ft

Lewis Range

Mt Stimson 10,142ft

Many Glacier

Grinnell Glacier

Logan Pass

Hidden Lake

Mt Jackson 10,052ft

Avalanche Lake

GLACIER NATIONAL PARK

Heavens Peak 8,987ft

Lake McDonald

GOING-TO-THE-SUN RD

West Glacier

Apgar

Scenic Drive

4 mi

4 km

GLACIER NATIONAL PARK 3 WAYS

HALF DAY

For a taste of Glacier's iconic scenery, head to the heart of the park at Logan Pass. Going-to-the-Sun Road takes you there, with plenty of overlooks to soak up the mountains, waterfalls, and U-shaped glacier-carved valleys. You can choose between two bus tour companies that provide narration and stop at scenic overlooks—meaning you can snap photos while letting the driver handle the road's traffic, curves, and cliffs. This is also an outstanding option for those with RVs or trailers that cannot go over Logan Pass. The itinerary below envisions starting on the west end of Going-to-the-Sun Road, but tours depart in either direction.

1 Board a tour bus that travels Going-to-the-Sun Road at **Apgar Visitor Center.**

2 Relish the scenery on the climb up Going-to-the-Sun Road, taking in the West Side Tunnel, Heavens Peak from **The Loop,** and Triple Arches.

3 The destination for your bus tour is **Logan Pass,** where you won't have to struggle for a parking spot as the buses are guaranteed parking. Check out the visitor center, walk the paved interpretive paths, and take your photo by the Continental Divide sign.

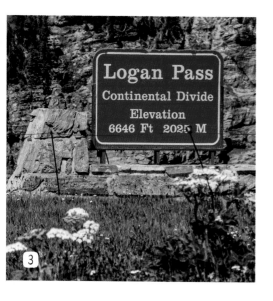

FULL DAY

Make reservations ahead of time for the boat tour (https://glacierparkboats.com) at Rising Sun, and start as early in the day as you can in order to beat the crowds.

1 Pack a picnic lunch and depart **Lake McDonald Lodge** by 7:30am to tour the west side of Going-to-the-Sun Road along McDonald Creek.

2 Once you reach Avalanche, stretch your legs on a boardwalk through a rain forest on **Trail of the Cedars.** You'll see black cottonwoods, hemlocks, and giant western red cedars growing along Avalanche Creek and the creek squeezing through a tight gorge. After the gorge, follow the trail through a narrow, forested valley to idyllic **Avalanche Lake.**

3 Continue your ascent of Going-to-the-Sun Road, climbing through the west-side tunnel and around The Loop. Stop at the **overlook** for **Bird Woman Falls** to admire the waterfall view. (Stop again at Big Bend if you're in the mood for more waterfalls.)

4 Pull over at the **Oberlin Bend Overlook** above Logan Creek to enjoy views of the west side mountains and U-shaped valley. Then, cross over Logan Pass (you'll be back later) and the Continental Divide, where Going-to-the-Sun Mountain dominates the view.

5 Descend down the east side of Logan Pass stopping at Jackson Glacier Overlook for views. Then head to **Sun Point** and its **picnic area** to have lunch. Before or after eating, walk to the windblown point for the panorama view.

6 Continue east to Rising Sun to catch an afternoon **boat tour** on St. Mary Lake. It will dock near the base of Baring Falls, and you'll have a few minutes to enjoy the falls and beach.

7 Drive east to **St. Mary Visitor Center** to take in the exhibits and a film about the park.

8 Retrace your route to head west on Going-to-the-Sun Road. Stop at **Wild Goose Island Overlook** for a photo of the tiny island in St. Mary Lake.

9 Continue climbing to Logan Pass. Go for an afternoon hike to **Hidden Lake Overlook.**

10 Descend the west side of Logan Pass back to Lake McDonald Lodge, and celebrate your day with dinner in **Russell's Fireside Dining Room.**

11 After dinner, end the day with a stroll to **Sprague Creek Picnic Area.** Find a patch of beach to sit on and watch the sunset.

AVOID THE CROWDS

Located in the southeast corner of Glacier, Two Medicine is favored for its less-developed ambiance, myriad hiking trails, and a string of three glaciated lakes.

1 Drive the Two Medicine Road along Lower Two Medicine Lake, and stop for a walk to **Running Eagle Falls,** a unique waterfall that pours from a top slot and from underground.

2 Continue up the road until you reach the ranger station. Turn right to head into Two Medicine Campground to claim a site. Unpack a snack or an early lunch at the nearby **Two Medicine Picnic Area.**

3 Drive to the Scenic Point trailhead and climb the switchbacks to **Scenic Point** to gaze over all three lakes in the Two Medicine Valley, plus the mountains and views stretching out on the plains. Afterward, jump into Two Medicine Lake to cool off on the way back to your campsite.

4 Enjoy dinner outside your tent at **Two Medicine Campground.** As you eat, scan the slopes of Rising Wolf Mountain for bighorn sheep, mountain goats, and sometimes bears.

More Ways to Avoid the Crowds

- Hiking to Rockwell Falls and Cobalt Lake
- Backpacking the Dawson-Pitamakin Loop

HIGHLIGHTS AND SCENIC DRIVES

LAKE MCDONALD

Catching water from Glacier's longest river, Lake McDonald is 10 mi (16.1 km) long, 1.5 mi (2.4 km) wide, and 472 feet (144 m) deep. It is the park's largest and deepest lake. Squeezed between Howe and Snyder Ridges, both lateral moraines, the 6,823-acre (2,761-hectare) lake sits where an ancient glacier gouged out a trough. Larch forests that turn gold in fall rim the shores. On the lake, visitors can fish, boat, paddle, or swim in its cold blue waters. Access the lakeshore via picnic areas, the Apgar boat ramp, or the many pullouts along Going-to-the-Sun Road.

Best Beaches

Smooth rounded rocks form Lake McDonald's beaches, which change size throughout the summer based on water level. Expect tiny beaches in June with high water and larger beaches for sitting, rock skipping, and swimming by August as the water level drops.

APGAR PICNIC AREA

Located on the southwest shore of Lake McDonald, this beach allows for swimming with a view uplake toward the Continental Divide.

FISH CREEK PICNIC AREA

On the northwest shore, the beach flanks Fish Creek with views across the lake to Snyder Ridge, Mt. Edwards, and Mt. Brown.

reflection on Lake McDonald (left); boat tour on Lake McDonald (right)

SPRAGUE CREEK PICNIC AREA

Near the southeast end of Lake McDonald, this beach forms a promontory that pushes out into the lake for views of Stanton Peak.

Boat Tour

Glacier Park Boat Company; 406/257-2426; https://glacierparkboats.com; several departures daily mid-May-Sept.; adult $23, child $11

At the boat dock behind Lake McDonald Lodge, hop on the historic *DeSmet* for a one-hour tour. With a 90-passenger capacity, the 1930s-vintage wooden boat motors to the lake's core, where surrounding snow-clad peaks pop into sight. Go for a prime seat on the top deck; bring a jacket for marginal weather. Book in advance by phone or buy tickets at the boat docks up to three days in advance.

★ GOING-TO-THE-SUN ROAD

Tunnels, switchbacks, arches, and a narrow two-lane highway cutting across precipitous slopes reveal feats of engineering. Cedar rain forests give way to windblown subalpine firs, broad lake valleys lead into glacial corridors, monstrous vertical cliff walls abut wildflower gardens, and waterfalls spew from every pore. Defying gravity, ragged peaks rake the sky, crowning all.

This National Historic Landmark and Historic Civil Engineering Landmark is a place to savor every nook and cranny. Oohs and aahs punctuate every sweep in the road as stunning scenery unfolds. Stopping at myriad pullouts along the road, many sightseers burn through scads of digital pixels. The sheer immensity of the glacier-chewed landscape leaves visitors gasping, "I can't fit it all in my photo."

To stretch your legs, well-signed short paths guide hikers through a dripping rain forest, along a glacial moraine, amid mountain goats, and beside a roaring waterfall. Those ready to put miles on their boots should tackle at least one of the longer high alpine trails, where you'll feel you've reached the apex of the world, sending your spirit soaring.

The Sun Road, as locals call it, is one place you won't want to miss. Its rugged beauty leaves a lasting impression.

Scenic Drive

DRIVING DISTANCE: 50 mi (81 km) one-way
DRIVING TIME: approx. 2 hours one-way (with no stops)
START: West Glacier
END: St. Mary

Going-to-the-Sun Road connects the towns of West Glacier and St. Mary via one of the most scenic highways in the United States. For some, scary tight curves that hug cliff walls produce white-knuckle driving. But for most, its beauty, diversity, color, flora, fauna, and raw wildness will leave an impression like no other. For that reason, many park visitors drive it more than once during their stay.

WEST SIDE

From the west, the Going-to-the-Sun Road cruises along **Lake McDonald,** the largest lake in the park. The road follows McDonald Creek, the longest river in the park, with stops to see its tumbling rapids and waterfalls before reaching **Avalanche,** where the **Trail of the Cedars** runs through a rain forest, the easternmost in the country.

When the road swings north, its

path climbs through engineering feats that garnered the road's designation as a National Civil Engineering Landmark. Its **West Tunnel** has two stunning alcoves framing **Heavens Peak.** Farther on, Going-to-the-Sun Road has one massive hairpin turn, which is known as **The Loop.**

Above The Loop, the road cuts through cliffs with views of the ribbonlike **Bird Woman Falls** and stairstep **Haystack Falls.** The **Weeping Wall** wails profusely in June, enough to douse cars driving the inside lane, but in August, drips slow to a trickle.

After **Big Bend,** drive slowly uphill to see **Triple Arches** (no pullout) at the very narrow S-turns. As the road arcs up the final mile to Logan Pass, a wheelchair-accessible path goes to **Oberlin Bend Overlook,** the best spot for photographing the road's west side and the knifelike **Garden Wall**—so named for the rainbow white cow parsnip, pink spirea, yellow columbine, and blue gentian, among others, that bloom in the meadows below its top cliffs—on the Continental Divide.

LOGAN PASS AND HIDDEN LAKE OVERLOOK

Located 32 mi (51.5 km) from the West Entrance, Logan Pass sits atop the **Continental Divide** at 6,646 feet (2,026 m) and rules an alpine wonderland of wildflower meadows and snowfields. With its altitude and location between mountainous hulks, the weather can be chilly even in midsummer. Explore the visitor center and scan surrounding slopes for goats, bighorn sheep, and bears. In late July, the pink alpine laurel, paintbrush, and monkeyflower reach their prime. Meadows at this elevation are fragile, with short-lived flora, so stick

Bird Woman Falls from Going-to-the-Sun Road (top); Garden Wall (middle); Weeping Wall (bottom)

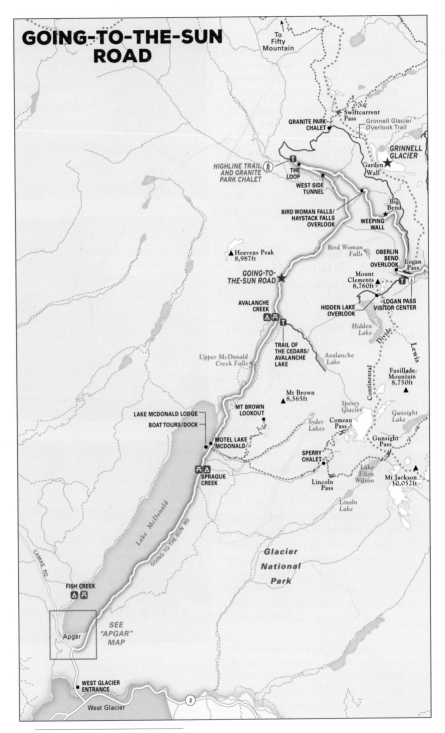

GOING-TO-THE-SUN ROAD

To Fifty Mountain

Swiftcurrent Pass

GRANITE PARK CHALET

Grinnell Glacier Overlook Trail

GRINNELL GLACIER

HIGHLINE TRAIL AND GRANITE PARK CHALET

THE LOOP

WEST SIDE TUNNEL

Garden Wall

Big Bend

BIRD WOMAN FALLS/ HAYSTACK FALLS OVERLOOK

WEEPING WALL

▲ Heavens Peak 8,987ft

Bird Woman Falls

OBERLIN BEND OVERLOOK

Logan Pass

GOING-TO-THE-SUN ROAD

Mount Clements 8,760ft

LOGAN PASS VISITOR CENTER

AVALANCHE CREEK

HIDDEN LAKE OVERLOOK

TRAIL OF THE CEDARS/ AVALANCHE LAKE

Hidden Lake

Upper McDonald Creek Falls

Avalanche Lake

Continental Divide

Lewis

▲ Mt Brown 8,565ft

Fusillade Mountain 8,750ft ▲

MT BROWN LOOKOUT

Sperry Glacier

Gunsight Lake

LAKE MCDONALD LODGE

BOAT TOURS/DOCK

Syder Lakes

Comeau Pass

MOTEL LAKE MCDONALD

SPERRY CHALET

Gunsight Pass

SPRAGUE CREEK

Lincoln Pass

Lake Ellen Wilson

Mt Jackson 10,052ft

Linoln Lake

Lake McDonald

GOING-TO-THE-SUN RD

Glacier National Park

CAMAS RD

FISH CREEK

Apgar

SEE "APGAR" MAP

WEST GLACIER ENTRANCE

2

West Glacier

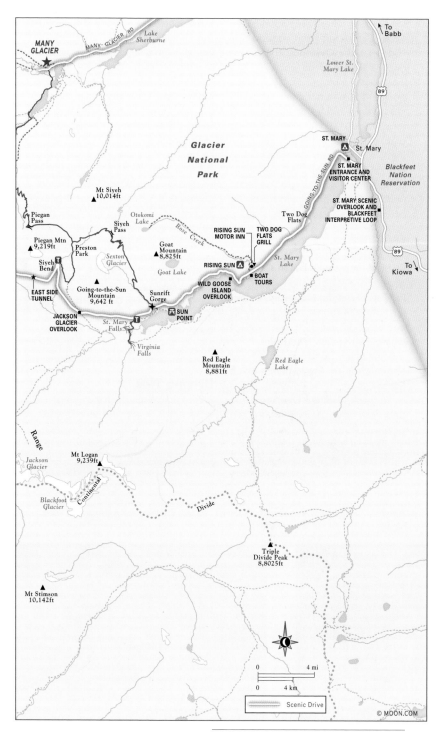

MANY GLACIER

Lake Sherburne

MANY GLACIER RD

To Babb

Lower St. Mary Lake

89

Glacier National Park

St. Mary Lake

ST. MARY

St. Mary

ST. MARY ENTRANCE AND VISITOR CENTER

Blackfeet Nation Reservation

ST. MARY SCENIC OVERLOOK AND BLACKFEET INTERPRETIVE LOOP

89

To Kiowa

Mt Siyeh 10,014ft

Otokomi Lake

Rose Creek

RISING SUN MOTOR INN

TWO DOG FLATS GRILL

Two Dog Flats

GOING-TO-THE-SUN RD

Piegan Pass

Siyeh Pass

Goat Mountain 8,825ft

RISING SUN

Piegan Mtn 9,219ft

Preston Park

Sexton Glacier

Goat Lake

WILD GOOSE ISLAND OVERLOOK

BOAT TOURS

St. Mary Lake

Siyeh Bend

EAST SIDE TUNNEL

Going-to-the-Sun Mountain 9,642 ft

Sunrift Gorge

JACKSON GLACIER OVERLOOK

St. Mary Falls

SUN POINT

Virginia Falls

Red Eagle Mountain 8,881ft

Red Eagle Lake

Range

Jackson Glacier

Mt Logan 9,239ft

Blackfoot Glacier

Continental

Divide

Triple Divide Peak 8,8025ft

Mt Stimson 10,142ft

0   4 mi

0   4 km

Scenic Drive

© MOON.COM

to the paths. There are two must-do trails that depart from Logan Pass: **Hidden Lake Overlook** (page 75) and the **Highline Trail** (page 76). This is one of the most popular spots in the park; in midsummer, the parking lot fills by 8am. If the parking lot is full, forgo Logan Pass for the time being and return later in the day. Although there are pullouts 0.5 mi (0.8 km) east and west of the pass, the shoulderless road does not afford safe walking to the pass, and tromping across the fragile meadows is taboo.

EAST SIDE

From Logan Pass, the road drops by the cascades of **Lunch Creek,** a good place to sit on the rock wall to look up at **Piegan Mountain.** Below, the **East Side Tunnel,** dug out entirely by hand, pops with a downhill view of **Going-to-the-Sun Mountain.**

After **Siyeh Bend,** where a trailhead leads to **Piegan** and **Siyeh Passes,** the route drops into the trees to **Jackson Glacier Overlook,** the best view of a glacier (with the aid of binoculars) from Going-to-the-Sun Road. More views are available in the next several pullouts east.

The road follows along **St. Mary Lake.** The often-windy **Sun Point** marks the site of the park's former Going-to-the-Sun Chalets. Walk five minutes on the trail from the parking lot to the top of the rock promontory jutting into St. Mary Lake. Spectacular views from there take in Going-to-the-Sun Mountain, Fusillade Mountain, and the Continental Divide.

Midway down St. Mary Lake, the road arrives at **Wild Goose Island Overlook.** It's one of the most photographed spots, and you'll see tiny Wild Goose Island dwarfed in the lake's blue waters, with the Continental Divide as the backdrop.

Around a bluff, **Rising Sun** has visitor services, including a boat tour, while **Two Dog Flats** lures elk, coyotes, and bears to grassland meadows bordered by aspen groves. The Going-to-the- Sun Road terminates in the town of **St. Mary.**

Driving Tips

Although you can drive the Sun Road in two hours with no stops, most visitors take all day. Construction, sightseeing, and traffic slow travel. Don't be anxious about it; just sit back and enjoy the view. Pack drinking

---

curves on Going-to-the-Sun Road (left); historic red buses touring Going-to-the-Sun Road (right)

water, snacks, and lunch to avoid frustration. Most restaurants around Glacier sell box or sack lunches.

For big waterfall shows and snow left from winter, drive it in late June or early July. For alpine wildflowers, go in late July or early August. For fewer crowds, go mid-September-mid-October. From July through August, expect crowds around Avalanche, The Loop, Oberlin Bend, Logan Pass, Lunch Creek, Siyeh Bend, St. Mary Falls, and Sun Point. To avoid the hordes, drive in early morning or early evening, when lighting is better for photography and wildlife is more active. In midsummer, the Logan Pass parking lot fills 8am-5pm. Some parking slots are reserved for one-hour parking for those who just want a quick experience, but the park service controls the entrance, admitting a car only when one departs.

Both ends of Going-to-the-Sun Road have entrance stations, at **West Glacier** and **St. Mary**. Staffed during daylight hours in summer and on weekends only fall-spring, the stations hand out national park maps and the *Waterton-Glacier Guide*, the park's newspaper, updated twice annually.

Snow buries the Sun Road in winter. The usual vehicle closure runs from Lake McDonald Lodge to St. Mary late October-spring, but cross-country skiers and snowshoers trek the lowland corridors where avalanche danger is minimal.

Bus Tours

You can leave the driving to someone else by taking a bus tour. Tour buses are also guaranteed parking at Logan Pass, so you don't have to deal with the parking lot crowds in summer.

RED BUS TOUR
855/733-4522; www.glaciernationalparklodges.com; full-day and half-day tours daily mid-June-mid-Oct.; adult $46-106, child half price, reservations required

In historic style, red jammer buses tour visitors over Going-to-the-Sun Road in vintage 1930s White Motor Company sedans operated by **Xanterra.** On good-weather days, the jammers (tour bus drivers known for their storytelling) roll the canvas tops back for spectacular views of the Continental Divide. Without a roof, it's one of the most scenic ways to feel the expanse of the glacier-carved terrain. Tours depart from Lake McDonald Lodge, Rising Sun Motor Inn, Apgar Visitor Center, and St. Mary Visitor Center.

SUN TOURS
406/732-9220 or 800/786-9220; www.glaciersuntours.com; June-Sept.; adult $60-70, child 6-12 $35

A Blackfeet-led tour provides a different perspective, with emphasis on Indigenous cultural and natural history. Sun Tours drives air-conditioned 25-passenger coaches with extra-big windows for taking in the massive mountains on Going-to-the-Sun Road. Four-hour Logan Pass tours depart daily from St. Mary (9:30am) and go up the east side of Going-to-the-Sun Road to Logan Pass and down the west side to Big Bend before returning. Make reservations at least one day in advance. West-side tours depart Apgar Visitor Center at 9am.

ST. MARY
St. Mary Lake

The second-largest lake in the park, St. Mary Lake fills a much narrower valley than its larger counterpart, Lake McDonald. At 9 mi (14.5 km) long and 292 feet (89 m) deep, it forms a blue platform out of which several stunning red argillite peaks rise. Its width shrinks in The Narrows to less than 0.5 mi (0.8 km), where buff-colored Altyn limestone resisted erosion. These strata contain the most ancient exposed rock in the park. Going-to-the-Sun Road follows the lakeshore for its last (or first, depending on the direction you're going) few miles.

BOAT TOUR

Glacier Park Boat Company; 406/257-2426; https://glacierpark-boats.com; several departures daily mid-June-early Sept.; adult $34, child $17

At the Rising Sun boat dock, catch a 90-minute ride on *Joy II* or *Little Chief* to brave St. Mary Lake's choppy waters. Views of Sexton Glacier and Wild Goose Island can't be beat, but be ready for some healthy wind (you'll be protected inside). See Baring Falls at a stop, or take a guided two-hour hike to St. Mary Falls. Book in advance by phone or buy tickets at the boat docks up to three days in advance.

St. Mary Scenic Overlook and Blackfeet Interpretive Loop

Two miles (3.2 km) south of St. Mary on U.S. 89, the St. Mary Scenic Overlook has an impressive panoramic view of the upper St. Mary Valley, St. Mary Lake, and Glacier's peaks. The 0.2-mi (0.3-km) paved, wheelchair-accessible Blackfeet Interpretive Loop begins from the overlook's parking area at a sculpture of a woman and a travois. The route tours metal tepee sculptures at overlooks, while interpretive signage tells stories of the Blackfeet. On the highway, look for signs that say "Turnout ½ mile."

★ MANY GLACIER

On Glacier's east side, Many Glacier is idyllic, filled with rugged scenery. Mountains graze the sky and drop abruptly to wide-open grassland prairies. Below sheer cliffs, elk browse. Aspen leaves chatter in only a hint of breeze.

From valley floors, a wild panorama of Glacier's peaks runs across the western skyline, dominated by red sediments and milky sapphire lakes. Ice fields cling for dear life to cliffs as the summer sun shrinks them each year. It's a place of extravagant color, where tumbling waterfalls and pink, purple, white, and yellow wildflowers intoxicate the eyes.

The morning sunrise gleams gold across the rampart of peaks. Loons call across glassy lakes. Grizzly bears forage on hillsides, clawing at the ground for glacier lily bulbs. By evening, when the trails vacate, the sunset paints royal hues above the Continental Divide. Dark descends, with a multitude of stars. And if you're lucky, the **northern lights** dance across the sky.

Officially called the Swiftcurrent Valley, Many Glacier is what locals call the area due to the string of small glaciers that populate its peaks: Grinnell, Salamander, Gem, North Swiftcurrent, and South Swiftcurrent. **Grinnell Glacier** is the most accessible glacier in the park, reached via an 11-mi (17.7 km) round-trip hike (page 81).

An easy walking trail circles **Swiftcurrent Lake,** a mountain-rimmed pool preferred by moose. Paddlers can rent kayaks and rowboats or ride a tour boat on Swiftcurrent and

boat tour on St. Mary Lake

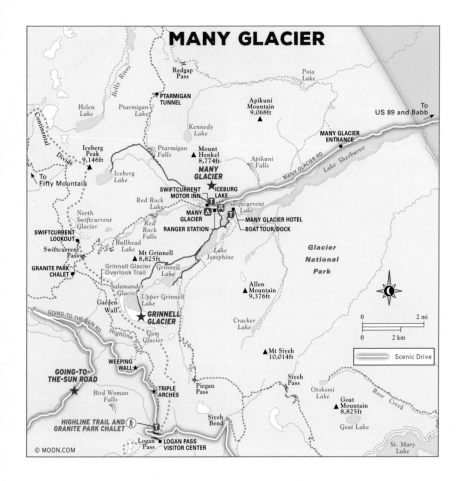

MANY GLACIER

Josephine Lakes, which shortens the walk to milky turquoise **Grinnell Lake.** At the end of the day, take in the sunset over the Continental Divide and watch on moonless nights for a sky full of stars and the northern lights.

Many Glacier Road
DRIVING DISTANCE: 12 mi (19.3 km) one-way
DRIVING TIME: 25 minutes one-way
START: Babb, east of Many Glacier Entrance
END: Swiftcurrent Motor Inn

The 12-mi-long (19.3-km) Many Glacier Road (Glacier Rte. 3; open

May-Oct.) is a stunning drive into **Swiftcurrent Valley.** Drive slowly to spot wildlife and avoid any animals if they cross the road. From Babb, the road follows Swiftcurrent Creek upstream across Blackfeet Nation lands. Watch for **bears,** particularly around dusk.

After the road rises to reach Sherburne Dam (mi 4.8/km 7.7), it follows the reservoir's north shore, crossing into the park over the cattle grate, but you won't reach the park entrance station for another 3 mi (4.8 km). Check the shoreline for deer, bears, and sometimes errant cows. Wildflower meadows with early July's pink sticky geraniums and lupine line the road. Scenic stops have views of **Sherburne Reservoir** and up the valley to **Grinnell Glacier.**

At the end of the road, you'll reach **Many Glacier Hotel** (mi 11.5/km 18.5), the picnic area (mi 12.1/km 19.5), and ranger station and campground (mi 12.3/km 19.8). It terminates at Swiftcurrent Motor Inn and trailheads.

Be aware: In 2021, Many Glacier Road will have a huge construction project that will cause long delays to repair roadbed damage, and the road will only be open mid-May–mid-September.

Boat Tour

Glacier Park Boat Company; 406/257-2426; http://glacierparkboats.com; several departures daily mid-June–mid-Sept.; round-trip adult $34, child $17

In Many Glacier, jump on a pair of historic wooden boats for a two-lake tour. Catch the 1961-vintage *Chief Two Guns* at Swiftcurrent Lake's boat dock behind Many Glacier Hotel. In 75 minutes, you'll cruise across the lake, hike five minutes over a hill, hop aboard the 1945 *Morning Eagle* for a cruise on Lake Josephine, and return. Don't forget your camera, although you may have difficulty cramming the view into the lens. Two of the launches offer guided round-trip walks to **Grinnell Lake** (2 mi/3.2 km), and the earliest boat has a ranger-led hike to **Grinnell Glacier.** Tours sell out, but you can make reservations by phone or in person at the dock at least one day in advance.

Hikers also use the boats as **shuttles** to cut down trail mileage. You can catch one-way return boats (half price) at the Lake Josephine upper dock; pay cash as you board. You may have to wait for a few launches

Blackfeet Interpretive Loop at St. Mary Scenic Overlook (top); Many Glacier at sunrise (middle); wildflowers in Many Glacier (bottom)

boat tour in Many Glacier

to get on, but the captain runs the boat until all hikers are shuttled.

TWO MEDICINE

Quiet and removed, Glacier's southeast corner harbors a less-traveled wonderland. It's a favorite part of the park for many locals.

It's away from the harried corridor of Going-to-the-Sun Road with its endless line of cars. With no hotel in Two Medicine, you'll find trails far less clogged on day hikes than at Many Glacier. Just because it sees fewer people, however, does not make it less dramatic.

A string of three lakes curves through the Two Medicine Valley below **Rising Wolf Mountain,** a red hulking monolith. Even though glaciers vacated this area within the past 150 years, their footprints are left in swooping valleys, cirques with blue lakes, and toothy spires. **Two Medicine Lake** shimmers in a valley strewn with hiking trails.

Running Eagle Falls

Shortly after entering the park at Two Medicine, a wheelchair-accessible packed-surface interpretive trail (0.3 mi/0.5 km one-way) leads to a view of Running Eagle Falls, named for a female Blackfeet warrior. The falls drops in two parts, one over the lip and the other through an underground chute. During June high water, so much flow spills over the lip that it nearly covers up the water spewing from the underground chute. But by August, the upper falls trickles or dries up, with only the falls coming through the passageway in the rock wall.

Two Medicine Lake

The largest of three lakes in the Two Medicine area, Two Medicine Lake is the highest road-accessible lake in Glacier, sitting almost 1 mi (1.6 km) high and flanked by peaks rich in Blackfeet history. Its waters collect snowmelt from peaks over 8,000 feet (2,438 m) high but devoid of glaciers. The lakes are all that remain of the 1,000-foot-thick (305-m) ice field that filled the valley and flowed out onto the prairie to the east, past the town Browning. To explore Two Medicine Lake, jump on the historic *Sinopah* tour boat, or if the waters are calm, paddle its shoreline, swim in its chilly clear waters, or fish for brook trout.

BOAT TOUR

Glacier Park Boat Company; 406/257-2426; http://glacierparkboats.com; five departures daily June-mid-Sept.; adult $17 round-trip, child half price

The *Sinopah* started service on Two Medicine Lake in 1927 and has never left its waters. The 45-foot (13.7-m),

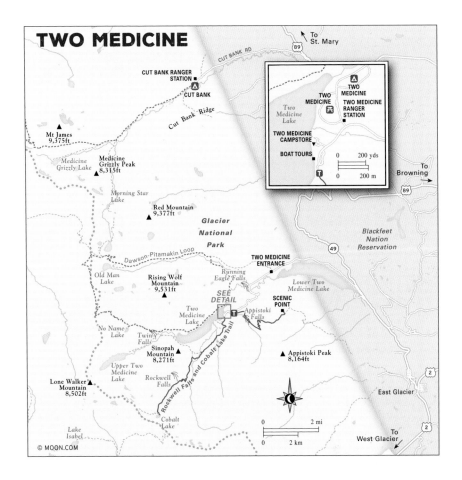

49-passenger wooden boat cruises up-lake for 45-minute tours while the captain narrates history, trivia, and natural phenomena. Two trips also incorporate a guided hike to **Twin Falls** (0.9 mi/1.4 km one-way). Make reservations by phone at least at least a day in advance; you can also buy tickets at the dock three days in advance.

Hikers use the tour boat as a **shuttle** to shorten mileages on trails. You can pay half price in cash for one-way return rides upon boarding at the head of the lake. If too many people are waiting, the boat runs extra trips to retrieve all hikers waiting at the upper dock.

Blackfeet Peaks

From the beach at Two Medicine Lake, you can see a trio of mountains: **Sinopah** across the lake, **Lone Walker** in the distance behind the lake's head, and the most prominent feature in Two Medicine Valley, **Rising Wolf** (9,513 ft/2,900 m), on the north shore. Rising Wolf's sheer mass is larger than any other peak in the park.

Lone Walker is named after a chief of the Small Robes band of Piegans, a tribe of the Blackfeet. He

WATERTON LAKES NATIONAL PARK

Bordering Glacier in Canada, Waterton Lakes National Park serves as the entrance to Glacier's remote north country. Together, the two national parks are the world's first International Peace Park and International Dark Sky Park. They are also a Biosphere Reserve and World Heritage Site. In summer 2017, the Kenow Fire burned 47,700 acres (19,394 ha) of the park, which included many trails, a campground, backcountry campsites, picnic areas, and roads, but not Waterton Townsite, which houses motels, restaurants, a campground, boat tours, and visitor services.

The **Waterton Lakes Visitor Information Centre** (Windflower Ave., Waterton Townsite; 403/859-5133; www.pc.gc.ca) provides information, maps, permits, and licenses. The entrance gate is open 24/7 year-round (staffed early May-early Oct.). To enter, purchase a **Parks Canada day pass** (C$7-20; May-Oct.).

HIGHLIGHTS
Chief Mountain International Highway
This two-nation scenic road circles Chief Mountain, sacred to the Blackfeet, and crosses through Glacier and Waterton.

Boat Tour
at the marina at junction of Mount View Rd. and Waterton Ave.; 403/859-2362; www.watertoncruise.com; May-early Oct.; adult C$55 round-trip, child C$27, under age 4 free
Hop aboard the historic *MV International* for a ride on the deepest lake in the Canadian Rockies. You'll float across the international boundary to Goat Haunt, USA, in Glacier.

Prince of Wales Hotel
844/868-7474 or 403/859-2231; www.glacierparkcollection.com; early June-mid-Sept
This 1927 hotel maintains British ambience thanks to kilt-wearing bellhops and afternoon high tea.

Cameron Falls
near the junction of Cameron Falls Dr. and Evergreen Ave.
This roadside falls on Cameron Creek splits several directions in its plunge to the valley floor.

BEST HIKES
Crypt Lake
10.6 mi (17 km) round-trip
A boat ride leads to the trailhead, where switchbacks ascend to what looks like impassable cliffs. A hidden tunnel curls into a hanging valley holding an alpine lake cowering below peaks in Glacier.

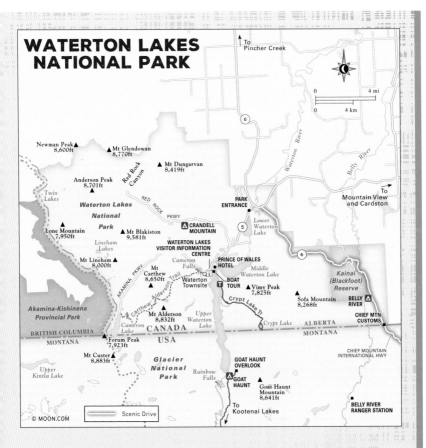

WATERTON LAKES NATIONAL PARK

To Pincher Creek

Newman Peak 8,600ft
Mt Glendowan 8,770ft
Mt Dungarvan 8,419ft
Anderson Peak 8,701ft
Red Rock Canyon
Twin Lakes
Waterton Lakes National Park
RED ROCK PKWY
Lone Mountain 7,950ft
Mt Blakiston 9,581ft
Lineham Lakes
Mt Lineham 8,000ft
AKAMINA PKWY
Mt Carthew 8,650ft
Cameron Falls
Waterton Townsite
Carthew-Alderson Trail
Mt Alderson 8,832ft
Cameron Lake
Forum Peak 7,923ft
Mt Custer 8,883ft
BRITISH COLUMBIA
MONTANA
Akamina-Kishinena Provincial Park
CANADA
USA
Upper Kintla Lake
Glacier National Park
Rainbow Falls
PARK ENTRANCE
Waterton River
Belly River
To Mountain View and Cardston
CRANDELL MOUNTAIN
Lower Waterton Lake
WATERTON LAKES VISITOR INFORMATION CENTRE
PRINCE OF WALES HOTEL
Middle Waterton Lake
BOAT TOUR
Vimy Peak 7,825ft
Crypt Lake Tr
Upper Waterton Lake
Crypt Lake
ALBERTA
MONTANA
Sofa Mountain 8,268ft
Kainai (Blackfoot) Reserve
BELLY RIVER
CHIEF MTN CUSTOMS
CHIEF MOUNTAIN INTERNATIONAL HWY
GOAT HAUNT OVERLOOK
GOAT HAUNT
Goat Haunt Mountain 8,641ft
To Kootenai Lakes
BELLY RIVER RANGER STATION
© MOON.COM
Scenic Drive

0   4 mi
0   4 km

6
5
6

Goat Haunt, USA

Accessible only by boat or on foot, Goat Haunt is a launchpad onto Glacier's remote northern trails. Destinations include Rainbow Falls (1.4 mi/2.3 km round-trip), Goat Haunt Overlook (1.9 mi/3.2 km round-trip), and Kootenai Lakes (5.6 mi/9 km round-trip).

TRANSPORTATION

From St. Mary, take U.S. 89 north through Babb, Montana. North of Babb, turn left onto **Chief Mountain International Highway** (Hwy. 17), which leads to the Canadian border, where the road becomes AB 6.

At the north terminus, turn west onto Highway 5 and south to the **Waterton Entrance Station.** The road's season and hours are linked to the Canadian and U.S. immigration and customs stations at the border (open daily mid-May-Sept., 7am-10pm June-Labor Day, 9am-6pm May and Sept.). The drive is 30 mi (48 km) total and takes one hour.

From Banff National Park, the fastest route heads east on the Trans-Canada Highway from the town of Banff to Calgary

CONTINUED ON NEXT PAGE

(128 km/80 mi, 90 minutes). From Calgary, head south on AB 2 toward Fort Macleod for 113 mi (181 km). Then turn west onto CA 3 to Pincher Creek, and turn south onto AB 6 for to the park entrance. The drive from Calgary to Waterton is 149 mi (240 km) and takes about 3.5 hours.

Prince of Wales Hotel at Waterton Lakes National Park

befriended Hugh Monroe, the first person of European descent to meet the Blackfeet. Lone Walker's daughter, Sinopah, married Monroe, who was eventually officially admitted to the band and given the name Rising Wolf. Many of Sinopah and Rising Wolf's descendants still live on the Blackfeet Reservation.

NORTH FORK

Home to scenic lakes for paddling, hiking, and camping, this remote area in the northwest of the park is accessible only by rough potholed and washboard dirt roads. This is rugged country with no services, no cell reception, and mostly vault toilets, but it's prized for those same reasons. The area can only be reached by driving north of Apgar outside the park and entering through the remote Polebridge Entrance (27 mi/43 km, 1 hour on mostly dirt road). From the Polebridge Entrance, rough roads of very slow driving reach Kintla Lake (12 mi/19 km, 1 hour) or Bowman Lake (6 mi/10 km, 35 minutes). In summer, access roads can close due to congested traffic. Use the Recreational Access Display (www.nps.gov/applications/glac/dashboard) for status or consult with the Apgar Visitor Center before driving up. Quiet primitive campgrounds are at Bowman Lake, Kintla Lake,

Logging Creek, and Quartz Creek. Trailers and vehicles longer than 21 feet (6.4 m) are not permitted on any North Fork roads in Glacier.

BEST HIKES

GOING-TO-THE-SUN ROAD
Trail of the Cedars and Avalanche Lake
DISTANCE: 0.9-mi (1.4-km) loop to 6.1 mi (9.8 km) round-trip
DURATION: 0.5-3 hours
ELEVATION GAIN: none-477 feet (none-145 m)
EFFORT: easy-moderate
TRAIL SURFACE: accessible boardwalk and hard-surface on the Trail of the Cedars; dirt, roots, rocks for Avalanche Lake
TRAILHEAD: across the Sun Road from Avalanche Picnic Area and shuttle stop

With interpretive signs, the Trail of the Cedars boardwalk, reconstructed in 2018, guides walkers and wheelchairs on a loop that crosses two footbridges over Avalanche Creek. The route tours the lush rain forest, where fallen trees become nurse logs, fertile habitat for hemlocks and tiny foamflowers. Immense black cottonwoods furrowed with deep-cut bark and huge 500-year-old western red cedars dominate the forest. At Avalanche Gorge, the creek slices through red rocks. To finish the 0.9-mi (1.4-km) loop, continue on the hard-surface walkway past large burled cedars to return to the trailhead.

The trailhead to Avalanche Lake departs from the southeast end of Trail of the Cedars. Turn uphill for the short grunt to the top of the water-carved Avalanche Gorge. Be extremely careful: Too many fatal accidents have occurred from slipping here. From the gorge, the trail climbs steadily through woods littered with glacial erratics. Some of these large boulders strewn when the glacier receded still retain scratch marks left from the ice. At the top, 1.9 mi (3.1 km) from the trailhead, a cirque with steep cliffs and tumbling waterfalls cradles the lake. An additional 0.7-mi (1.1-km) path goes to the lake's less-crowded head, where anglers find better fishing.

High season sees streams of people. Avoid midday crowds by hiking this trail earlier or later in the day, but make noise for bears.

Hidden Lake Overlook
DISTANCE: 2.6 mi (4.2 km) round-trip to overlook, 5 mi (8 km) round-trip to lake
DURATION: 2-4 hours round-trip
ELEVATION GAIN: 482 feet (147 m)
EFFORT: moderate
TRAIL SURFACE: wide boardwalk with stairs and rocky dirt
TRAILHEAD: behind Logan Pass Visitor Center and shuttle stop

Regardless of crowds, Hidden Lake Overlook is a spectacular hike. Avoid long lines of hikers by going shortly after sunrise or in the evening. The trail is often buried under feet of snow until mid-July or later, but tall poles mark the route. Once the trail melts out, a boardwalk climbs the first half through alpine meadows

TOP HIKE
HIGHLINE TRAIL AND GRANITE PARK CHALET

DISTANCE: 7.4 mi (11.9 km) to Granite Park Chalet, 11.4 mi (18.3 km) to The Loop
DURATION: 5-6 hours to The Loop
ELEVATION GAIN: 975 feet (297 m) up; 3,395 feet (1,035 m) down
EFFORT: strenuous
TRAIL SURFACE: narrow, dirt and rocky
TRAILHEAD: across Going-to-the-Sun Road from Logan Pass parking lot and shuttle stop

Many first-time hikers stop every 10 feet to take photos on this hike, which scares severe acrophobes with its exposed thousand-foot drop-offs. The trail drops from **Logan Pass** through a cliff walk above the Sun Road before crossing a flower land that gave the Garden Wall arête its name. At 3 mi (4.8 km), nearly all the elevation gain is packed into one climb: **Haystack Saddle** appears to be the top, but it is only halfway. After the high point, the trail drops and swings through several large bowls before passing **Bear Valley** to reach **Granite Park Chalet** atop a knoll at 6,680 feet (2,036 m). Due to steep, snow-filled avalanche paths, the park service keeps the trailhead at Logan Pass closed usually into early July. Be aware: Changes may happen regarding the first section of the Highline. These may include mak-

ing the trail one-way only from Logan Pass, adding an exit trail to Big Bend, and using a timed permit entry.

Stronger Highline hikers can add on side trails to **Grinnell Glacier Overlook** (a steep 1.6 mi/2.6 km round-trip) and **Swiftcurrent Lookout** (4.2 mi/6.8 km round-trip). To exit the area, some hikers opt to hike out over Swiftcurrent Pass to **Many Glacier** (7.6 mi/12.2 km) and catch shuttles; backpackers continue on to **Fifty Mountain** (11.9 mi/19.2 km farther) and **Goat Haunt** (22.5 mi/36.2 km farther). Most day hikers head down **The Loop Trail** (4 mi/6.4 km) to catch the shuttle.

The chalet (July-early Sept., overnight reservations required) does not have running water. Carry your own, filter water from the stream below the chalet, or purchase bottled water. Day hikers may use the outdoor picnic tables or chalet dining room but do not have access to the kitchen. On a rainy day, a warm fire offers respite from the bluster and a chance to dry out.

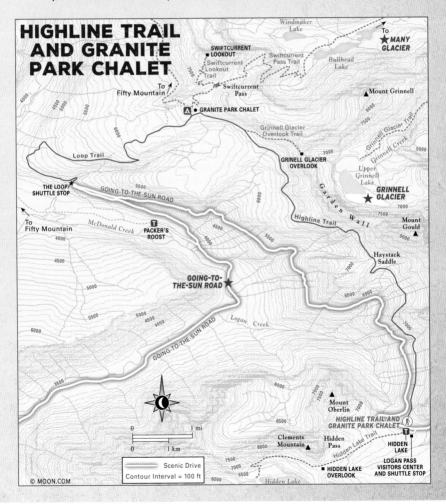

Trail of the Cedars boardwalk at Avalanche

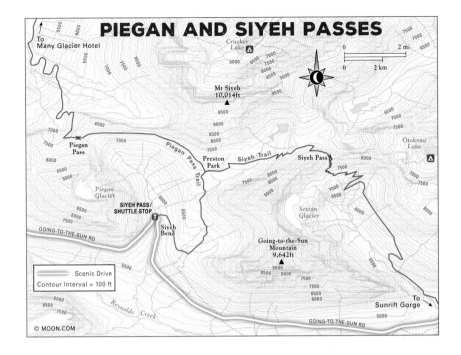

PIEGAN AND SIYEH PASSES

where fragile shooting stars and alpine laurel dot the landscape with pink. The trail ascends through argillite: Look for evidence of mud-cracked and ripple-marked rocks from the ancient Belt Sea. Above, **Mount Clements** reveals various sea sediments in colorful layers.

The upper trail climbs past moraines, waterfalls, mountain goats, and bighorn sheep. At Hidden Pass on the Continental Divide, the trail reaches the platform overlooking Hidden lake's blue waters. For ambitious hikers or anglers, the trail continues 1.2 mi (1.9 km) down to the lake. Just remember: What drops 776 feet (237 m) must come back up. After late September, bring ice cleats for walking the trail.

Piegan Pass/Siyeh Pass

DISTANCE: 8.8 mi (14.2 km) round-trip, 11.5 mi (18.5 km) to Many Glacier, or 10 mi (16.1 km) point to point

DURATION: 4-6 hours
ELEVATION GAIN: 1,739 feet (530 m)/2,278 feet (694 m)
EFFORT: moderate-strenuous
TRAIL SURFACE: dirt path with roots and rocks
TRAILHEAD: Piegan Pass Trailhead at Siyeh Bend and Siyeh Bend shuttle stop

This trail is often snowbound until early July. After climbing 2 mi (3.2 km) through subalpine forest and turning north at the first trail junction, the trail breaks out into **Preston Park,** bursting with purple fleabane, blue gentians, white valerian, and fuchsia paintbrush. During the climb, spy four glaciers: **Piegan, Jackson, Blackfoot,** and **Sperry,** the latter seen through trees. As the trail waltzes through the wildflower meadows of **Preston Park,** a signed trail junction splits the Piegan Pass Trail (left) from the Siyeh Pass Trail (right).

Shortly after the junction, the

Piegan Pass Trail heads into the seemingly barren alpine zone as it crosses the base of Siyeh Peak. But miniature flowers bloom and serve as food for pikas. The trail sweeps around a large bowl where two steep snowfields often linger until mid-July to **Piegan Pass.** The pass, which is named for the Pikuni or Piegan people of the Blackfeet Nation, sneaks a close look at the Continental Divide. Rather than returning to Siyeh Bend (8.8 mi/14.2 km round-trip), some hikers opt for continuing on to Many Glacier Hotel (11.5 mi/18.5 km from Piegan Pass Trailhead) to link with shuttles to return.

Or, take the **Siyeh Pass Trail** from Preston Park. When switchbacks ascend above the tree line, the elevation gain provides a look back at the hanging valley in which Preston Park sits. The switchbacks appear to lead to a saddle, which is **Siyeh Pass.** But eight more turns climb above the pass before swinging through a cliff to the divide between Boulder and Baring Creeks. Snow can bury the steep switchbacks south of the divide until mid-July. **Sexton Glacier** hunkers protected from the afternoon sun by Going-to-the-Sun Mountain (accessible via a 1-mi/1.6-km spur trail). The trail descends in 3,446 feet (1,050 m) of elevation past bighorn sheep and a multicolored cliff band before traversing the flanks of Goat Mountain and dropping a couple hot miles through the 2015 Reynolds Creek Fire to the lower trailhead and shuttle stop at the Sunrift Gorge on Going-to-the-Sun Road. From Piegan Pass Trailhead to Sunrift Gorge is 10 mi (16.1 km) total.

Preston Park (top); Virginia Falls (middle); Iceberg Lake in Many Glacier (bottom)

St. Mary and Virginia Falls
DISTANCE: 2-3.4 mi (3.2-5.5 km) round-trip

DURATION: 1-2 hours round-trip
ELEVATION GAIN: 216 feet (66 m)
EFFORT: easy
TRAIL SURFACE: dirt path with roots and rocks
TRAILHEAD: St. Mary Falls Trailhead or St. Mary Falls shuttle stop

In midsummer, this trail sees a constant stream of people. Two trailheads depart from Going-to-the-Sun Road. The west trailhead descends from the shuttle stop. The east trailhead launches from the vehicle parking lot. Both trails connect with the St. Mary Lake Trail leading to the falls. Between the trailheads and St. Mary Falls, the 2015 Reynolds Creek Fire burned the forest, opening up views of surrounding mountains and the St. Mary River. On hot days, hike it in the morning.

The trail drops 1 mi (1.6 km) through several well-signed junctions en route to St. Mary Falls, a multi-drop falls that cascade through a mini-gorge into blue-green pools. After crossing the wooden bridge at St. Mary Fall, the trail switchbacks up 0.7 mi (1.1 km) to Virginia Falls, a broad veil-type waterfall spewing mist. A short spur climbs to the base of Virginia Fall. Be wary of slippery rocks and strong, cold currents at both falls. Nesting near both waterfalls, water ouzels (American dippers) are dark gray birds easily recognized by their dipping action, up to 40 bends per minute.

MANY GLACIER
★ Grinnell Glacier
DISTANCE: 11 mi (17.7 km) round-trip
DURATION: 6 hours round-trip
ELEVATION GAIN: 1,619 feet (493 m)
EFFORT: moderate-strenuous
TRAIL SURFACE: narrow, dirt, rocky, rock steps
TRAILHEADS: on the south side of Many Glacier Hotel, at Swiftcurrent Picnic Area, or via the tour boat

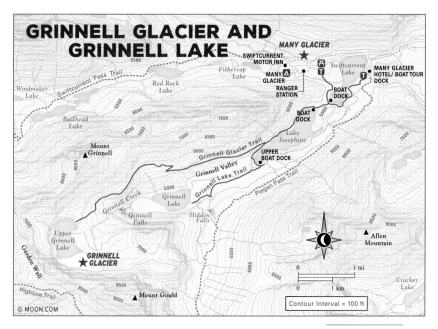

Grinnell Lake

In early summer, a large steep snowdrift frequently bars the path into the upper basin until early July; check the status before hiking. The most accessible glacier in the park, Grinnell Glacier still requires stamina as most of its elevation gain packs within 2 mi (3.2 km). Many hikers take the boat shuttle, cutting the length to 7.8 mi (12.6 km) round-trip, or just trimming 2.5 mi (4 km) off the return. To hike the entire route from the picnic area, follow Swiftcurrent Lake's west shore to the boat dock. From Many Glacier Hotel, round the southern shore to meet up with the same dock. Bop over the short hill and hike around Lake Josephine's north shore.

Toward Josephine's west end, the Grinnell Glacier Trail diverges uphill. As the trail climbs through multicolored rock strata, Grinnell Lake's milky turquoise waters come into view below. Above, you'll spot Gem Glacier and Salamander Glacier, both shrunken to static snowfields, long before Grinnell Glacier appears. The trail ascends on a cliff stairway where a waterfall douses hikers before passing a rest stop with outhouses. A steep grunt up the moraine leads to a stunning view. Trot through the maze of paths crossing the bedrock to Upper Grinnell Lake's shore, but do not walk out on the glacier's ice, as it harbors deadly hidden crevasses.

Grinnell Lake

DISTANCE: 2.2-7.8 mi (3.5-12.6 km) round-trip
DURATION: 1-4 hours round-trip
ELEVATION GAIN: minimal
EFFORT: easy
TRAIL SURFACE: dirt and rocks
TRAILHEADS: on the south side of Many Glacier Hotel, at Swiftcurrent Picnic Area, or via the tour boat

For a 2.2-mi (3.5-km) round-trip walk, catch the tour boat across Swiftcurrent Lake and Lake Josephine to hike to Grinnell Lake. For a longer hike, begin at Many Glacier Hotel, following the trail winding around Swiftcurrent Lake to the boat dock opposite the hotel. A third starting point begins at Many Glacier picnic area, where the trail follows Swiftcurrent Lake to that same boat dock.

From the boat dock, pop over the hill to Josephine Lake, where the trail hugs the north shore until it splits off to Grinnell Glacier. Stay on the lower trail to wrap around Josephine's west end to the Grinnell Lake junction. Turn right and follow the trail over a swinging bridge. At the lakeshore, enjoy Grinnell's milky turquoise waters and the giant falls across the lake spilling from Grinnell Glacier.

Iceberg Lake

DISTANCE: 10.4 mi (16.7 km) round-trip
DURATION: 5 hours round-trip
ELEVATION GAIN: 1,193 feet (364 m)
EFFORT: moderate
TRAIL SURFACE: narrow, dirt, roots, rocks
TRAILHEAD: behind Swiftcurrent Motor Inn cabins in Many Glacier

One of the top hikes in Glacier, the trail to Iceberg Lake begins with a short, steep jaunt straight uphill, with no time to warm up your muscles gradually. Within 0.4 mi (0.64) you reach a junction. Take note of the directional sign here, and watch for it when you come down. On the return, some hikers zombie-walk right on past it.

At the junction, go left; the trail maintains an easy railroad grade to the lake. Make noise on this trail, known for frequent bear sightings. Wildflowers line the trail in July: bear grass, bog orchids, penstemon, and thimbleberry. One mile (1.6 km) past the junction, the trail rounds a red argillite outcropping with views of the valley. As the trail swings north, it enters a pine and fir forest and crosses Ptarmigan Falls at 2.6 mi (4.2 km), a good break spot where aggressive ground squirrels will steal your snacks. Do not feed them; feeding only trains them to be more forceful. Just beyond the falls, the Ptarmigan Tunnel Trail veers right. Stay straight to swing west through multiple avalanche paths. After crossing a creek, the trail climbs the final bluff, where a view of stark icebergs against blue water unfolds. Brave hikers dive into the lake, but be prepared to have the frigid water suck the air from your lungs.

Scenic Point in Two Medicine

TWO MEDICINE
Scenic Point
DISTANCE: 7.4 mi (11.9 km) round-trip
DURATION: 4 hours round-trip
ELEVATION GAIN: 2,124 feet (647 m)
EFFORT: moderate-strenuous
TRAIL SURFACE: narrow, dirt, roots, rocks
TRAILHEAD: milepost 6.9 up Two Medicine Road

Scenic Point is one short climb with big scenery. The trail launches up through a thick subalpine fir forest. A short side jaunt en route allows a peek at Appistoki Falls. As switchbacks line up like dominoes, stunted firs give way to silvery dead and twisted limber pines. Broaching the ridge, the trail enters seemingly barren alpine tundra. Only alpine bluebells and pink mats of several-hundred-year-old moss campion cower in crags.

On the ridge, the trail traverses a north-facing slope; avoid the early summer steep snowfield by climbing a worn path that goes above it before descending to Scenic Point. To reach the actual Scenic Point above the trail, cut off at the sign, stepping on rocks to avoid crushing fragile alpine plants. At the top, views

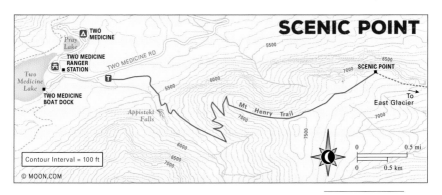

plunge several thousand feet straight down to Lower Two Medicine Lake and across the plains. Return the way you came.

Rockwell Falls and Cobalt Lake

DISTANCE: 6.8–15.8 mi (10.9–25.4 km) round-trip
DURATION: 4–8 hours round-trip
ELEVATION GAIN: minimal-2,518 feet (minimal-767 m)
EFFORT: easy-strenuous
TRAIL SURFACE: narrow, dirt, roots, rocks
TRAILHEAD: adjacent to Two Medicine boat dock

Follow the gentle South Shore Trail along Two Medicine Lake past beaver ponds and bear-scratched trees to Paradise Creek, crossing on a swinging bridge. At 2.3 mi (3.7 km), turn left at the signed junction. The trail wanders through avalanche paths with uprooted trees shredded like toothpicks. At 3.4 mi (5.5 km), you reach Rockwell Falls. Spur trails explore the falls.

Continuing on to Cobalt Lake, the trail climbs up several switchbacks into an upper basin, crossing the creek. It ascends at a moderate pitch for the last 2 mi (3.2 km). Tucked in the uppermost corner of the basin, Cobalt Lake sits below mountain-goat cliffs.

GUIDED HIKES
Glacier Guides
11970 U.S. 2 E., West Glacier; 406/387-5555; http://glacierguides. com; mid-May–Sept.

Glacier Guides runs the trail-guiding concession in the park. They lead day hikes, backpacking, and overnight chalet trips. For day hiking, reservations are required, and rates include the guide service, a deli lunch, and transportation to the trailhead. Solo travelers can hook up with the daily group day hikes (July–early Sept.; $120 pp), scheduled to a different destination each day. Backpacking trips depart every week for 3–6-day adventures; rates run around $225 per day and include the guide service, transportation to and from the trailhead, meals, and snacks.

Ranger-Guided Hikes

National Park Service naturalists guide hikes in summer to varied destinations. Check the current schedules online or in the park newspaper for meeting times, locations, and days. Several of the most popular guided hikes include Avalanche Lake, St. Mary Falls, and Grinnell Glacier. The hikes are free and do not require reservations; however, you may need reservations with **Glacier Park Boat Company** (406/257-2426; http://glacierparkboats.com) and to pay a fee for the boat shuttle for hikes that use it.

BACKPACKING

Glacier National Park's backpacking is unrivaled, with miles of well-marked scenic trails. Sixty-six designated backcountry campgrounds spread campers out to avoid crowds. Long-distance trekkers can tackle more than 100 mi (161 km) of Continental Divide Trail in 7-10 days.

Permits (adults $7 pp/night) for backpacking trips are in high demand. Pick them up 24 hours in advance in person at the **Apgar Backcountry Permit Office** (406/888-7859 May-Oct.; 406/888-7800 Nov.-Apr.), **St. Mary Visitor Center** (406/888-7800; late May-late Sept.), or **Many Glacier Ranger Station** (406/888-7800; late May-late Sept.). Lines begin forming around 6am. For advance reservations, apply online starting in mid-March (www.nps.gov/glac; $40).

For guided backpacking trips, contact **Glacier Guides** (406/387-5555; http://glacierguides.com).

DAWSON-PITAMAKIN LOOP
18.4 mi (29.6 km)

The Dawson-Pitamakin Loop takes a top-of-the-world traverse between high passes on the Continental Divide, where bighorn sheep summer. Launch this three-day trek in either direction, starting from the trailhead at Two Medicine Campground. Camp a night each at Old Man Lake and No Name Lake. The route is snow-free some summers by early July, but advance reservations are only available after mid-July.

GUNSIGHT PASS
28 mi (45 km)

From Jackson Glacier Overlook on Going-to-the-Sun Road, hike west for four days over Gunsight Pass and Lincoln Pass to finish at Lake McDonald Lodge. Shuttles access both trailheads, making logistics easy. Spend one night in each locale: Gunsight Lake, Lake Ellen Wilson, and Sperry Chalet. With the short hike on the third day, you'll have time to trek up through Comeau Pass to Sperry Glacier.

FIFTY MOUNTAIN
32 mi (52 km)

This four-day Continental Divide trek starts at Logan Pass to traipse along the Garden Wall to reach the backcountry campsites below Granite Park Chalet and Fifty Mountain, two spectacular camps near subalpine wildflower meadows surrounded by peaks. It finishes with a romp across West Flattop to the Flattop Camp and then a descent to Packer's Roost. Snow can be tricky in July with a steep snowfield before Ahern Pass and a dangerous snow bridge at Cattle Queen, and advance permits are not available until August.

Dawson-Pitamakin Loop (left); Gunsight Pass hike (right)

To use the shuttles, you'll need to add on 1.4 mi (2.3 km) uphill to reach The Loop on Going-to-the-Sun Road.

NORTHERN CIRCLE
52 mi (84 km)

Hike the Northern Circle in either direction to take in prime fishing lakes and high passes. The loop makes logistics easy. The classic route starts at the Iceberg Trailhead and ends at the Swiftcurrent Trailhead. The route crosses through Ptarmigan Tunnel (open mid-July) into the Belly River Area to stay at Elizabeth and Glenns Lakes. Then, it climbs over Stoney Indian Pass to Stony Indian Lake for a night before dropping and ascending to the Continental Divide to camp at Fifty Mountain and Granite Park Chalet. Complete the loop by popping over Swiftcurrent Pass. The trek takes 5-7 days; choose between 12 backcountry campgrounds on or near the route. Get walk-in permits for July, but advance reservations for Fifty Mountain and Stoney Indian Lake are only available starting August 1.

BIKING

Glacier is a tough place to cycle. There are no shoulders, roads are narrow and curvy, and drivers gawk at scenery instead of the road, all putting cyclists in precarious positions. With that caveat, for a dedicated cyclist, nothing compares with bicycling Going-to-the-Sun Road, one of the United States' premier routes.

GOING-TO-THE-SUN ROAD

Going-to-the-Sun Road is an unforgettable bicycle trip. While the 3,500-foot (1,067 m) climb up the west side seems intimidating, it's not steep, just a constant uphill grind amid stunning scenery. During construction in the 1920s, the road grade stayed at 6 percent because cars of

bicycling Going-to-the-Sun Road

the era required rigorous shifting at a steeper grade; that helps maintain a minimal incline for cyclists.

Because the Sun Road is so narrow, it is not the place for a family ride, except when the road is closed to cars. While laws do not mandate helmets, wear one anyway, considering most drivers are gaping at the views rather than paying attention to the road. Be sure to carry plenty of water. Before heading out, check your brake pads, as the screaming downhill off the Continental Divide can wear them down to nubbins. Both mountain bikes and road bikes are appropriate here, but with skinny tires, be wary of obstacles: debris, grates, rockfall, and ice.

Locals also celebrate the full moon with a bone-chilling night ride. It's dangerous (injuries and one fatality have occurred), but an otherworldly experience. At dusk or at night, biking requires tail reflectors and a front light.

Spring and Fall
Locals relish spring riding when the Sun Road is closed to cars. Cycling begins in early April as soon as snowplows free the pavement while the west-side road remains closed to vehicles from Lake McDonald Lodge or Avalanche, and the east side remains closed from Rising Sun. Riders climb up as far as plowing operations permit. By May, it is such a popular activity that free bicycle-carrying **shuttles** (mid-May-road opening to vehicles, 9am-5pm weekends only) run from Apgar and Lake McDonald Lodge to the Avalanche road closure to expand parking options. Mother's Day often brings out wee ones on tricycles, training wheels, tagalongs, and trailers. Call or consult the park website (406/888-7800; www.nps.gov/glac)

to check on access, as construction or spring plowing limits cycling some days. In fall, as portions of the road close again to vehicles, cycling sans cars resumes until snow arrives.

Summer
In summer, when the road opens to vehicles, strong riders who are comfortable being pinched between cliffs and cars head for Logan Pass. Some riders return the way they came; others continue on to the other side. Local racers make a 142-mi (229-km) loop (Going-to-the-Sun Road, U.S. 89, MT 49, and U.S. 2) in one day; tourers take two days.

Cyclists must be prepared to ride the narrow, shoulderless road with a constant stream of cars. Due to heavy midday traffic, biking is not permitted 11am-4pm daily June 15-Labor Day in two sections on the west side: along Lake McDonald between the Apgar Road junction and Sprague Creek, and climbing uphill between Avalanche Campground and Logan Pass. If starting from the west side, head out from Lake McDonald by 6:30am for adequate time to pedal to Logan Pass. In early summer, long daylight hours allow for riding after 4pm, when traffic lessens. The east side has no restrictions, but is still easier to ride early or late in the day with fewer cars on the road. Some free shuttle buses are equipped with bicycle racks in case you need a lift. Catch the shuttles only at official stops.

APGAR BIKE TRAIL
Especially good for families, a level, paved bicycle trail connects West Glacier with Apgar. Approximately 2 mi (3.2 km) long, the Apgar Bike Trail begins on the north side of the West Glacier Bridge. After dropping

through the woods, it crosses through the National Park Service employee housing area before entering the forest again, where it continues on to Apgar, connecting the village, visitor center, and campground. Be cautious at two road crossings en route.

RENTALS
GLACIER OUTFITTERS
Apgar; 406/219-7466; www.goglacieroutfitters.com

PADDLING

- -

Glacier has instituted strict boating and paddling guidelines in order to protect its pristine waters from aquatic invasive species. The lakes are only open in summer and only available by **permit** to boaters and paddlers who have passed an inspection, and permiting requirements make bringing a powerboat from home impractical for most short-term visitors.

Due to vehicle length (21 ft/6.4 m) and height (10 ft/3 m) restrictions, towed boats and some rooftop-carried boats may not cross Going-to-the-Sun Road between Avalanche and Sun Point. Although river kayakers drool at the rapids on McDonald Creek, the creek is closed to all boating due to nesting harlequin ducks.

LAKE MCDONALD
Electric-powered and hand-propelled watercraft can get a same-day inspection and permit to launch immediately without quarantining. Get inspections daily at **St. Mary Visitor Center** (7am-4:30pm daily June-Sept.) or in Apgar for **Lake McDonald** (7am-9pm daily mid-May-Oct., shorter hours May and late Sept.-Oct.).

Apgar
Lake McDonald (open mid-May-Oct.) has only one boat ramp in Apgar, but hand-carried craft can launch from Sprague Creek Picnic Area or several pullouts along the lake. When the lake is placid, these locations make for prime morning and evening paddling.

MANY GLACIER
Glacier's east-side lakes offer outstanding paddling, but the larger lakes are subject to big winds. Be aware of changing conditions for safety. The park's east-side lakes open June-September and are only available by permit to boaters and paddlers who have passed an inspection. Non-trailered electric-powered and hand-propelled watercraft can get a same-day inspection and permit to launch immediately. Jet Skis and gas-powered motorboats are banned.

Many Glacier has smaller lakes that are more protected from big winds, surrounded by stunning scenery and sometimes moose. Only nonmotorized boats are permitted: sailboats, kayaks, rowboats, paddleboards, and canoes.

Swiftcurrent Lake
Kayakers can cross Swiftcurrent Lake and paddle the connecting slow-moving **Cataract Creek** upstream to **Lake Josephine**, where a shoreline loop makes a scenic tour. The public boat ramp

on Swiftcurrent Lake sits east of the picnic area. Get inspections and permits at the **Many Glacier Ranger Station** (7am-4:30pm daily; free).

TWO MEDICINE

On calm days, kayaks, canoes, and paddleboards tour the shoreline of **Two Medicine Lake.** But it is one of the windiest lakes in the park, so boaters need to keep an eye on waves; if whitecaps pop up, get off the lake. Some paddlers prefer the tiny **Pray Lake** in the campground for its more protected water instead. Two Medicine Road terminates at the public boat ramp, so it's easy to find. Hand-propelled watercraft and non-trailered electric-powered boats are allowed, but Jet Skis and gas-engine motorboats are not.

Stop at the **Two Medicine Ranger Station** (7am-4:30pm daily) to get your watercraft inspected and get your **permit** (free) before launching. Boating season runs June-late September.

RENTALS

Glacier Park Boat Company operates watercraft rentals at Lake McDonald, Many Glacier, and Two Medicine boat docks. Rentals available include canoes, double kayaks,

boat rental dock at Many Glacier

and small motorboats, and at Lake McDonald, paddleboards. Paddles and life jackets are included.

**LAKE MCDONALD
LODGE BOAT DOCK
406/888-5727 or 406/257-2426;
https://glacierparkboats.com;
$15-28/hour**

**MANY GLACIER HOTEL
BOAT DOCK
406/257-2426; http://
glacierparkboats.com; daily mid-June-mid-Sept.; $18-22/hour; for use
on Swiftcurrent Lake only**

**TWO MEDICINE BOAT DOCK
406/257-2426; www.
glacierparkboats.com; $16-23/hour**

WINTER SPORTS

Some roads and trails in the park make for nice cross-country skiing and snowshoeing routes. For route descriptions and maps, pick up *Skiing and Snowshoeing* in the visitor centers or online (www.nps.gov/glac). Skiers and snowshoers should be well equipped and versed in winter travel safety before venturing out.

GOING-TO-THE-SUN ROAD

Since winter buries Going-to-the-Sun Road with snow from Lake McDonald Lodge to St. Mary, the road attracts cross-country skiers and snowshoers November-early April. Touring up the gated road's lower elevations goes through relatively avalanche-free

cross-country skiing on Going-to-the-Sun Road

zones. The gentle grade makes for good gliding suitable for beginners. For snowshoers, etiquette requires blazing a separate snowshoe trail rather than squishing the parallel ski tracks flat.

Between Rising Sun and Avalanche Creek, Going-to-the-Sun Road sees significant avalanche activity and is best avoided. When Logan Pass opens in June, skiers and snowboarders can hike up the Hidden Lake Overlook trail for turns on the lingering snowpack.

In McDonald Valley, ski tours lead past McDonald Creek and Upper McDonald Creek Falls to **Avalanche Campground** (6 mi/9.7 km one-way). Some skiers head up to **Snyder Lakes** (8.4 mi/13.5 km round-trip), but be ready for the narrow trail descending through tight trees on the way back down. Blue-sky days attract hearty snowshoers to the steep trek up to **Mount Brown Lookout** (9.9 mi/15.9km round-trip).

AROUND APGAR

Winter converts the roads and trails around Apgar into easy cross-country ski and snowshoe paths late November-early April. Quiet and scenic, road skiing makes for easy route-finding with little avalanche danger at lower elevations. Roads are plowed into Apgar and up Lake McDonald's south shore. Beyond plowing, popular ski tours follow roads and trails to **Fish Creek Campground,** among other routes.

GUIDES

GLACIER ADVENTURE GUIDES
406/892-2173; www.glacieradventureguides.com
Glacier Adventure Guides leads full-day and overnight trips for cross-country touring, backcountry skiing, and snowshoeing. If you're a solo traveler, it's the best way to get accompanied into the backcountry with avalanche-certified guides to find pristine powder stashes. Lunch, snacks, and some equipment are included, although ski rentals need to be picked up outside the park in Flathead Valley. For deep backcountry, ski in to an igloo to spend the night.

PARK-RUN TOURS
The National Park Service guides free weekend snowshoe tours from **Apgar Visitor Center** (406/888-7800) January-mid-March. Call for departure times for the two-hour walks to look for animal tracks. Interpretive rangers point out how flora and fauna adapt to harsh winters. Hikers should wear winter footwear, dress in layers, and bring water. Rent snowshoes from the park service.

FOOD

Glacier is a place for good home-style cooking, where tasty fresh-baked fruit pies are still the rage, rather than upscale or international fare. Seasonal restaurants cater to summer visitors; hours can shorten in spring or fall, and only a few remain open in winter.

Many eateries and camp stores are operated by **Xanterra** (855/733-4522; www.glaciernationalparklodges.com; daily mid-June-mid-Sept.) No reservations are accepted, so you may have to wait for a table in midsummer. Menus rely on local, fresh, and organic sourcing served with healthy, gluten-free, vegan, and child options plus choices for toppings and portions. The restaurants serve craft cocktails, beer, and wine.

STANDOUTS
Russell's Fireside Dining Room
288 Lake McDonald Lodge Loop; 855/733-4522; daily mid-May-late Sept.
At Lake McDonald Lodge, the headliner dining room is Russell's Fireside Dining Room, decorated with painted Native American chandeliers and full of historical ambience. The north windows have a peekaboo lake view, but during dinner the blinds usually need to be pulled down as the hot sun blazes in. Breakfast (6:30am-10am; $9-18) is a choice of continental buffet, full buffet, or menu entrées. Lunch (11:30am-2pm; $10-18) serves small plates, burgers, sandwiches, salads, and pasta. Dinner (5pm-9:30pm; $17-30) can go casual with burgers,

Ptarmigan Dining Room

salads, and pasta or full-on dining with charcuterie, shared appetizers, and plated entrées of fish or meats.

Ptarmigan Dining Room
Many Glacier Hotel, milepost 11.5, Many Glacier Rd.; front desk 406/732-4411; early June-mid-Sept.
In Many Glacier Hotel, the Ptarmigan Dining Room underwent a renovation that unmasked the original railroad beams and took the restaurant back to its historic look. Massive windows look out on Swiftcurrent Lake, Grinnell Point, and Mount Wilbur. For the best views to watch the bears, ask to sit near the north windows facing Mount Altyn. For breakfast (6:30am-10am; $12-18), choose between a continental buffet or hot entrée buffet. Lunch (11:30am-2:30pm; $10-22) serves pasta, salads, sandwiches, and burgers. Dinner (5pm-9:30pm; $12-44) has prime rib, Wagyu steak, duck, fish, or more casual burgers, pasta, and salads. Grab small plates, sandwiches, salads, and pasta in the adjacent **Swiss Room** bar (11:30am-10pm; $8-21).

GLACIER NATIONAL PARK FOOD

NAME	LOCATION	TYPE
Eddie's Café & Mercantile	Apgar	sit-down restaurant
★ Russell's Fireside Dining Room	Lake McDonald Lodge	sit-down restaurant
Lucke's Lounge	Lake McDonald Lodge	sit-down bar
Jammer Joe's Grill and Pizzeria	Lake McDonald Lodge	sit-down restaurant
Two Dog Flats Grill	Rising Sun	sit-down restaurant
★ Ptarmigan Dining Room	Many Glacier Hotel	sit-down restaurant
'Nell's	Swiftcurrent Motor Inn, Many Glacier	sit-down restaurant
Heidi's Snack Shop	Many Glacier Hotel	convenience store
Swiftcurrent Campstore	Swiftcurrent Motor Inn, Many Glacier	convenience store
Two Medicine Campstore	Two Medicine	convenience store

BEST PICNIC SPOTS

Except for Sun Point, fires are permitted in fire rings at the picnic areas below. Bring your own firewood, or purchase at camp stores, since gathering it is prohibited.

Lake McDonald
APGAR PICNIC AREA
Southwest corner of Lake McDonald, off Going-to-the-Sun Road
Apgar Picnic Area offers a beautiful up-lake view to the Continental Divide. The picnic area has beach access, and there are picnic tables, flush toilets, and fire rings with grills.

On weekends and holidays, plan to nab a table early.

Going-to-the-Sun Road
AVALANCHE CREEK PICNIC AREA
Across Going-to-the-Sun Road from Avalanche Creek Campground
Picnic sites at Avalanche Creek are under cedar shade adjacent to McDonald Creek, but due to bears, do not leave your picnic gear unattended. The picnic area has larger rebuilt vault-toilet restrooms. Fires in the fire rings with grills are permitted.

SUN POINT PICNIC AREA
Sun Point Picnic Area has great views

FOOD	PRICE	HOURS
casual American	moderate	8am-10pm daily May-mid-Sept.
traditional American	moderate-splurge	6:30am-10am, 11:30am-2pm, and 5pm-9:30pm daily mid-May-late Sept.
casual American and drinks	moderate	11:30am-10pm daily mid-May-late Sept.
family-friendly American and pizza	moderate	11am-9pm (closes earlier in Sept.) daily mid-May-late Sept.
casual American	moderate	6:30am-10am and 11am-10pm daily mid-June-mid-Sept.
traditional American	moderate-splurge	6:30am-10am, 11:30am-2:30pm, 5pm-9:30pm early June-mid-Sept.
casual American	moderate	6:30am-10pm mid-June-mid-Sept.
limited groceries	budget	6am-9:30pm daily mid-June-mid-Sept.
limited groceries, camping and hiking supplies	budget	7am-10pm daily mid-June-mid-Sept.
snacks and light lunches	budget	8:30am-6pm daily summer

up St. Mary Valley to the Continental Divide, but watch the paper plates, as the wind can howl. Trails lead to Sun Point and Baring Falls. It has vault toilets. Fires are not permitted.

Many Glacier
MANY GLACIER PICNIC AREA
Many Glacier Rd. milepost 12.2
Many Glacier's small picnic area crams with picnickers toting binoculars to scan for bears on Mount Altyn. It's a popular picnic site and can be crowded in midsummer. If you want to roast marshmallows in one of the fire pits, buy firewood at the Swiftcurrent Campstore.

Two Medicine
TWO MEDICINE PICNIC AREA
Below Rising Wolf Mountain, Two Medicine picnic area is adjacent to the campground. With running water and flush toilets, it is in a scenic spot right on the shore of Two Medicine Lake amid cottonwoods. Most of the sites have some trees, which provide a good windbreak on days when the wind howls, but scant shade on hot days. Sites include a picnic table and a fire ring with a grill, but buy firewood from the camp store.

GLACIER NATIONAL PARK CAMPGROUNDS

NAME	LOCATION	SEASON
Apgar Campground	Apgar	May-mid-Oct.
Fish Creek Campground	Lake McDonald	June-early Sept.
Sprague Creek Campground	Lake McDonald	mid-May-mid-Sept
Kintla Lake Campground	North Fork	June-mid-Sept.
Bowman Lake Campground	North Fork	late May-early Sept.
Quartz Creek Campground	North Fork	July-Nov.
Logging Creek Campground	North Fork	July-Sept.
Avalanche Campground	Going-to-the-Sun Road	mid-June-early Sept.
★ Rising Sun Campground	St. Mary Lake	late May-mid-Sept.
St. Mary Campground	St. Mary	mid-May-mid-Sept.
★ Many Glacier Campground	Many Glacier	late May-mid-Sept.
★ Two Medicine Campground	Two Medicine	late May-late Sept.
Cut Bank Campground	Two Medicine	June-mid-Sept.

SITES AND AMENITIES	RV LIMIT	PRICE	RESERVATIONS
25 tent and RV sites, 169 tent-only sites, drinking water, flush toilets, dump station	25 sites for RVs up to 40 ft (12.2 m)	$20	only for group campsites
80 tent and RV sites, 98 tent-only sites, drinking water, flush toilets, showers, dump station	18 sites for RVs up to 35 ft (10.7 m), 62 sites for RVs up to 27 ft (8.2 m)	$23	yes
25 tent and RV sites, drinking water, flush toilets	RVs up to 21 ft (6.4 m)	$20	no
13 tent and RV sites, drinking water, pit toilet	21 ft (6.4 m) maximum vehicle length, no trailers	$15	no
48 tent and RV sites, drinking water, vault toilets	21 ft (6.4 m) maximum vehicle length, no trailers	$15	no
7 tent and RV sites, pit toilets	21 ft (6.4 m) maximum vehicle length, no trailers	$10	no
7 primitive sites	21 ft (6.4 m) maximum vehicle length, no trailers	$10	no
87 tent and RV sites, drinking water, flush toilets	RVs up to 26 ft (7.9 m)	$20	no
83 tent and RV sites, drinking water, flush toilets, showers, dump station	RVs up to 25 ft (7.6 m)	$20	no
183 tent and RV sites, drinking water, flush toilets, showers, dump station	RVs up to 35 ft (10.7 m)	$23	yes
110 tent and RV sites, drinking water, flush toilets, dump station	some sites for RVs up to 35 ft (10.7 m), most sites RVs up to 21 ft (6.4 m)	$23	yes
13 tent and RV sites, 86 tent-only sites, drinking water, flush toilets, dump station	13 sites for RVs up to 32 ft (9.7 m)	$20	no
14 primitive sites	only very small RVs	$10	no

CAMPING

Reservations

Most of Glacier's 13 campgrounds are first-come, first-served. Reservations (877/444-6777; www.recreation.gov) are accepted for **Fish Creek, St. Mary,** and **Many Glacier** starting six months in advance. Reserve group campsites 12 months in advance for **St. Mary** and **Apgar** campgrounds.

Tips

Rather than moving campgrounds frequently, you are better off staying in one campground and driving to other locations to experience the park. Many of the park campsites fill early, some before 8am, and packing up to move and get a new campsite is stressful. Online, look at the campground status page (www.

nps.gov/applications/glac/cgstatus/cgstatus.cfm) to assess the current fill time for the campgrounds. You can also look up fill times for past years on each campground's individual page to help you gauge when to arrive.

STANDOUTS
Rising Sun Campground
6 mi (9.7 km) west of St. Mary; late May-mid-Sept.; $20

Located only 12 mi (19.3 km) east of Logan Pass and 6 mi (9.7 km) west of St. Mary, Rising Sun Campground tucks on the lower hillside of Otokomi Mountain by St. Mary Lake. The sun drops down early behind Goat Mountain, creating a long twilight at the campground. While the 2015 Reynolds Creek Fire bypassed the larger trees in the lower campground, it left burnt trees on the hillside above the upper campsites. The 83-site campground is a few minutes' walk to a restaurant, a camp store, and hot showers. Beach access is across Going-to-the-Sun Road, with a picnic area, boat ramp, and boat tours. The Otokomi Lake trailhead is behind the adjacent inn. RVs can only be 25 feet (7.6 m). Midsummer, the campground can fill by 9am.

Many Glacier Campground
end of Many Glacier Rd.; late May-mid-Sept.; $23

Many Glacier Campground packs 110 treed sights at the base of Grinnell Point. As the most coveted campground in the park, reservations are essential. In 2021, all campsites will be in the reservation system.

Two Medicine Campground on Pray Lake

For 2022, half of the sites can be reserved in advance, but for first-come, first-served campsites plan to arrive by 7am. A few sites can fit RVs up to 35 feet (10.7 m), but most fit RVs only up to 21 feet (6.4 m). Nearby trails depart for Red Rock, Bullhead, and Iceberg Lakes as well as Ptarmigan Tunnel and Swiftcurrent Pass. From the picnic area, a five-minute walk down the road, trails depart to Lake Josephine and Grinnell Lake, Grinnell Glacier, and Piegan Pass. Across the parking lot, Swiftcurrent Motor Inn has a restaurant, laundry, hot showers, and a camp store. If bears frequent the campground, tent camping may be restricted, with only hard-sided vehicles allowed. In 2022, primitive camping (mid-Sept.-Oct.; $10) will have pit toilets and no water.

Two Medicine Campground
406/888-7800; late May-late Sept.; $20
Two Medicine Campground yields views of bears foraging on Rising Wolf Mountain, especially from the A and C loops. Riverfront sites are 95, 99, and 100. In early summer, ruby-crowned kinglets call out "teacher, teacher" from the trees. The campground surrounds the calmer waters of small Pray Lake, a good place for paddling, fishing, or chilly swimming. With 99 sites, the campground may have availability later in the day than campgrounds nearer Going-to-the-Sun Road, but it can fill up midsummer before 11am. Tenters should choose sheltered sites due to abrupt high winds that can flatten poles. Flush toilets, water, and a dump station are provided. The North Shore Trail departs right from the campground, leading in both directions around Rising Wolf Mountain. A seven-minute walk or a few-minute drive connects with the boat tour and rental dock. Only 13 sites can handle RVs up to 32 feet (9.7 m). Primitive camping (late Sept.-Oct.; $10) has pit toilets and no water.

LODGING

Accommodations have en suite bathrooms, unless otherwise indicated. Lodges generally do not have TVs or air-conditioning. Add the 7 percent state bed tax to rates.

Reservations
Advance reservations for all in-park lodgings are **imperative,** especially for July and August. Contact **Xanterra** (855/733-4522; www.glaciernationalparklodges.com) 13 months in advance for Many Glacier Hotel, Lake McDonald Lodge, Rising Sun Motor Inn, Swiftcurrent Motor Inn, and Apgar Village Inn. Make reservations 13-16 months ahead with **Pursuit Glacier Park Collection** (844/868-7474; www.glacierpark-collection.com) for Apgar Village Lodge and Motel Lake McDonald. For Granite Park Chalet and Sperry Chalet, make reservations in early January through **Belton Chalets** (406/387-5654 or 888/345-2649; www.graniteparkchalet.com or www.sperrychalet.com).

Tips
For your best chance at getting a reservation, book the **first day of the month** when reservations open, as inside-park lodging often fills fast. Flexibility in dates can also help

GLACIER NATIONAL PARK LODGING

NAME	LOCATION	SEASON
Apgar Village Inn	Apgar	late May-mid-Sept.
Apgar Village Lodge and Cabins	Apgar	late May-late Sept.
★ Lake McDonald Lodge	Lake McDonald	mid-May-late Sept.
Motel Lake McDonald	Lake McDonald	mid-June-mid-Sept.
Rising Sun Motor Inn	Going-to-the-Sun Road	mid-June-mid-Sept.
★ Granite Park Chalet	Going-to-the-Sun Road	early July-early Sept.
★ Sperry Chalet	Going-to-the-Sun Road	early July-early Sept.
★ Many Glacier Hotel	Many Glacier	early June-mid-Sept.
Swiftcurrent Motor Inn	Many Glacier	mid-June-mid-Sept.

secure a reservation. Sometimes, you can pick up a last-minute reservation from a cancellation. Call to check on these rather than looking online.

STANDOUTS
Lake McDonald Lodge
288 Lake McDonald Lodge Loop; reservations 855/733-4522, front desk 406/888-5431; www.glaciernationalparklodges.com; mid-May-late Sept.; $118-515

A National Historic Landmark, Lake McDonald Lodge graces the southeast lake shore. Centered around a massive stone fireplace and hunting lodge-themed lobby full of trophy specimens hung by John Lewis, the original owner, the complex has four types of accommodations: main lodge rooms, cabin rooms, Cobb House suites, and Snyder Hall. A $3 million renovation in 2016-17 revamped some cabins and lodge

OPTIONS	PRICE
guest rooms, some with kitchenettes; family units that sleep up to six	rooms starting at $185
20 motel rooms; 28 rustic cabins, some with kitchens	rooms starting at $120
main lodge rooms; cabin rooms; Cobb House two-room suites; Snyder Hall with shared bathrooms	rooms starting at $118
motel rooms	rooms starting at $180
motel rooms	rooms starting at $182
hike-in camper chalet (no road access) with 12 rooms that sleep 2-6 people each; shared vault toilets; no running water; linen service available ($25)	$120 first person in room, $82 per added person
hike-in camper lodge (no road access) with private rooms that sleep 2-6 people each (bedding included); shared vault toilets; running cold water; basic meals included	$240 for first person in room, $160 per additional person in room
guest rooms and suites	rooms starting at $220
cabins, with private or shared bathrooms; motel rooms	rooms starting at $120

rooms. Dial back your expectations to the mid-1900s with telephones as the only in-room amenities, and you'll be delighted with the location and historical ambience. Some lakeside rooms have views. Most rooms are small with bathrooms converted from original closets. Upstairs rooms lack elevator access. Snyder Hall has shared bathrooms. Cobb House has two-room suites with televisions. Wireless internet is available in the lobby and reading room.

Granite Park Chalet

Hike-in from Logan Pass or The Loop on Going-to-the-Sun Road; 406/387-5654 or 888/345-2649; www.graniteparkchalet.com; $120 first person in room, $82 per added person

Granite Park Chalet sits atop a knoll with a 360-degree view and bear-watching. This rustic chalet, which has 12 guest rooms sleeping 2-6 people each and outdoor vault toilets, functions like a hostel:

Bring your own sleeping bag, eating utensils, and food to cook in the kitchen. With **no running water,** you must haul water for cooking and washing from 5 minutes away. As an option, purchase linen service ($25 for sheets, a pillow, and blankets), preorder freeze-dried food ($2-15/item), and buy environmentally friendly disposable plates and utensils. Reach the chalet from Logan Pass (7.4 mi/11.9 km), The Loop (4 mi/6.4 km), or Swiftcurrent (7.6 mi/12.2 km). Book in early January.

Sperry Chalet

Hike-in from Lake McDonald Lodge or Jackson Glacier Overlook on Going-to-the-Sun Road; 406/387-5654 or 888/345-2649; www.sperrychalet.com; $240 first person in room, $160 per added person

With views plunging down to Lake McDonald, this full-service chalet provides meals (dinner, breakfast, and sack lunch) and guest rooms with fresh linens and bedding. But the chalet still offers a rustic experience, with trekking outside to vault toilets in a separate building. Most visitors opt to stay for two nights to allow for hiking to Sperry Glacier (6.9 mi/11.1 km round-trip) on their middle day. Access is strenuous, by trail from Lake McDonald Lodge (6.2 mi/10 km, 3,500 ft/1,067 m elevation gain) or Jackson Glacier Overlook (14 mi/23 km) over two high passes. Book in early January.

Many Glacier Hotel

milepost 11.5, Many Glacier Rd.; reservations 855/733-4522 or front desk 406/732-4411; www.glacier-nationalparklodges.com; early June-mid-Sept.; $220-590

A National Historic Landmark, Many Glacier Hotel is the largest of the park's historic lodges and the most popular due to its stunning location. Set on Swiftcurrent Lake, the immense hotel cowers below surrounding peaks. The lodge centers around its massive four-story lobby with a huge fireplace. Some guest rooms and suites (some with decks) face the lake, while east-side guest rooms get the sunrise, with a unique morning wake-up call as the horses jangle to the corral. A Swiss theme pervades the hotel, with bellhops dressed in lederhosen and gingerbread cutout deck railings. An extensive rehabilitation was completed 2017, but the baths are still small (many were created from the original closets) and no elevators access the upper floors. Rooms have phones, and the lobby has limited wireless internet. A restaurant, lounge, convenience store, and gift shop are on-site.

Lake McDonald Lodge

INFORMATION AND SERVICES

For services, **Apgar,** near the West Glacier Entrance, is the biggest in-park hub, with a restaurant, camp store, two inns, a boat ramp, swimming beaches, visitor center, campground, picnic area and more. Most of Apgar opens May-September only.

St. Mary is the eastern portal to Going-to-the-Sun Road and the other main hub for services. At the junction of the Sun Road and the Blackfeet Highway (U.S. 89), the town clusters at the park boundary along the highway. Only the visitor center and St. Mary Campground are within the park; more services, such as restaurants and grocery stores, are on the Blackfeet Reservation outside the park.

Entrance Stations

Glacier has four main entrance stations. Despite staffing only during daylight hours, the entrances are open 24 hours per day. If they are not staffed, you can buy a park entrance pass at the self-serve kiosk just past the station. Seven-day passes cost $35 per vehicle, $30 per motorcycle, and $20 per biker, hiker, or pedestrian in summer; winter rates drop to $25, $20, and $15. All entrance stations hand out park maps and the summer or winter edition of the park's newspaper. For those headed to the remote North Fork area of the park, the **Polebridge Ranger Station** serves as an entrance and is staffed during the summer with a self-pay kiosk also available.

West Glacier Entrance
Year-round
Crossing the West Glacier Bridge over the Middle Fork of the Flathead River officially is the entry to Glacier National Park. After the bridge, a parking pullout allows for photo-documenting your travel with the park sign. With 60 percent of Glacier's visitors entering here, be prepared for long lines on weekends and in summer. The West Glacier entrance station, which is usually staffed during daylight hours in summer and on weekends off-season, serves as the west entrance to Going-to-the-Sun Road.

St. Mary Entrance
Year-round
The east entrance for Going-to-the-Sun Road is St. Mary. This entrance station is staffed during daylight hours daily in summer and on weekends only fall-spring. It is usually open year-round, with winter access only as far as St. Mary Campground.

Many Glacier Entrance
May-Oct.
On the Many Glacier Road, the Many Glacier Entrance is usually staffed daily but drops to weekends in spring and fall.

Two Medicine Entrance
Mid-May-Oct.
On Two Medicine Road, the Two Medicine Entrance is staffed during daylight hours daily in the summer. During shoulder seasons, staffing is reduced to weekends only.

Visitor Centers

All three of Glacier's visitor centers are small. But you can get maps, ranger program information, *Junior Ranger Activity Guides,* and information on current conditions especially on Going-to-the-Sun Road. They each have Glacier National Park Conservancy **bookstores** (406/892-3250; http://glacier.org), which also sells books online. Shuttles service all three visitor centers, too.

Apgar Visitor Center
Going-to-the-Sun Rd.; 406/888-7800; 8am-6pm daily mid-June-Aug., shorter hours mid-May-mid-June, Sept.-early Oct., weekends only in winter
Tucked in the woods at the four-way intersection two minutes north of Glacier's West Glacier Entrance, the small Apgar Visitor Center is the place to find maps, Junior Ranger Program activity guides, trail and road conditions, fishing

CONTINUED ON NEXT PAGE

and boating information, and ranger program schedules for guided walks, astronomy programs, and evening amphitheater presentations. The parking lot accommodates big RVs, and you can leave your car all day to hop shuttles or meet up for concession-operated tours. The **Apgar Backcountry Permit Office** (406/888-7859 May-Oct., 406/888-7800 Nov.-Apr.; 7am-4:30pm daily May-Sept., 8am-4pm daily Oct.) is opposite the old red schoolhouse in Apgar. This is the main office for acquiring permits for overnight backpacking or paddling trips. Rush hour is the first 3 hours of each morning in July and August; lines begin forming at 6am.

Logan Pass Visitor Center

406/888-7800; 9am-7pm daily mid-June-Aug., shorter hours Labor Day-mid-Sept.

The one place everyone wants to go is Logan Pass, but its visitor center is a small, seasonal outpost with an information desk, a few displays, and a bookstore. The parking lot crowds by 8am. Flush toilets are available downstairs and vault toilets at the parking lot. The center has a water bottle refill station, but no food or beverage sales. Due to the elevation, expect harsher weather including wind, rain, and snow even in August. Don't be surprised if you left the lowlands in sunny summer only to arrive at Logan Pass in winter.

St. Mary Visitor Center

406/888-7800; 8am-5pm daily late May-early Oct., until 6pm July-mid-Aug.

Located at the St. Mary entrance to Glacier National Park, the St. Mary Visitor Center is the largest visitor center in the park. It houses a bookstore and displays on Indigenous cultural history. Inside the center, find **backcountry permits** (7am-4:30pm daily late May-late Sept.). The theater hosts slide presentations, evening naturalist programs, and the popular Two Medicine Lake Singers and Dancers (tickets required). Astronomy programs that celebrate this International Dark Sky Park take place outdoors, where you can see night sky features from the **St. Mary Observatory** telescope on two high-resolution screens.

Cell Service and Internet

Glacier has very limited cell service reception and public Wi-Fi. Plan to download apps, maps, podcasts, and pdfs you will need before you arrive. Limited cell reception is in Apgar on the southwest end of Lake McDonald (but not around Lake McDonald Lodge) and St. Mary; cell service is not available on most of Going-to-the-Sun Road and Logan Pass. Many Glacier, Two Medicine, and the North Fork also have no cell reception. Limited public Wi-Fi is available at Apgar and St. Mary visitor centers. Guests staying in lodges have access to limited Wi-Fi in lobbies.

TRANSPORTATION

Getting There

From Banff National Park

There are two routes from Banff National Park to Glacier National Park. For the **eastern route,** head east on the Trans-Canada Highway from the town of Banff to Calgary (80 mi/128 km; 90 minutes). From Calgary, head south for 113 mi (181 km) on AB 2 toward Fort Macleod. Continue from Fort Macleod south through Cardston to the Carway-Piegan border crossing (7am-11pm daily year-round). From Calgary to the border takes about 3 hours (165 mi/266 km). After crossing the Canadian-U.S. border onto U.S. 89, drive 25 minutes (19 mi/26 km) to St. Mary for Going-to-the-Sun Road's east entrance. To enter the park at Many Glacier, after crossing the border, drive U.S. 89 to Babb and turn right onto the Many Glacier Road to reach Many Glacier Hotel or Swiftcurrent in 40 minutes (22 mi/35 km). Total drive time from Calgary to Many Glacier or St. Mary is about 4 hours.

For the **western route,** travel south

on BC 93 through Kootenay National Park and British Columbia toward Cranbrook. At 3.7 mi (6 km) before Cranbrook, merge with CA 3 heading 36 mi (58 km) east toward Elko. Take BC 93 south at Elko for 24 mi (39 km) toward Roosville on the Canadian-U.S. border (24 hours daily year-round). After crossing, continue south 63 mi (101 km) on U.S. 93 through Eureka to Whitefish. Drive with caution: Deer frequent the road between Eureka and Whitefish, earning it the nickname "Deer Alley." In downtown Whitefish, U.S. 93 turns south again at the third stoplight. Drive 2 mi (3.2 km) to the junction with MT 40 with signs for Glacier. Turn left onto MT 40, which joins U.S. 2 just before Columbia Falls, and reaches West Glacier. Expect 6.5 hours driving time from Banff.

Gas
Inside the Park
There are **no gas stations** inside the park.

Outside the Park
In West Glacier, gas is available year-round with a credit card at **Glacier Highland** across from the train depot. Two gas stations are in **St. Mary** on U.S. 89, one on either side of the junction with Going-to-the-Sun Road. Babb has a gas station across from Thronson's General Store. **East Glacier,** outside the park southeast of Two Medicine, also has gas stations.

Parking
Apgar and St. Mary Visitor Centers
Two-lane highways and roads dominate the West Glacier and Apgar area. Most roads are paved, although dirt and gravel byways reach river accesses. In Apgar, three small parking lots are in the village, and you can also park at the picnic area and boat dock. The largest parking lot, where RVs will find room, is at Apgar Visitor Center; a paved path connects to the village.

The St. Mary Visitor Center is also a shuttle stop: To avoid parking hassles at Logan Pass, park your car here all day for free and catch the free shuttle up Going-to-the-Sun Road.

Logan Pass
In midsummer, the Logan Pass parking lot fills by 8am. Some parking slots are reserved for one-hour parking for those who just want a quick experience, but the park service controls the entrance, admitting a car only when one departs. If the parking lot is full, forgo Logan Pass for the time being and return later in the day. While pullouts are 0.5 mi (0.8 km) east and west of the pass, the shoulderless road does not afford safe walking to the pass, and tromping across the fragile meadows is taboo.

Trailheads
Popular trailheads pack out with parking by 8am in summer. These include the trailheads at Avalanche, The Loop, Logan Pass, and St. Mary Falls on Going-to-the-Sun Road.

Road Closures
Snow buries the Going-to-the-Sun Road in winter. The usual vehicle closure runs from Lake McDonald Lodge to St. Mary late October-spring.

Some of Glacier's roads can close in summer due to weather or when traffic gets congested. These include Going-to-the-Sun Road and the Many Glacier Road. Use the Recreational Access Display (www.nps.gov/applications/glac/dashboard) to learn the real-time status of the roads.

Shuttles
Going-to-the-Sun Road
406/888-7800; www.nps.gov/glac; 9am-5pm daily July-late Sept.; free
Going-to-the-Sun Road shuttles enable point-to-point hiking on some of Glacier's most spectacular trails. Due to their popularity, waiting lines of an hour or more often form to board. But going car-free to trailheads outweighs disappointments of full parking lots. The shuttles do not come with interpretive guides. The shuttles

CONTINUED ON NEXT PAGE

CONTINUED FROM PREVIOUS PAGE

stop at designated locations: trailheads, campgrounds, picnic areas, lodges, and Logan Pass. Get on or off at any of the stops denoted by interpretive signs, each one featuring a different animal print. For Logan Pass, be sure to take a day pack with water, snacks, and extra clothing for fast-changing weather. Some shuttles also have bike racks, and most are wheelchair-accessible.

On the west side, shuttles depart every 15-30 minutes. For heading east, Avalanche serves as a transfer stop, where you can then board a shuttle to Logan Pass. From Apgar Visitor Center to Logan Pass takes 90 minutes or more; from Avalanche takes 45 minutes or longer. From locations on the Sun Road, you can also take shuttles to Apgar and back.

On the east side, shuttles depart every 30-40 minutes to run between St. Mary Visitor Center and Logan Pass, where you can transfer to west side shuttles for the Lake McDonald Valley. The ride to Logan Pass takes about one hour with stops.

Due to COVID-19 restrictions, shuttles did not operate in summer 2020. But the shuttle system is undergoing change: check online (www.nps.gov/glac) for current status. The shuttle is slated for expansion, adding longer hours, more stops, and maybe a fee.

Many Glacier: Xanterra Shuttle

855/733-4522; www.glaciernational-parklodges.com; 4 times each way daily early June-mid-Sept.; $7-14 one-way, first-come, first-served

Best for connecting with the Going-to-the-Sun Road shuttles, this service for point-to-point hikers on the Highline and Piegan Pass Trails links Many Glacier Hotel and Swiftcurrent Motor Inn with St. Mary Visitor Center.

Two Medicine: Pursuit Shuttle

844/868-7474; www.glacierparkcollection.com; June-Sept.; $15-30 one-way

Pursuit Glacier Park Collection runs shuttles on the east side of the park between St. Mary, Two Medicine, and East Glacier. Make reservations before 24 hours in advance or pay driver in cash when you board.

bear on snowy Going-to-the-Sun Road

West Entrance

Moraine Lake

BANFF
NATIONAL PARK

BANFF NATIONAL PARK ENCOMPASSES SOME OF THE WORLD'S most magnificent scenery. The snowcapped peaks of the Rocky Mountains form a spectacular backdrop for glacial lakes, fast-flowing rivers, and endless forests.

Deer, moose, elk, mountain goats, bighorn sheep, black and grizzly bears, wolves, and cougars inhabit the park's vast wilderness, while the human species is concentrated in the picture-postcard towns of Banff and Lake Louise. The town of Banff is near the park's southeast gate, 80 mi (128 km) west of Calgary. The village of Lake Louise, northwest of Banff along the Trans-Canada Highway, sits close to its namesake lake, which is regarded as one of the seven natural wonders of the world. The lake is rivaled for sheer beauty only by Moraine Lake, down the road. Just north of Lake Louise, the Icefields Parkway begins its spectacular course alongside the Continental Divide to Jasper National Park.

One of the greatest draws of this 2,564-square-mi (6,641-sq-km) park is the accessibility of its natural wonders. Most highlights are close to the road system, but adventurous visitors can follow an excellent network of hiking trails to alpine lakes, along glacial valleys, and to spectacular viewpoints where crowds are scarce and human impact has been minimal.

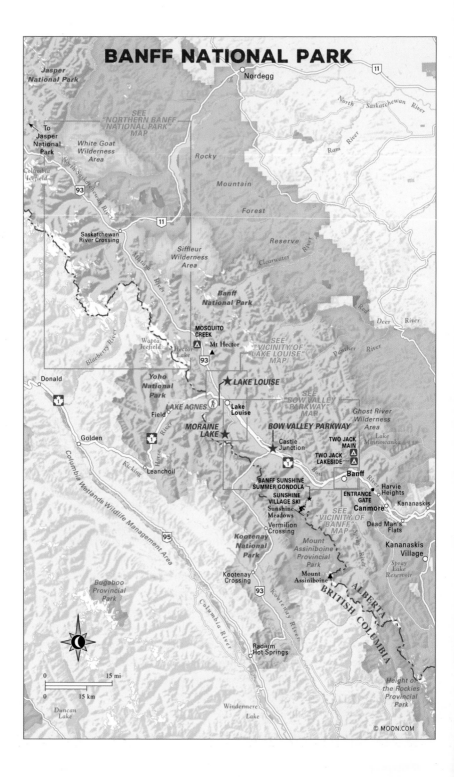

BANFF NATIONAL PARK

Jasper National Park

Nordegg

11

SEE "NORTHERN BANFF NATIONAL PARK" MAP

White Goat Wilderness Area

To Jasper National Park

Columbia Icefield

Rocky

North Saskatchewan River

Ram River

93

North Saskatchewan River

Saskatchewan River Crossing

11

Mountain

Siffleur Wilderness Area

Forest

Reserve

Clearwater River

Red Deer River

Banff National Park

Panther River

MOSQUITO CREEK

SEE "VICINITY OF LAKE LOUISE" MAP

Mt Hector

93

Wapta Icefield

Hector Lake

Blaeberry River

Donald

Yoho National Park

LAKE LOUISE

SEE "BOW VALLEY PARKWAY" MAP

LAKE AGNES

Field

Lake Louise

Ghost River Wilderness Area

Lake Minnewanka

Golden

MORAINE LAKE

BOW VALLEY PARKWAY

Castle Junction

Leanchoil

Kicking Horse River

TWO JACK MAIN

TWO JACK LAKESIDE

Banff

Harvie Heights

BANFF SUNSHINE SUMMER GONDOLA

ENTRANCE GATE

Kananaskis

Columbia Wetlands Wildlife Management Area

95

SUNSHINE VILLAGE SKI

Sunshine Meadows

Canmore

Dead Man's Flats

Vermilion Crossing

Kootenay National Park

Mount Assiniboine Provincial Park

Kananaskis Village

Bugaboo Provincial Park

Kootenay Crossing

Mount Assiniboine

Spray Lake Reservoir

ALBERTA

93

Kootenay River

BRITISH COLUMBIA

Columbia River

Radium Hot Springs

Duncan Lake

Windermere Lake

Height of the Rockies Provincial Park

0   15 mi
0   15 km

© MOON.COM

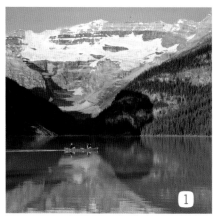

TOP 3

⭐ **1. LAKE LOUISE:** Famous Lake Louise has hypnotized visitors with its beauty for more than 120 years (page 129).

⭐ **2. MORAINE LAKE:** This body of water qualifies as a double must-see, with the deep blue of the lake itself and the glaciated peaks surrounding it (page 134).

⭐ **3. BOW VALLEY PARKWAY:** This scenic drive between Banff and Lake Louise provides views of abundant wildlife and many worthwhile stops (page 135).

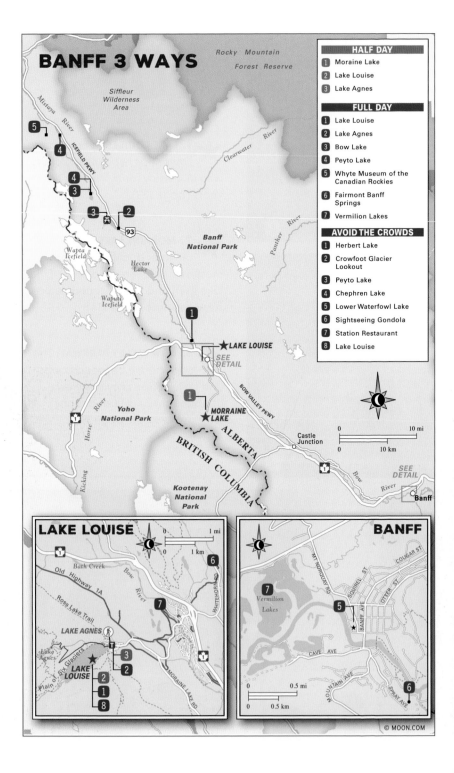

BANFF 3 WAYS

HALF DAY
1. Moraine Lake
2. Lake Louise
3. Lake Agnes

FULL DAY
1. Lake Louise
2. Lake Agnes
3. Bow Lake
4. Peyto Lake
5. Whyte Museum of the Canadian Rockies
6. Fairmont Banff Springs
7. Vermilion Lakes

AVOID THE CROWDS
1. Herbert Lake
2. Crowfoot Glacier Lookout
3. Peyto Lake
4. Chephren Lake
5. Lower Waterfowl Lake
6. Sightseeing Gondola
7. Station Restaurant
8. Lake Louise

Rocky Mountain Forest Reserve

Siffleur Wilderness Area

Mistaya River

ICEFIELD PKWY

Clearwater River

93

Banff National Park

Panther River

Wapta Icefield

Hector Lake

Waputi Icefield

★ LAKE LOUISE

SEE DETAIL

Yoho National Park

Horse River

Kicking Horse River

MORRAINE LAKE

BOW VALLEY PKWY

ALBERTA

BRITISH COLUMBIA

Castle Junction

Bow River

SEE DETAIL

Banff

Kootenay National Park

0   10 mi
0   10 km

LAKE LOUISE

0   1 mi
0   1 km

Bath Creek

Bow River

Old Highway 1A

Ross Lake Trail

WHITEHORN

LAKE AGNES

Lake Agnes

Plain of Six Glaciers

LAKE LOUISE

MORAINE AVE RD

BANFF

Vermilion Lakes

MT NORQUAY RD

COUGAR ST

SQUIRREL ST

OTTER ST

BANFF AVE

CAVE AVE

MOUNTAIN AVE

SPRAY AVE

0   0.5 mi
0   0.5 km

© MOON.COM

BANFF NATIONAL PARK 3 WAYS

HALF DAY

Banff National Park encompasses a large area, so if you only have a half day, concentrate your time on the Lake Louise area, which is under an hour's drive from the town of Banff.

1 The parking lot at **Moraine Lake** is often full well before dawn, but early risers who climb to the top of the Rockpile are rewarded with the first rays of sun hitting one of the world's most beautiful lakes.

2 At nearby **Lake Louise,** a lakeside trail offers the best views, or take to the turquoise waters in a canoe.

3 Afterward, hike to **Lake Agnes** and enjoy tea and muffins at the historic backcountry teahouse.

FULL DAY

1 Rise early and head north from Banff to **Lake Louise** (plan on arriving before 6am to ensure a parking spot), and watch the first rays of light hit the surrounding mountains.

2 Lace up for a three-hour round-trip hike to **Lake Agnes,** where there is a delightful teahouse.

3 Take a one-hour scenic drive up the Icefields Parkway, stopping at **Bow Lake** to enjoy a picnic lunch at the day use area.

4 Continue to the viewpoint at **Peyto Lake** and check out what color it is—its hues change according to season.

5 Return to Banff and wander along bustling Banff Avenue. Explore local history at the **Whyte Museum of the Canadian Rockies.**

6 Enjoy dinner at the iconic **Fairmont Banff Springs** hotel. Dine at the Lookout Patio for wonderful valley views, or splurge at 1888 Chop House.

7 After dinner, take advantage of the long days of summer to enjoy a late evening stroll or drive along **Vermilion Lakes.**

AVOID THE CROWDS

Millions of visitors who descend on Banff National Park every year gravitate to downtown Banff and famous lakes such as Louise and Moraine. In fact, Moraine Lake is so popular that access is closed when the parking lot is full—which is often as early as 5am. An alternative is the itinerary below, around 125 mi (200 km) round-trip from Lake Louise (or 186 mi/300 km from Banff). Make reservations ahead of time for dinner at Station Restaurant in Lake Louise.

1 Strike out early from Banff or Lake Louise heading north along the Icefields Parkway, and make your first stop **Herbert Lake,** a delightful spot that perfectly frames the snowcapped peaks of the Continental Divide.

2 Farther north, stop at the **lookout** for the **Crowfoot Glacier,** with its distinctively shaped glacial claws clinging to the steep slopes of Crowfoot Mountain.

3 Continuing north, **Peyto Lake** is a beautiful body of water backdropped by rugged peaks.

4 Stop near Waterfowl Lakes Campground to access the trailhead for a one-hour each way hike to the glacial waters of **Chephren Lake.**

5 **Lower Waterfowl Lake** is a good turnaround point along the Icefields Parkway. Be sure to admire the lake's beautiful turquoise waters before heading back south toward Lake Louise.

6 Return to Lake Louise by mid-afternoon and you'll have missed most of the crowds riding the **Sightseeing Gondola.**

7 Head to dinner at Lake Louise's **Station Restaurant** to enjoy fine Canadian dining in an elegant setting.

8 End your day with an evening stroll along the shoreline of **Lake Louise.**

walking along the Louise Lakeshore

HIGHLIGHTS

TOWN OF BANFF

Many visitors planning a trip to the national park don't realize that the town of Banff is a bustling commercial center. The town's location is magnificent. It is spread out along the **Bow River,** extending to the lower slopes of Sulphur Mountain to the south and Tunnel Mountain to the east. In one direction is the towering face of Mount Rundle, and in the other, framed by the buildings along Banff Avenue, is Cascade Mountain. Hotels and motels line the north end of Banff Avenue, while a profusion of shops, boutiques, cafés, and restaurants hugs the south end. Also at the south end, just over the Bow River, is the Park Administration Building. Here the road forks—to the right is the historic Cave and Basin Hot Springs, to the left the Fairmont Banff Springs and Banff Gondola. Some people are happy walking along the crowded streets or shopping in a unique setting; those more interested in some peace and quiet can easily slip into pristine wilderness just a five-minute walk from town.

Whyte Museum of the Canadian Rockies

111 Bear St.; 403/762-2291; www. whyte.org; 10am-5pm daily; adult C$10, senior C$9, child C$5

The Whyte Foundation was established in the mid-1950s by local artists Peter and Catharine Whyte to help preserve artistic and historical material relating to the Canadian Rockies. Their Whyte Museum of the Canadian Rockies opened in 1968 and has continued to grow ever since. It now houses the world's largest collection of Canadian Rockies literature and art. Included in the archives are more than 4,000 volumes, oral tapes of early pioneers and outfitters, antique postcards, old cameras, manuscripts, and a large photography collection. The highlight is the photography of Byron Harmon, whose black-and-white studies of mountain geography have shown people around the world the beauty of the Canadian Rockies. The downstairs gallery features changing art exhibitions. The museum also houses the library and archives of the Alpine Club of Canada. On the grounds are several heritage homes and cabins formerly occupied by local pioneers.

MUSEUM TOURS

The Whyte Museum hosts interesting walking tours during the summer. The most popular of these is the **Heritage Homes Tour** (11:30am daily summer; C$10 per person), which allows an opportunity for visitors to take a closer look at the historic residences located among the trees behind the museum, including that of Peter and Catharine Whyte.

Buffalo Nations Luxton Museum

1 Birch Ave.; 403/762-2388; www. buffalonationsmuseum.com; 10am-7pm daily in summer, 11am-5pm daily rest of year; adult C$10, senior C$9, child C$5

Looking like a stockade, the Buffalo Nations Luxton Museum overlooks the Bow River across from Central Park. It is dedicated to the heritage of the First Nations who once inhabited the Canadian Rockies and adjacent prairies. The museum was developed by prominent local resident Norman Luxton in the early 1900s. At that time it was within the Indian Trading Post, an adjacent gift shop that still stands. The museum contains memorabilia from Luxton's lifelong relationship with the Stoney people, including an elaborately decorated tepee, hunting equipment, arrowheads dating back 4,000 years, stuffed animals, original artwork, peace pipes, and traditional clothing. Various aspects of First Nations culture—such as ceremonial gatherings, living in a tepee, and weaving—are also displayed. The Indian Trading Post is one of Banff's more distinctive gift shops and is definitely worth a browse.

Cave and Basin National Historic Site
403/762-1566; 10am-5pm daily summer, noon-4pm Wed.-Sun. rest of year; adult C$7.80, senior C$7, child C$4.80

At the end of Cave Avenue, the Cave and Basin National Historic Site is the birthplace of Banff National Park and of the Canadian National Parks system. Here, in 1883, three men employed by the Canadian Pacific Railway (CPR) stumbled on the hot springs and were soon lounging in the hot water—a real luxury in the Wild West. Bathhouses were installed in 1887, and bathers paid C$0.10 for a swim. Ironically, the soothing minerals in the water that had attracted millions of people to bathe here eventually caused the pools' demise. The minerals, combined with chlorine, produced sediments that ate away at the concrete structure until the pools were deemed unsuitable for swimming in 1993. Although the pools are now closed to swimming, the site is still one of Banff's most popular attractions. A narrow tunnel winds into the dimly lit cave, and short trails lead to the cave entrance and through a unique environment created by the hot water from the springs.

Banff Upper Hot Springs
Mountain Ave.; 403/762-1515; 9am-11pm daily mid-May-mid-Oct., 10am-10pm Sun.-Thurs. and

Banff Avenue

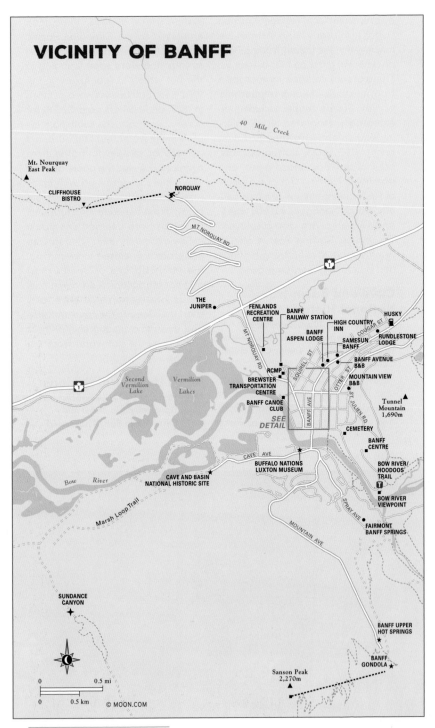

VICINITY OF BANFF

40 Mile Creek

Mt. Nourquay
East Peak

CLIFFHOUSE
BISTRO

NORQUAY

MT. NORQUAY RD

THE
JUNIPER

FENLANDS
RECREATION
CENTRE

BANFF
RAILWAY STATION

HIGH COUNTRY
INN

COUGAR ST

HUSKY

MT NORQUAY RD

BANFF
ASPEN LODGE

SAMESUN
BANFF

RUNDLESTONE
LODGE

BANFF AVENUE
B&B

SQUIRREL ST

MOUNTAIN VIEW
B&B

OTTER ST

RCMP

BREWSTER
TRANSPORTATION
CENTRE

ST. JULIEN RD

Second
Vermilion
Lake

Vermilion
Lakes

BANFF CANOE
CLUB

BANFF AVE

Tunnel
Mountain
1,690m

SEE
DETAIL

CEMETERY

BANFF
CENTRE

CAVE AVE

Bow River

BUFFALO NATIONS
LUXTON MUSEUM

BOW RIVER/
HOODOOS
TRAIL

CAVE AND BASIN
NATIONAL HISTORIC SITE

BOW RIVER
VIEWPOINT

Marsh Loop Trail

SPRAY AVE

FAIRMONT
BANFF SPRINGS

MOUNTAIN AVE

SUNDANCE
CANYON

BANFF UPPER
HOT SPRINGS

N

0   0.5 mi
0   0.5 km
© MOON.COM

Sanson Peak
2,270m

BANFF
GONDOLA

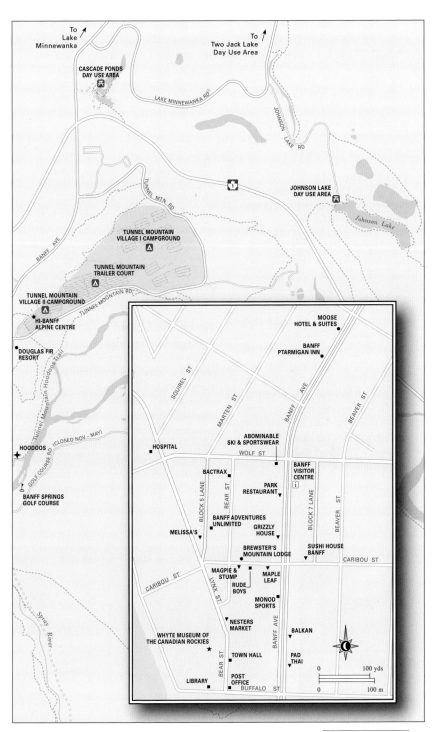

To Lake Minnewanka

To Two Jack Lake Day Use Area

CASCADE PONDS DAY USE AREA

LAKE MINNEWANKA RD

JOHNSON LAKE RD

JOHNSON LAKE DAY USE AREA

Johnson Lake

TUNNEL MTN RD

TUNNEL MOUNTAIN VILLAGE I CAMPGROUND

BANFF AVE

TUNNEL MOUNTAIN TRAILER COURT

TUNNEL MOUNTAIN VILLAGE II CAMPGROUND

TUNNEL MOUNTAIN RD

HI-BANFF ALPINE CENTRE

DOUGLAS FIR RESORT

Tunnel Mountain Hoodoo Trail

HOODOOS

GOLF COURSE RD (CLOSED NOV - MAY)

BANFF SPRINGS GOLF COURSE

Spray River

SQUIREL ST

MARTEN ST

BANFF AVE

BEAVER ST

MOOSE HOTEL & SUITES

BANFF PTARMIGAN INN

ABOMINABLE SKI & SPORTSWEAR

HOSPITAL

WOLF ST

BACTRAX

BEAR ST

BLOCK 5 LANE

PARK RESTAURANT

BANFF VISITOR CENTRE

BLOCK 7 LANE

BEAVER ST

BANFF ADVENTURES UNLIMITED

GRIZZLY HOUSE

MELISSA'S

BREWSTER'S MOUNTAIN LODGE

SUSHI HOUSE BANFF

CARIBOU ST

CARIBOU ST

MAGPIE & STUMP

MAPLE LEAF

LYNX ST

RUDE BOYS

MONOD SPORTS

NESTERS MARKET

BANFF AVE

BALKAN

WHYTE MUSEUM OF THE CANADIAN ROCKIES

BEAR ST

PAD THAI

TOWN HALL

0   100 yds

LIBRARY

POST OFFICE

BUFFALO ST

0   100 m

10am-11pm Fri.-Sat. mid-Oct.-mid-May; C$8 adults, C$6.80 seniors and children

The Banff Upper Hot Springs were first developed in 1901. The present building was completed in 1935, with extensive renovations made in 1996. Water flows out of the bedrock at 116.6°F (47°C) and is cooled to 104°F (40°C) in the main pool.

Banff Gondola

403/762-2523; 8:30am-9pm daily in summer, shorter hours rest of year; adult C$70, child C$35

The easiest way to get high above town without breaking a sweat is on the Banff Gondola. The four-person cars rise 2,300 feet (700 m) in eight minutes to the summit of 7,500-foot (2,285-m) **Sulphur Mountain.** From the observation deck at the upper terminal, the breathtaking view includes the town, the Bow Valley, Cascade Mountain, Lake Minnewanka, and the Fairholme Range. Inside the upper terminal are interactive displays, a theater, and three eateries. Bighorn sheep often hang around below the upper terminal. The short **Sulphur Mountain Boardwalk** leads along a ridge to a restored weather observatory. Between 1903 and 1931, long before the gondola was built, Norman Sanson was the meteorological observer who collected data at the station. During this period he made more than 1,000 ascents of Sulphur Mountain, all in the line of duty.

From downtown, the gondola is 1.9 mi (3 km) south along Mountain Avenue. May-October, **Pursuit** (403/762-6700 or 866/606-6700; www.banffjaspercollection.com) provides free shuttle service to the gondola from downtown hotels.

A 3.4-mi (5.5-km) hiking trail to the summit begins from the Upper Hot Springs parking lot. Although it's a long slog, you have the option of a gondola ride down (C$35 one-way).

Vermilion Lakes

This series of three shallow lakes forms an expansive montane wetland supporting a variety of mammals and more than 200 species of birds. The entire area is excellent for wildlife viewing, especially in winter when it provides habitat for elk, coyotes, and the occasional wolf. Vermilion Lakes Drive, paralleling the Trans-Canada Highway immediately west of Banff,

upper terminal, Banff Gondola (left); Lake Minnewanka (right)

provides the easiest access to the area.

Lake Minnewanka

Minnewanka (Lake of the Water Spirit) is the largest body of water in Banff National Park. Mount Inglismaldie (9,720 ft/2,964 m) and the Fairholme Range form an imposing backdrop. The reservoir was first constructed in 1912, and additional dams were built in 1922 and 1941 to supply hydroelectric power to Banff. Even if you don't feel up to an energetic hike, it's worth parking at the facility area and going for a short walk along the lakeshore. You'll pass a concession selling snacks and drinks along the way, the tour boat dock, and reach an area with picnic tables—the perfect place for a picnic. You should continue farther around the lake, as well—with the added benefit of escaping the crowds. The lake is also great for fishing.

Banff Lake Cruise (403/762-3473; 4-8 times daily late May-early Oct.; adult C$64, child C$32) is a 90-minute cruise to the far reaches of the lake, passing the Devil's Gap formation.

SUNSHINE MEADOWS

Sunshine Meadows, straddling the Continental Divide, is a unique and beautiful region of the Canadian Rockies. It's best known as home to **Sunshine Village,** a self-contained alpine resort accessible only by gondola from the valley floor. But for a few short months each summer, the area is clear of snow and becomes a wonderland for hiking. Large amounts of precipitation create a lush cover of vegetation—over 300 species of wildflowers alone have been recorded here.

From Sunshine Village, trails radiate across the alpine meadow, which is covered in a colorful carpet of fireweed, glacier lilies, mountain avens, white mountain heather, and forget-me-nots (the meadows are in full bloom mid-July-early Aug.). The most popular destination is **Rock Isle Lake,** an easy 1.6-mi (2.5-km) jaunt from the upper village that crosses the Continental

Rock Isle Lake, Sunshine Meadows

YOHO NATIONAL PARK

Yoho, a Cree word that translates to amazement, is a fitting name for this park on the western slopes of the Canadian Rockies.

Its wild and rugged landscape holds spectacular waterfalls, extensive ice fields, a lake to rival those in Banff, and one of the world's most intriguing fossil beds. In addition, you'll find some of the finest hiking in all Canada on the park's 186-mi (300-km) trail system.

The Trans-Canada Highway bisects the 324,450-acre (131,300-ha) park on its run between Lake Louise (Alberta) and Golden (British Columbia). Yoho borders Banff National Park, making it an easy add-on to a Glacier, Banff, and Jasper trip. Unless you're traveling straight through and not stopping or have a Discovery Pass for all of Canada's national parks, you'll need a National Parks Day Pass (adult C$10.20) to visit Yoho.

Within the park are lodges, road-accessible campgrounds, and the small railway town of Field, where you'll find basic services. Yoho is open year-round, although road conditions in winter can be treacherous, and occasional closures occur on Kicking Horse Pass. The road out to Takakkaw Falls is closed through winter, and it often doesn't reopen until late June.

HIGHLIGHTS
Emerald Lake
One of the jewels of the Canadian Rockies, this beautiful lake is surrounded by a forest of Engelmann spruce, as well as many peaks more than 9,840 feet (3,000 m) high. It is covered in ice most of the year but comes alive with activity for a few short months in summer when hikers take advantage of the magnificent surroundings.

Takakkaw Falls
Takakkaw Falls is the most impressive waterfall in the Canadian Rockies. The falls are fed by the Daly and Des Poilus Glaciers of the Waputik Icefield, which straddles the Continental Divide. Meaning "wonderful" in the language of the Cree, Takakkaw tumbles 830 feet (254 m) over a sheer rock wall at the lip of the Yoho Valley, creating a spray bedecked by rainbows. It can be seen from the parking lot, but it's well worth the easy 10-minute stroll over the Yoho River to appreciate the sight in all its glory.

Lake O'Hara
Nestled in a high bowl of lush alpine meadows, Lake O'Hara, 6.8 mi (11 km) from the nearest public road, is surrounded by dozens of smaller alpine lakes and framed by spectacular peaks permanently mantled in snow. The entire area is webbed by a network of hiking trails radiating in all directions, making it the premier hiking region

CONTINUED ON NEXT PAGE

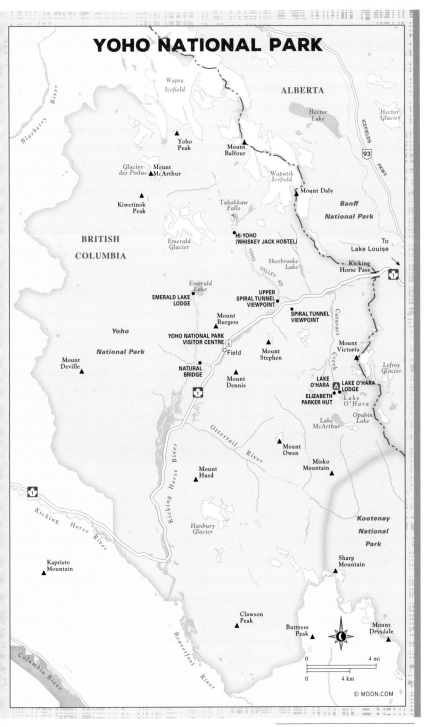

YOHO NATIONAL PARK

Wapta Icefield

ALBERTA

Hector Lake

Hector Glacier

ICEFIELDS

93

▲ Yoho Peak

▲ Mount Balfour

Glacier des Poilus Mount ▲ McArthur

Waputik Icefield

▼ Mount Daly

▲ Kiwetinok Peak

Takakkaw Falls

Banff

National Park

● HI-YOHO (WHISKEY JACK HOSTEL)

Emerald Glacier

BRITISH

COLUMBIA

Emerald Lake

YOHO VALLEY RD

Sherbrooke Lake

To Lake Louise

Kicking Horse Pass

1

EMERALD LAKE LODGE

UPPER SPIRAL TUNNEL VIEWPOINT ■

■ SPIRAL TUNNEL VIEWPOINT

▲ Mount Burgess

YOHO NATIONAL PARK VISITOR CENTRE ℹ

○ Field

▲ Mount Stephen

Cataract Creek

▲ Mount Victoria

Lefroy Glacier

Yoho

National Park

▲ Mount Deville

NATURAL BRIDGE

1

▲ Mount Dennis

LAKE O'HARA ⛺

▲ LAKE O'HARA LODGE

ELIZABETH PARKER HUT

Lake O'Hara

Opabin Lake

Ottertail River

Lake McArthur

▲ Mount Hurd

▲ Mount Owen

Misko Mountain ▲

1

Kicking Horse River

Kicking Horse River

Hanbury Glacier

Kootenay

National

Park

▲ Kapristo Mountain

Sharp Mountain ▲

▲ Clawson Peak

Buttress Peak ▲

Mount Drysdale ▲

Beaverfoot River

Columbia River

0   4 mi

0   4 km

© MOON.COM

in the park. What makes this destination all the more special is that a quota system limits the number of visitors. It's possible to walk to Lake O'Hara, but most visitors take the shuttle bus (www.reservation.pc.gc.ca; mid-June–early Oct.) along a road closed to the public. To book a seat, register online in February for the lottery. Several overnight options are available at the lake, including the **Elizabeth Parker Hut** (403/678-3200; www.alpineclubofcanada.ca), **Lake O'Hara Lodge** (250/343-6418; www.lakeohara.com), and a campground (www.reservation.pc.gc.ca), but each should be booked well in advance.

SCENIC DRIVE

As with all other parks of the Canadian Rockies, you don't need to travel deep into the backcountry to view Yoho's most spectacular features—many are visible from the roadside.

Yoho Valley Road

Fed by the Wapta Icefield in the far north of the park, the **Yoho River** flows through this spectacularly narrow valley, dropping more than 660 feet (200 m) in the last 0.6 mi (1 km) before its confluence with the Kicking Horse River. The road leading up the valley, which is usually open and snow-free by late June, passes the park's main campground, climbs a *very* tight series of switchbacks (watch for buses reversing through the middle section), and emerges at **Upper Spiral Tunnel Viewpoint,** which offers a different perspective on the aforementioned tunnel. A further 0.2 mi (400 m) along the road is a **pullout** for viewing the confluence of the Yoho and Kicking Horse Rivers—a particularly impressive sight as the former is glacier-fed and therefore silty, while the latter is lake-fed and clear. Yoho Valley Road ends 8.7 mi (14 km) from the main highway at **Takakkaw Falls.**

HIKES

Emerald Lake

DISTANCE: 3.2 mi (5.2 km) round-trip
DURATION: 1.5 hours round-trip
ELEVATION GAIN: minimal
RATING: easy
TRAILHEAD: Emerald Lake parking lot, 5.6 mi (9 km) from Highway 1

One of the easiest yet most enjoyable walks in Yoho is around the park's most famous lake. The trail encircles the lake and can be hiked in either direction. The best views are from the western shoreline, where a massive avalanche has cleared away the forest of Engelmann spruce. Across the lake from this point, Mount Burgess can be seen rising an impressive 8,530 feet (2,599 m). Traveling in a clockwise direction, beyond the avalanche slope, the trail to Emerald Basin veers off to the left, crossing a small bridge at the 1.4-mi (2.2-km) mark. Beyond the lake's inlet, the vegetation changes dramatically. A lush forest of towering western red cedar creates a canopy, protecting moss-covered fallen trees, thimbleberry, and bunchberry extending to the water's edge. Just over 0.6 mi (1 km) from the bridge, the trail divides: The left fork leads back to the parking lot via a small forest-encircled pond, or continue straight ahead through the grounds of Emerald Lake Lodge. Park staff lead a guided hike around the lake every Saturday morning, departing at 10am from the parking lot trailhead.

Iceline Trail

DISTANCE: 4 mi (6.4 km) one-way
DURATION: 2.5 hours one-way
ELEVATION GAIN: 2,260 feet (690 m)
RATING: moderate-strenuous
TRAILHEAD: HI-Yoho (Whiskey Jack Hostel); park in the Takakkaw Falls lot across the road from the hostel

The Iceline is one of the most spectacular day hikes in the Canadian Rockies. The length given is from HI-Yoho to the highest point along the trail (7,380 ft/2,250 m). From the hostel, the trail begins a steep and steady 0.6-mi (1-km) climb to a point where two options present themselves: The Iceline Trail is to the right, and Yoho Lake is to the left. After another 20 minutes of walking, the Iceline Trail option enters its highlight—a 2.5-mi (4-km) traverse of a moraine below Emerald Glacier. Views across the valley improve as the trail climbs to its crest and passes a string of small lakes filled with glacial meltwater. Many day hikers return from this point, although officially the trail continues into Little Yoho River Valley.

Opabin Plateau Circuit

DISTANCE: 3.7 mi (5.9 km) round-trip
DURATION: 2 hours round-trip
ELEVATION GAIN: 820 feet (250 m)
RATING: easy-moderate
TRAILHEAD: Shoreline Trail; access via reserved summer shuttle bus (www.reservation.pc.gc.ca)

This plateau high above the tree line and dotted with small lakes is one of the most picturesque destinations in the Canadian Rockies. Two trails lead up to the plateau, which itself is laced with trails. The most direct route is the Opabin Plateau West Circuit, which branches right from the Shoreline Trail 0.2 mi (300 m) beyond Lake O'Hara Lodge. It then passes Mary Lake, climbs steeply, and reaches the plateau in about 1.2 mi (2 km). Opabin Prospect is an excellent lookout along the edge of the plateau. From this point, take the right fork to

CONTINUED ON NEXT PAGE

continue to the head of the cirque and Opabin Lake. This section of trail passes through a lightly forested area of larch that comes alive with color the second week of September. From Opabin Lake, the East Circuit traverses the lower slopes of Yukness Mountain, passing Hungabee Lake, then descending steeply to Lake O'Hara and ending back along the Shoreline Trail 0.4 mi (600 m) east of Lake O'Hara Lodge.

FOOD AND LODGING

Truffle Pigs Bistro

100 Centre St.; 250/343-6303; 8am-10am, and 11pm-9pm daily; C$19-34

In downtown Field, Truffle Pigs Bistro is one of those unexpected finds that make traveling such a joy. In the evening this place really shines, with dishes as meaty as bacon-wrapped beef tenderloin to start and as simple as seared salmon served with local vegetables for a main.

Emerald Lake Lodge

Emerald Lake; 250/343-6321 or 800/663-6336; www.crmr.com; from C$575 s or d

Emerald Lake Lodge is a gracious, luxury-class accommodation along the southern shore of one of the Canadian Rockies' most magnificent lakes. The original lodge was built in 1902 in the same tradition as the Fairmont Chateau Lake Louise and Fairmont Banff Springs—as a playground for wealthy railway travelers. No original buildings remain (although the original framework is used in the main building); instead, guests lap up the luxury of richly decorated duplex-style units and freestanding cabins. Each spacious unit is outfitted in a heritage theme and has a wood-burning fireplace, private balcony, and luxurious bathroom. A restaurant, lounge, and café are on-site.

INFORMATION

The main source of information about the park is the **Yoho National Park Visitor Centre** (250/343-6783 or 250/343-6783; 9am-5pm daily May-mid-Oct., until 7pm daily in summer) on the Trans-Canada Highway at Field. For more information, check out the **Parks Canada** website (www.pc.gc.ca/yoho).

GETTING THERE

The Trans-Canada Highway passes through the heart of Yoho National Park; it's 52 mi (83 km) from the town of Banff to Field. Public transportation to and around the park is limited—you will need to have your own vehicle or a rental. For park road conditions, call 403/762-1450.

Divide while only gaining 330 feet (100 m) of elevation. **Mount Assiniboine** (11,870 ft/3,618 m), known as the "Matterhorn of the Rockies," is easily distinguished to the southeast. Various viewpoints punctuate the descent to an observation point overlooking the lake. From here, options include a loop around **Grizzly and Larix Lakes** (page 142) and a traverse along **Standish Ridge.** If the weather is cooperating, it won't matter which direction you head (so long as it's along a formed trail); you'll experience the Canadian Rockies in all their glory.

It's possible to walk the 3.7-mi (6-km) restricted-access road up to the meadows, but a more practical alternative is to take the **Banff Sunshine Summer Gondola** (403/705-4000; www.banffsunshinemeadows.com; 8am-6pm daily late June-mid-Sept.; adult C$45, senior C$42, child C$23). To get to the base of the gondola from Banff, follow the Trans-Canada Highway 5.6 mi (9 km) west to Sunshine Village Road, which continues a similar distance along Healy Creek to the Sunshine Village parking lot.

JOHNSTON CANYON
Bow Valley Parkway

Johnston Creek drops over a series of spectacular waterfalls here, deep within the chasm it has carved into the limestone bedrock. The canyon is not nearly as deep as Maligne Canyon in Jasper National Park—100 feet (30 m) at its deepest, compared to 165 feet (50 m) at Maligne—but the catwalk that leads to the lower falls has been built through the depths of the canyon rather than along its lip, making it seem just as spectacular. The **lower falls** are 0.6 mi (1 km) from the Bow

the lower falls in Johnston Canyon

Valley Parkway, while the equally spectacular **upper falls** are a farther 1 mi (1.6 km) upstream. Beyond this point are the **Ink Pots,** shallow pools of spring-fed water. While in the canyon, look for fast-moving black swifts zipping through the air.

★ LAKE LOUISE

In summer, about 10,000 visitors per day make the journey from the Bow Valley floor up to Lake Louise, famous for its stunning turquoise coloring. By 9am the tiered parking lot is often full. (During summer, free shuttles operate from the overflow campground along the Trans-Canada Highway east of town.). An alternative to the road is one of two hiking **trails** that begin in the village and end at the public parking lot. From here several paved trails lead to the lake's eastern shore. From these vantage points the dramatic setting can be fully appreciated. The lake is 1.5 mi (2.4 km) long, 1,640 feet (500 m) wide, and up to 295 feet (90 m) deep. Its cold

Lake Louise

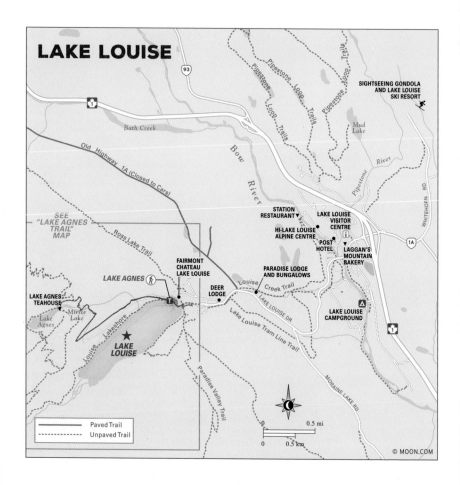

LAKE LOUISE

Paved Trail
Unpaved Trail

© MOON.COM

waters reach a maximum temperature of 39°F (4°C) in August.

Near the **Fairmont Chateau Lake Louise,** which is a tourist attraction in itself, you'll find some of the park's best hiking, canoeing, and horseback riding. The snow-covered peak at the back of the lake is **Mount Victoria** (11,350 ft/3,459 m), which sits on the Continental Divide. Mount Victoria, first climbed in 1897, remains one of the park's most popular peaks for mountaineers. Although the difficult northeast face (facing the château) was first successfully ascended in 1922, the most popular and easiest route

to the summit is along the southeast ridge, approached from Abbot Pass.

Sightseeing Gondola

9am-4pm daily May-Sept., until 5pm in summer; adult C$38, child C$17
During summer, the main ski lift at the **Lake Louise Ski Resort** (403/522-3555 or 877/253-6888; www.skilouise.com) whisks visitors up the face of Mount Whitehorn to Whitehorn Lodge in either open chairs or enclosed gondola cars. At an altitude of more than 1.2 mi (2 km) above sea level, the view from the top—across the Bow Valley, Lake Louise, and the

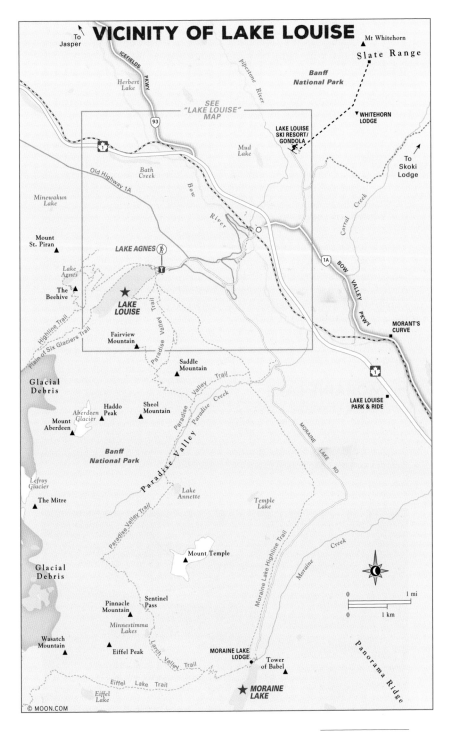

VICINITY OF LAKE LOUISE

To Jasper

ICEFIELDS PKWY

Herbert Lake

93

Pipestone River

SEE "LAKE LOUISE" MAP

Mud Lake

Banff National Park

Mt Whitehorn

Slate Range

LAKE LOUISE SKI RESORT/ GONDOLA

WHITEHORN LODGE

To Skoki Lodge

Old Highway 1A

Bath Creek

Bow River

1A

BOW VALLEY PKWY

Corral Creek

Minewakun Lake

Mount St. Piran

LAKE AGNES

Lake Agnes

The Beehive

Highline Trail

Plain of Six Glaciers Trail

★ LAKE LOUISE

Fairview Mountain

Paradise Valley Trail

Saddle Mountain

Paradise Valley Trail

MORANT'S CURVE

1

LAKE LOUISE PARK & RIDE

Glacial Debris

Aberdeen Glacier

Haddo Peak

Sheol Mountain

Mount Aberdeen

Banff National Park

Paradise Valley

Paradise Creek

Paradise Valley Trail

MORAINE LAKE RD

Lefroy Glacier

The Mitre

Lake Annette

Temple Lake

Moraine Lake Highline Trail

Moraine Creek

Glacial Debris

Mount Temple

Moraine Creek

Pinnacle Mountain

Sentinel Pass

Minnestimma Lakes

Larch Valley Trail

N

0   1 mi
0   1 km

Wasatch Mountain

Eiffel Peak

Eiffel Lake Trail

Eiffel Lake

MORAINE LAKE LODGE

Tower of Babel

★ MORAINE LAKE

Panorama Ridge

© MOON.COM

Continental Divide—is among the most spectacular in the Canadian Rockies. Short trails lead through the forests, across open meadows, and, for the energetic, to the summit of Mount Whitehorn, more than 1,970 vertical feet (600 vertical m) above. Visitors are free to walk these trails, but it pays to join a **guided walk** if you'd like to learn about the surrounding environment. After working up an appetite (and working off breakfast), head to the teahouse in the **Whitehorn Lodge,** try the outdoor barbecue, or, back at the base area, enjoy lunch at the **Lodge of the Ten Peaks,** the resort's impressive post-and-beam day lodge. Ride-and-dine packages are an excellent deal: Pay an extra few dollars and have a buffet breakfast (8am-11am) included with the gondola ride. Free shuttles run from Lake Louise accommodations to the day lodge.

★ MORAINE LAKE

Although less than half the size of Lake Louise, Moraine Lake is just as spectacular and worthy of just as much time. It is up a winding road 8 mi (13 km) off Lake Louise Drive. Its rugged setting, nestled in the Valley of the Ten Peaks among the towering mountains of the main ranges, has provided inspiration for millions of people around the world. Despite its name, the lake was not dammed by a glacial moraine; in fact, the large rock pile that blocks its waters was deposited by major rockfalls from the Tower of Babel to the south.

The lake often remains frozen until June, and the access road is closed all winter. A trail leads along the lake's northern shore, and canoes are rented for C$120 per hour from the concession below **Moraine Lake Lodge.** Climb onto the **Rockpile** beyond the parking lot for the most magnificent lake-and-mountain view you could possibly imagine.

Parking at Moraine Lake is even more limited than at Lake Louise. If you arrive at the beginning of the Moraine Lake Road after 6am most days, expect the road to be closed until vehicles begin leaving. This bears repeating: If you want to see Moraine Lake during July and August, arrive before 6am or park at the Lake Louise Park & Ride lot and take the shuttle.

Moraine Lake

SCENIC DRIVES

★ BOW VALLEY PARKWAY

DRIVING DISTANCE: 32 mi (51 km) one-way
DRIVING TIME: 1 hour one-way
START: Banff
END: Lake Louise

Two roads link Banff to Lake Louise. The Trans-Canada Highway is the quicker route and more popular with through traffic. The other is the more scenic 32-mi (51-km) Bow Valley Parkway, which branches off the Trans-Canada Highway 3.1 mi (5 km) west of Banff. Cyclists will appreciate this paved road's two long, divided sections and low speed limit (37 mph/60 kph). Along this route are several impressive viewpoints,

picnic areas, good hiking, lodges, campgrounds, and one of the park's best restaurants. Between March and late June, the southern end of the parkway (as far north as Johnston Canyon) is closed 6pm-9am daily for the protection of wildlife.

As you enter the parkway, you pass a short side road to creekside **Fireside** picnic area. At **Backswamp Viewpoint,** you can look upstream to the site of a former dam, now a swampy wetland filled with aquatic vegetation. Farther along the road is another wetland at **Muleshoe.** Across the parkway is a 0.6-mi (1-km) trail that climbs to a viewpoint overlooking the valley. (The slope around this trail is infested with wood ticks during late spring and early summer,

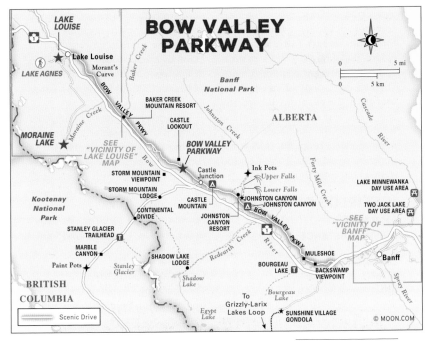

so be sure to check yourself carefully after hiking in this area.) To the east, **Hole-in-the-Wall** is visible. This large-mouthed cave was created by the Bow Glacier, which once filled the valley.

Beyond Muleshoe the road inexplicably divides for a few car lengths. The road then passes through particularly hilly terrain, part of a massive rockslide that occurred approximately 8,000 years ago. The parkway also goes past **Johnston Canyon,** notable for its waterfalls and inkpots, and the former site of the 1800s boomtown **Silver City.**

Beyond Silver City, the aptly named **Castle Mountain** comes into view. It's one of the park's most recognizable peaks and most interesting geographical features. The road skirts the base of the mountain, passes **Castle Junction** (with gas, groceries, and accommodations), and climbs a small hill to **Storm Mountain Viewpoint,** which provides more stunning views and a picnic area. The next commercial facility is **Baker Creek Mountain Resort** (403/522-3761), where the mountain-style restaurant is an excellent spot for a meal. Then it's on to another viewpoint at **Morant's Curve,** from where rail line, river, and mountains combine for perfect symmetry. After passing another picnic area, the Bow Valley Parkway rejoins the Trans-Canada Highway at Lake Louise.

ICEFIELDS PARKWAY (BANFF)

DRIVING DISTANCE: 76 mi (122 km) one-way
DRIVING TIME: 2 hours one-way
START: Lake Louise
END: Sunwapta Pass

The 143-mi (230-km) Icefields Parkway, between Lake Louise and Jasper, is one of the most scenic, exciting, and inspiring mountain roads ever built. From Lake Louise this paved route parallels the Continental Divide, following in the shadow of the highest, most rugged mountains in the region. The first 76 mi (122 km) to Sunwapta Pass (the boundary between Banff and Jasper National Parks) can be driven in two hours, and the entire parkway in four hours. But it's likely you'll want to spend at least a day, probably more, stopping at each of the 13 viewpoints, hiking the trails, watching the abundant wildlife, and just generally enjoying one of the world's most magnificent landscapes. Along the section within Banff National Park are two lodges, three hostels, three campgrounds, and one gas station.

Although the road is steep and winding in places, it has a wide shoulder, making it ideal for an extended bike trip. Allow seven days to pedal north from Banff to Jasper, staying at hostels or camping along the route. This is the preferable direction to travel by bike because the elevation at the town of Jasper is more than 1,640 feet (500 m) lower than either Banff or Lake Louise.

The parkway remains open year-round, although winter brings with it some special considerations. The road is often closed for short periods for avalanche control. Check road conditions in Banff or Lake Louise before setting out. And be sure to fill up with gas; no services are available between November and April.

Lake Louise to Crowfoot Glacier
The Icefields Parkway forks right from the Trans-Canada Highway just north of Lake Louise. The impressive

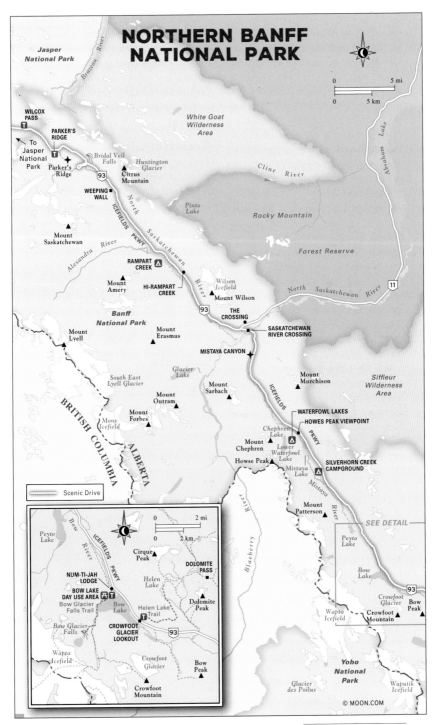

NORTHERN BANFF NATIONAL PARK

Jasper National Park

WILCOX PASS

To Jasper National Park

PARKER'S RIDGE

Parker's Ridge

Bridal Veil Falls

Cirrus Mountain

Huntington Glacier

WEEPING WALL

ICEFIELDS PKWY

Mount Saskatchewan

North Saskatchewan River

Alexandra River

White Goat Wilderness Area

Cline River

Pinto Lake

Rocky Mountain

Forest Reserve

Abraham Lake

0   5 mi
0   5 km

RAMPART CREEK

HI-RAMPART CREEK

Mount Amery

Wilson Icefield

Mount Wilson

THE CROSSING

SASKATCHEWAN RIVER CROSSING

North Saskatchewan River

11

Banff National Park

Mount Lyell

Mount Erasmus

MISTAYA CANYON

Glacier Lake

Mount Murchison

Siffleur Wilderness Area

South East Lyell Glacier

Mount Outram

Mount Sarbach

Mount Forbes

Mons Icefield

Chephren Lake

WATERFOWL LAKES

HOWES PEAK VIEWPOINT

Mount Chephren

Lower Waterfowl Lake

Howse Peak

Mistaya Lake

SILVERHORN CREEK CAMPGROUND

ICEFIELDS PKWY

Mount Patterson

Mistaya River

SEE DETAIL

Peyto Lake

Bow Lake

93

BRITISH COLUMBIA

ALBERTA

Blaeberry River

Crowfoot Glacier

Crowfoot Mountain

Bow Peak

Scenic Drive

0   2 mi
0   2 km

Peyto Lake

Bow River

ICEFIELDS PKWY

Cirque Peak

DOLOMITE PASS

NUM-TI-JAH LODGE

Helen Lake

BOW LAKE DAY USE AREA

Bow Glacier Falls Trail

Bow Lake

Helen Lake Trail

Dolomite Peak

CROWFOOT GLACIER LOOKOUT

Bow Glacier Falls

93

Wapta Icefield

Crowfoot Glacier

Crowfoot Mountain

Bow Peak

Yoho National Park

Glacier des Poilus

Waputik Icefield

© MOON.COM

scenery begins immediately. Just 1.9 mi (3 km) from the junction is **Herbert Lake,** formed during the last ice age when retreating glaciers deposited a pile of rubble, known as a *moraine,* across a shallow valley and water filled in behind it. The lake is a perfect place for early-morning or early-evening photography, when the Waputik Range and distinctively shaped **Mount Temple** are reflected in its waters.

Traveling north, you'll notice numerous depressions in the steep, shaded slopes of the Waputik Range across the Bow Valley. The cooler climate on these north-facing slopes makes them prone to glaciation. Cirques were cut by small local glaciers. On the opposite side of the road, **Mount Hector** (11,130 ft/3,394 m), easily recognized by its layered peak, soon comes into view.

Hector Lake Viewpoint is 10 mi (16 km) from the junction. Although the lake itself is a long way from the highway, the emerald-green waters nestled below a massive wall of limestone form a breathtaking scene. **Bow Peak,** seen looking northward along the highway, is only 9,410 feet (2,868 m) high but is completely detached from the Waputik Range, making it a popular destination for climbers.

Crowfoot Glacier

The aptly named Crowfoot Glacier can best be appreciated from a lookout 10.6 mi (17 km) north of Hector Lake. The glacier sits on a wide ledge near the top of Crowfoot Mountain, from where its glacial claws cling to the mountain's steep slopes. The retreat of this glacier has been dramatic. In the 1960s, two of the claws extended to the base of the lower cliff. Today they are a shadow of their former selves, barely reaching over the cliff edge.

Bow Lake

The sparkling, translucent waters of Bow Lake are among the most beautiful that can be seen from the Icefields Parkway. The lake was

Bow Lake

created when moraines deposited by retreating glaciers dammed subsequent meltwater. On still days, the water reflects the snowy peaks, their sheer cliffs, and the scree slopes that run into the lake. At the southeast end of the lake, a day-use area offers waterfront picnic tables and a trail to a swampy area at the lake's outlet. At the upper end of the lake, you'll find the historic **Num-ti-jah Lodge** and the trailhead for a walk to **Bow Glacier Falls.**

The road leaves Bow Lake and climbs to **Bow Summit.** As you look back toward the lake, its true turquoise color becomes apparent, and the Crowfoot Glacier reveals its unique shape. At an elevation of 6,790 feet (2,069 m), this pass is one of the highest points crossed by a public road in Canada. It is also the beginning of the **Bow River,** the one you may have camped beside at Lake Louise or photographed flowing through the town of Banff.

Peyto Lake

From the parking lot at Bow Summit, a paved trail leads 0.3 mi (500 m) to one of the most breathtaking views you could ever imagine. Far below the viewpoint is Peyto Lake, an impossibly intense green lake whose hues change according to season. Before heavy melting of nearby glaciers begins (in June or early July), the lake is dark blue. As summer progresses, meltwater flows across a delta and into the lake. This water is laden with finely ground particles of rock debris known as rock flour, which remains suspended in the water. It is not the mineral content of the rock flour that is responsible for the lake's unique color, but rather the particles reflecting the blue-green sector of the light spectrum.

As the amount of suspended rock flour changes, so does the color of the lake.

The lake is one of many park landmarks named for early outfitter Bill Peyto. In 1898, Peyto was part of an expedition camped at Bow Lake. Seeking solitude (as he was wont to do), he slipped off during the night to sleep near this lake. Other members of the party coined the name Peyto's Lake, and it stuck.

Beside the Continental Divide

From Bow Summit, the parkway descends to a viewpoint directly across the Mistaya River from **Mount Patterson** (10,490 ft/3,197 m). Snowbird Glacier clings precariously to the mountain's steep northeast face, and the mountain's lower, wooded slopes are heavily scarred where rock and ice slides have swept down the mountainside.

As the parkway continues to descend and crosses Silverhorn Creek, the jagged limestone peaks of the Continental Divide can be seen to the west. **Mistaya Lake** is a 1.9-mi-long (3-km-long) body of water that sits at the bottom of the valley between the road and the divide, but it can't be seen from the parkway. The best place to view it is from the **Howse Peak Viewpoint** at Upper Waterfowl Lake. From here the high ridge that forms the Continental Divide is easily distinguishable.

To Saskatchewan River Crossing

A trail leads down to the swampy shore of **Upper Waterfowl Lake,** providing one of the park's best opportunities to view moose, which feed on the abundant aquatic vegetation. Rock and other debris that have been carried down nearby valley systems have built up, forming a wide alluvial fan, nearly blocking the Mistaya River and creating Upper Waterfowl Lake. **Lower Waterfowl Lake** gets all the attention for its beautiful turquoise hue. Continuing north is **Mount Murchison** (10,950 ft/3,337 m), on the east side of the parkway. Although not one of the park's highest mountains, this gray and yellow massif of Cambrian rock comprises 10 individual peaks, covering an area of 7,400 acres (3,000 ha).

From a parking lot 8.9 mi (14 km) northeast of Waterfowl Lakes Campground, a short trail descends into the montane forest to **Mistaya Canyon.** Here the effects of erosion can be appreciated as the Mistaya River leaves the floor of Mistaya Valley, plunging through a narrow-walled canyon into the North Saskatchewan Valley. The area is scarred with potholes where boulders have been whirled around by the action of fast-flowing water, carving deep depressions into the softer limestone bedrock below.

The **North Saskatchewan River** posed a major problem for early travelers and later for the builders of the Icefields Parkway. This swift-running river eventually drains into Hudson Bay. At 0.6 mi (1 km) past the bridge, you'll come to a panoramic **viewpoint** of the entire valley. From here the Howse and Mistaya Rivers can be seen converging with the North Saskatchewan at a silt-laden delta. This is also a junction with Highway 11 (also known as David Thompson Highway), which heads east, following the North Saskatchewan River. From this viewpoint, numerous peaks can be seen to the west. Two sharp peaks are distinctive: **Mount Outram** (10,680 ft/3,254 m) is the closer; the farther is **Mount Forbes** (11,975 ft/3,630 m), the highest peak in Banff National Park.

To Sunwapta Pass

On the north side of the North Saskatchewan River is the towering hulk of **Mount Wilson** (10,700 ft/3,261 m), named for Banff outfitter Tom Wilson. The Icefields Parkway passes this massif on its western flanks. A **pullout** just past Rampart Creek Campground offers good views of **Mount Amery** to the west and **Mounts Sarbach, Chephren,** and **Murchison** to the south. Beyond here is the **Weeping Wall,** a long cliff of gray limestone where a series of waterfalls tumbles more than 330 feet (100 m) down the steep slopes of **Cirrus Mountain.** In winter this wall of water freezes, becoming a mecca for ice climbers.

After ascending quickly, the road drops again before beginning a long climb to Sunwapta Pass. Halfway up the 1,180-vertical-foot (360-vertical-m) climb is a **viewpoint** well worth a stop (cyclists will definitely appreciate a rest). From here views extend down the valley to the slopes of **Mount Saskatchewan** and, on the other side of the parkway, Cirrus Mountain. Another **viewpoint,** farther up the road, has the added attraction of a view of **Bridal Veil Falls** across the valley.

A cairn at **Sunwapta Pass** (6,640 ft/2,023 m) marks the boundary between Banff and Jasper National Parks. It also marks the divide between the North Saskatchewan and Sunwapta Rivers, whose waters drain into the Atlantic and Arctic Oceans, respectively.

BEST HIKES

TOWN OF BANFF
Bow River/Hoodoos
DISTANCE: 3 mi (4.8 km) one-way
DURATION: 1-1.5 hours one-way
ELEVATION GAIN: minimal
RATING: easy
TRAIL SURFACE: unpaved
TRAILHEAD: Bow River Viewpoint, Tunnel Mountain Drive

From a viewpoint famous for its Fairmont Banff Springs outlook, the trail descends to the Bow River, passing under the sheer east face of Tunnel Mountain. It then follows the river a short distance before climbing into a meadow where deer and elk often graze. From this perspective the north face of Mount Rundle is particularly imposing. As the trail climbs, you'll hear the traffic on Tunnel Mountain Road long before you see it. The trail ends at a viewpoint above the hoodoos, strange-looking limestone-and-gravel columns jutting mysteriously out of the forest. An alternative to returning the same way is to catch the Banff Transit bus (every half hour; C$2) from Tunnel Mountain Campground.

BETWEEN BANFF AND LAKE LOUISE
Bourgeau Lake
DISTANCE: 4.7 mi (7.6 km) one-way
DURATION: 2.5 hours one-way
ELEVATION GAIN: 2,400 feet (730 m)
EFFORT: moderate
TRAIL SURFACE: unpaved
TRAILHEAD: signposted parking lot, Trans-Canada Highway, 1.9 mi (3 km) west of Sunshine Village Junction

This trail follows Wolverine Creek to a small subalpine lake nestled at the base of an impressive limestone amphitheater. Although the trail is moderately steep, plenty of distractions along the way are worthy of a stop (and rest). Back across the Bow Valley, the Sawback Range is easy to distinguish. As the forest of lodgepole pine turns to spruce, the trail passes under the cliffs of Mount Bourgeau

Bourgeau Lake

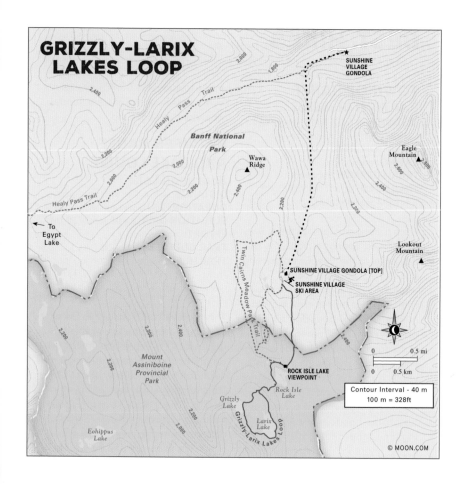

GRIZZLY-LARIX LAKES LOOP

SUNSHINE VILLAGE GONDOLA

Healy Pass Trail

Banff National Park

Wawa Ridge

Eagle Mountain

Healy Pass Trail

To Egypt Lake

Lookout Mountain

Twin Cairns Meadow Park Trail

SUNSHINE VILLAGE GONDOLA [TOP]

SUNSHINE VILLAGE SKI AREA

Mount Assiniboine Provincial Park

ROCK ISLE LAKE VIEWPOINT

Grizzly Lake

Rock Isle Lake

Larix Lake

Grizzly-Larix Lakes Loop

Eohippus Lake

0   0.5 mi
0   0.5 km

Contour Interval - 40 m
100 m = 328ft

© MOON.COM

and crosses Wolverine Creek (below a spot where it tumbles photogenically over exposed bedrock). After strenuous switchbacks, the trail climbs into the cirque containing Bourgeau Lake. As you explore the lake's rocky shore, you'll hear the colonies of noisy pikas, even if you don't see them.

Grizzly-Larix Lakes Loop
DISTANCE: 5.3 mi (8.5 km) round-trip
DURATION: 3 hours round-trip
ELEVATION GAIN: 350 feet (105 m)
EFFORT: easy-moderate
TRAIL SURFACE: unpaved

TRAILHEAD: Sunshine Village, reached by gondola from the valley floor 11 mi (18 km) from the town of Banff

The trail that loops around Grizzly and Larix Lakes is the most popular half-day outing in the **Sunshine Meadows** region. Following a broad gravel track from the center of Sunshine Village, you make a steady but brief climb to the Great Divide, passing through the last scattered stands of alpine fir into a treeless alpine landscape. On the 7,560-foot (2,305-m) summit, views stretch south

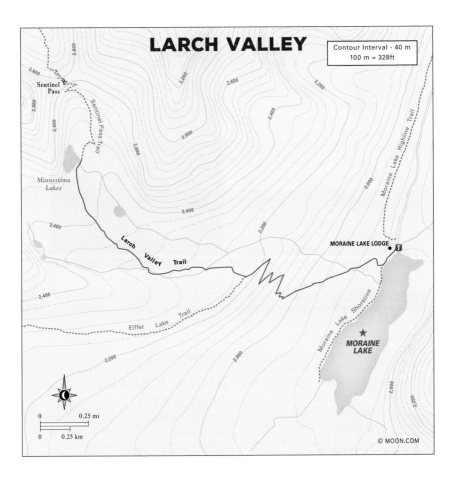

LARCH VALLEY

Contour Interval - 40 m
100 m = 328ft

Sentinel Pass

Sentinel Pass Trail

Minnestima Lakes

Larch Valley Trail

Eiffel Lake Trail

Moraine Lake Highline Trail

MORAINE LAKE LODGE

Moraine Lake Shoreline

★ MORAINE LAKE

0   0.25 mi

0   0.25 km

© MOON.COM

across the vast Sunshine Meadows to the distant pyramid of Mount Assiniboine. West of the divide, you descend to **Rock Isle Lake viewpoint,** one of the most photogenic scenes in the region. From this point, the trail climbs over a low, rocky hill to where the lake's outlet stream plunges down steep limestone slabs, and then drops through open forest and lush meadows filled with wildflowers. Soon the trail splits to begin a 1.5-mi (2.5-km) loop around Grizzly and Larix Lakes. Keep right and descend to Grizzly Lake. From the lake's inlet bridge, the trail turns left

and contours the lip of the basin to a fine viewpoint over the Simpson Valley. Larix, the larger of the two lakes, is just beyond the viewpoint.

Larch Valley
DISTANCE: 1.8 mi (2.9 km) one-way
DURATION: 1 hour one-way
ELEVATION GAIN: 1,310 feet (400 m)
EFFORT: moderate
TRAIL SURFACE: unpaved
TRAILHEAD: Moraine Lake, 8 mi (13 km) from Lake Louise Drive

In mid- to late September, when the larch trees have turned a magnificent gold and the sun is shining, few spots can match the beauty of this valley, but don't expect to find much solitude. Although the most popular time for visiting the valley is fall, it is a worthy destination all summer, when the open meadows are filled with colorful wildflowers. The trail begins just past Moraine Lake Lodge and climbs fairly steeply, with occasional glimpses of Moraine Lake below. After reaching the junction of the Eiffel Lake Trail, keep right, passing through an open forest of larch and into the meadow beyond. The range of larch is restricted within the park, and this is one of the few areas where they are prolific. Mount Fay (10,615 ft/3,235 m) is the dominant peak on the skyline, rising above the other mountains that make up the Valley of the Ten Peaks. Continue up a further 0.6 mi (1 km) to the two Minnestimma Lakes, where views back to the Ten Peaks are unforgettable. Due to the risk of human–wildlife conflicts in Larch Valley, there is often a restriction on this trail requiring hikers to be in groups of four or more.

Larch Valley

mountaineer James Outram once described as "a gem of composition and of coloring ... perhaps unrivalled anywhere."

ALONG ICEFIELDS PARKWAY
Helen Lake
DISTANCE: 3.7 mi (6 km) one-way
DURATION: 2.5 hours one-way
ELEVATION GAIN: 1,500 feet (455 m)
EFFORT: moderate
TRAIL SURFACE: unpaved
TRAILHEAD: across the Icefields Parkway from Crowfoot Glacier Lookout, 20 mi (33 km) northwest of the junction with the Trans-Canada Highway

The trail to Helen Lake is one of the easiest ways to access a true alpine environment from any highway within the park. The trail climbs steadily through a forest of Engelmann spruce and subalpine fir for the first 1.6 mi (2.5 km) to an avalanche slope, reaching the tree line and the first good viewpoint after 1.9 mi (3 km). The view across the valley is

LAKE LOUISE
Louise Lakeshore
DISTANCE: 1.2 mi (2 km) one-way
DURATION: 30 minutes one-way
ELEVATION GAIN: none
EFFORT: easy
TRAIL SURFACE: paved
TRAILHEAD: Lake Louise, 2.5 mi (4 km) from Trans-Canada Highway

Probably the busiest trail in all the Canadian Rockies, this one follows the north shore of Lake Louise from in front of the château to the west end of the lake. Here numerous braided glacial streams empty their silt-filled waters into Lake Louise. Along the trail's length are benches for sitting and pondering what English

Helen Lake trail (left); Bow Glacier Falls (right)

spectacular, with Crowfoot Glacier visible to the southwest. As the trail reaches a ridge, it turns sharply and passes through extensive meadows of wildflowers that are at their peak in late July and early August. The trail then crosses a stream and climbs to the glacial cirque where Helen Lake lies. Listen and look for hoary marmots along the last section of trail and around the lakeshore.

For those with the time and energy, it's possible to continue an additional 1.9 mi (3 km) to Dolomite Pass; the trail switchbacks steeply up a farther 330 vertical feet (100 vertical m) in less than 0.6 mi (1 km), then descends for a farther 0.6 mi (1 km) to Katherine Lake and beyond to the pass.

Bow Glacier Falls
DISTANCE: 2.1 mi (3.4 km) one-way
DISTANCE: 1 hour one-way
ELEVATION GAIN: 430 feet (130 m)
EFFORT: easy
TRAIL SURFACE: unpaved
TRAILHEAD: Num-ti-jah Lodge, Bow Lake, 22.3 mi (36 km) northwest of the Trans-Canada Highway

This hike skirts one of the most beautiful lakes in the region before ending at a narrow but spectacular waterfall. From the public parking lot in front of Num-ti-jah Lodge, follow the shore through to a gravel outwash area at the northwest end of the lake. Across the lake are reflected views of Crowfoot Mountain. The trail then begins a short but steep climb up the rim of a canyon before leveling out at the edge of a vast moraine of gravel, scree, and boulders. Pick your way through the 0.5 mi (800 m) of rough ground that remains to reach the base of Bow Glacier Falls. (The namesake glacier can be seen above the falls from the trailhead, but not from the falls themselves.)

Parker's Ridge
LENGTH: 1.5 mi (2.4 km) one-way
DURATION: 1 hour one-way
ELEVATION GAIN: 690 feet (210 m)
RATING: easy-moderate
TRAIL SURFACE: unpaved
TRAILHEAD: Icefields Parkway, 2.5 mi (4 km) south of Sunwapta Pass

From the trailhead on the west side of the highway, this wide path gains elevation quickly through open meadows and scattered stands of subalpine fir. This fragile environment is easily destroyed, so it's important that you stay on the trail. During the short alpine summer, these meadows are carpeted

TOP HIKE
LAKE AGNES

DISTANCE: 2.2 mi (3.6 km) one-way
DURATION: 1.5 hours one-way
ELEVATION GAIN: 1,312 feet (400 m)
EFFORT: moderate
TRAIL SURFACE: unpaved
TRAILHEAD: Lake Louise

This moderately strenuous hike is one of the park's most popular. It begins in front of the château, branching right near the beginning of the Louise

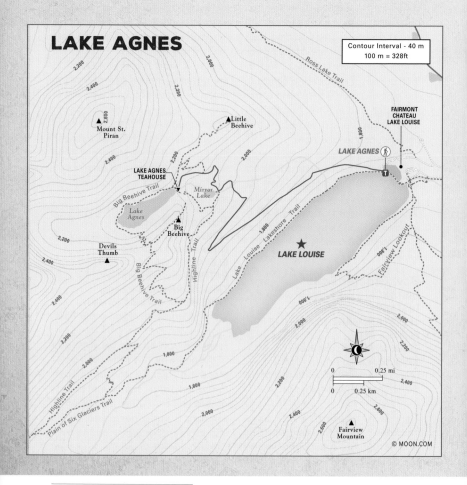

Lakeshore Trail. For the first 1.6 mi (2.5 km), the trail climbs steeply, switch-backing through a forest of subalpine fir and Engelmann spruce, crossing a horse trail, passing a lookout, and leveling out at tiny **Mirror Lake.** Here the old, traditional trail veers right (use it if the ground is wet or snowy), while a more direct route veers left to the **Plain of the Six Glaciers.** The final elevation gain along both trails is made easier by a flight of steps beside **Bridal Veil Falls.** The trail ends at its namesake subalpine lake, which is nestled in a hanging valley. It's also where you'll find the rustic **Lake Agnes Teahouse** (8am-5pm daily June-Sept.; cash only), which offers homemade soups, healthy sandwiches, and a wide assortment of teas.

From the teahouse, a 0.6-mi (1-km) trail leads to **Little Beehive** and impressive views of the Bow Valley. Another trail leads around the northern shore of Lake Agnes, climbing to **Big Beehive.**

with red heather, white mountain avens, and blue alpine forget-me-nots. From the summit of the ridge, you look down on the 1.2-mi-wide (2-km-wide) **Saskatchewan Glacier** spreading out below.

BACKPACKING

For those with relevant experience, heading into the backcountry of Banff National Park is a great way to escape the crowds encountered on day hikes. One of the most popular regions for a backcountry trip is **Egypt Lake,** a 7.5-mi (12-km) walk from the nearest road. Here you'll find a campground and covered shelter, from where trails lead to alpine lakes and passes high above the treeline. If you are not equipped for backcountry travel, lodges at Shadow Lake and the Skoki Valley provide the opportunity for everyone to visit these regions.

If you are planning an overnight camping trip into the backcountry, you *must* purchase a **backcountry camping permit** through the **Parks Canada Campground Reservation Service** (877/737-3783; www.reservation.pc.gc.ca; C$10 per person per night).

SHADOW LAKE
LENGTH: 8.9 mi (14.3 km) one-way
TRAILHEAD: Redearth Creek Parking Area, Trans-Canada Highway, 6.8 mi (11 km) west of Sunshine Village Junction

Shadow is one of the many impressive subalpine lakes along the Continental Divide and, for those staying at **Shadow Lake Lodge** (403/678-3200; www.shadowlakelodge.com; mid-June-Sept.; starting at C$400 s, C$730 d) or the backcountry campground, a popular base for day trips. The trail follows an abandoned fire road for 6.8 mi (11 km) before forking right and climbing into the forest. The campground is 1.2 mi (2 km) beyond this junction, and just 0.2 mi (300 m) farther is Shadow Lake Lodge. The lake is nearly 1.2 mi (2 km) long, and from its eastern shore trails lead to Ball Pass, Gibbon Pass, and Haiduk Lake.

SKOKI VALLEY
LENGTH:8.9 mi (14.3 km) one-way
TRAILHEAD: end of Fish Creek Road, off Whitehorn Road 1.1 mi (1.8 km) north of Lake Louise interchange

The trail into historic **Skoki Lodge** (403/256-8473 or 800/258-7669; www.skoki.com; late June-early Oct. and late Dec.-mid-Apr.; starting at C$240 pp) is only one of the endless

Shadow Lake Lodge

hiking opportunities tucked behind the Lake Louise winter resort. The first 2.1 mi (3.4 km) of the trail are along a gravel access road leading to Temple Lodge, part of the Lake Louise winter resort. Guests of Skoki Lodge ride a shuttle for this first stretch, lessening the hiking distance to 6.8 mi (11 km) one-way. From Temple Lodge, the trail climbs to Boulder Pass, passing a campground and Halfway Hut, above Corral Creek. The pass harbors a large population of pikas and hoary marmots. The trail then follows the north shore of Ptarmigan Lake before climbing again to Deception Pass, named for its false summit. It then descends into Skoki Valley, passing the Skoki Lakes and eventually reaching Skoki Lodge. Less than 1 mi (just over 1 km) beyond the lodge is a **campground,** an excellent base for exploring the region.

BIKING

Whether you have your own bike or you rent one from the many bicycle shops in Banff or Lake Louise, cycling in the park is for everyone. Popular routes for road biking include the roads to **Lake Minnewanka** (10 mi/16 km) and along the **Bow Valley Parkway** (32 mi/51 km).

Several trails radiating from Banff and ending deep in the backcountry have been designated as bicycle trails. Before heading into the backcountry, pick up the free *Mountain Biking and Cycling Guide* from the Banff or Lake Louise Visitor Centres. Riders are particularly susceptible to sudden bear encounters. Be alert and make loud noises when passing through heavy vegetation.

SUNDANCE CANYON

Sundance Canyon is a rewarding destination across the Bow River from downtown. Starting at Cave and Basin National Historic Site, this easy ride is 2.3 mi (3.7 km) one-way and is paved for the first 1.9 mi (3 km). The paved road is shared with hikers but not cars. Occasional glimpses of the Sawback Range are afforded by breaks in the forest. At the end of the paved section is a bike rack, from where you can continue on foot into a spectacular overhanging canyon formed by Sundance Creek's powerful waters.

SPRAY RIVER LOOP

This popular mountain biking route (7.4 mi/12 km round-trip) starts at the Fairmont Banff Springs Hotel and heads uphill, following the Spray River closely, for 3.7 mi (6 km). After crossing the river, it's downhill all the way to the Fairmont Banff Springs Golf Course. A worthwhile stop on the inbound leg is at a cliff face where Rundlestone used for the famous hotel's façade was quarried.

RENTALS

Renting front- and full-suspension mountain bikes runs approximately C$15-20 per hour and C$50-80 per day.

BACTRAX
225 Bear St., Banff; 403/762-8177; https://snowtips-bactrax.com

BANFF ADVENTURES UNLIMITED
211 Bear St., Banff; 403/762-4554; www.banffadventures.com

Spray River Loop (left); rafting down the Bow River (right)

PADDLING

BOW RIVER

On a quiet stretch of the Bow River at the north end of Wolf Street, **Banff Canoe Club** (403/762-5005; www. banffcanoeclub.com; 9am-9pm daily mid-June-Sept.; C$45 one hour, C$25 each additional hour) rents canoes and paddleboards. From here you can paddle upstream, or along **Forty Mile Creek** to First Vermilion Lake. It's an extremely peaceful way to leave the bustle of Banff behind, especially the Forty Mile Creek option, where beavers are often spotted at dusk.

WINTER SPORTS

From November to May, the entire park transforms itself into a winter playground covered in a blanket of snow. Three world-class winter resorts are in Banff National Park.

DOWNHILL SKIING

Apart from an abundance of snow, the resorts in Banff National Park have something else in common—spectacular views, which alone are worth the price of a lift ticket. Although the resorts operate independently, the **Ski Hub** (114 Banff Ave.; 403/762-4754; www.skibig3.com; 9am-8pm daily) represents all three and is the place to get information on multiday ticketing and transportation.

Norquay
403/762-4421; www.banffnorquay. com; early Dec.-early Apr.; lift tickets adult C$93, youth and senior C$72, child C$37

Norquay is a small but steep hill overlooking the town of Banff. There are some great cruising runs and a well-respected ski school, but also the experts-only North American Chair (the one you can see from town), which opens up the famous double-black-diamond Lone Pine run. A magnificent post-and-beam day lodge nestled below the main runs is flanked on one side by a wide deck that catches the afternoon sun, while holding a cafeteria, restaurant, and bar inside. A shuttle bus makes pickups from Banff hotels for the short 3.7-mi (6-km) ride up to the resort.

Sunshine Village
403/762-6500 or 877/542-2633; www.skibanff.com; late Nov.-late May; day passes adult C$127, senior C$99, youth C$99, child C$49

Perched high in the mountains on the Continental Divide, Sunshine Village has lots going for it—more than 20 feet (6 m) of snow annually, wide-open bowls, a season stretching for nearly 200 days, North America's only heated chairlift, and the only slopeside accommodations in the park. Aside from the infamous experts-only Delirium Dive, the area is best known for its excellent beginner and intermediate terrain. The total vertical rise is 3,510 feet (1,070 m), and the longest run (down to the lower parking lot) is 5 mi (8 km).

Lake Louise Ski Resort
403/522-3555 or 877/253-6888; www.skilouise.com; Nov.-mid-May; lift tickets adult C$124, senior C$95, youth C$95, child C$37

The Lake Louise Resort, Canada's second-largest winter resort, comprises 4,200 acres (1,700 ha) of gentle trails, mogul fields, long cruising runs, steep chutes, and vast bowls filled with famous Rocky Mountain powder.

The resort spreads over four distinct mountain faces. The front side has a vertical drop of 3,280 feet (1,000 m) and is served by eight lifts, including four high-speed quads and western Canada's only six-passenger chairlift.

Free shuttle buses run regularly from Banff and Lake Louise accommodations to the hill.

Lake Louise Ski Resort

KOOTENAY NATIONAL PARK

If you're driving to or from the west side of Glacier National Park, you will pass through Kootenay National Park (National Parks Day Pass adult C$10.20) on your way to Banff or Lake Louise. You could just admire the mountain vistas from the road, but if you want to take a break from driving, here are a few options for where to stop.

Radium Hot Springs

250/347-9485; 9am-11pm daily in summer, noon-9pm daily the rest of the year; adult C$7, senior and child C$6

Located just 1.9 mi (3 km) from the point where Highway 93 crosses into the park from the south, this hot spring pool gushes with mineral waters. A soak here makes a great antidote for drive-stiffened muscles.

Scenic Viewpoints

For a quick stretch in some beautiful scenery, stop at one or all of the following viewpoints along Highway 93:

- **Olive Lake,** just east of Sinclair Pass

- **Hector Gorge,** north of Kootenay Crossing

- **Numa Falls,** where the Vermilion River tumbles over exposed bedrock

Marble Canyon and the Paint Pots

Get a close-up look at two different natural features—Marble Canyon, an ice-carved, marble-streaked canyon, and the Paint Pots, circular ponds stained red, orange, and yellow by oxide-bearing springs—by following short trails that can both be completed in an hour or less.

Stanley Glacier

If you have a bit more time, hike up to Stanley Glacier (2.6 mi/4.2 km one-way), which will take around three hours round-trip. The stunning views are worth every step.

Numa Falls

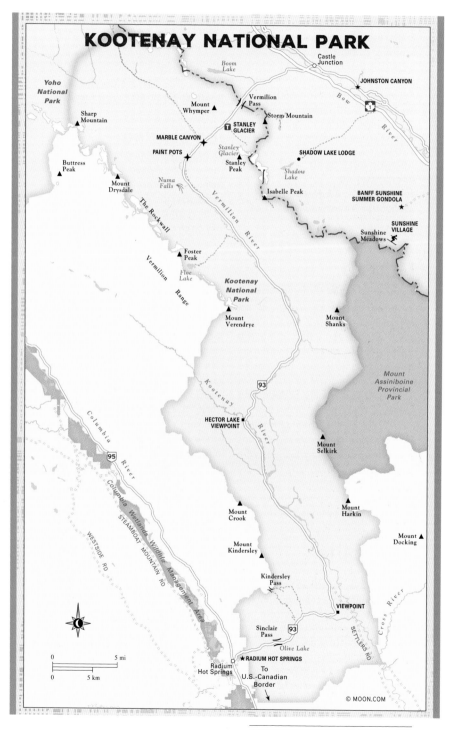

KOOTENAY NATIONAL PARK

Yoho National Park

Boom Lake

Castle Junction

JOHNSTON CANYON

Bow River

Mount Whymper

Vermilion Pass

Storm Mountain

Sharp Mountain

STANLEY GLACIER

MARBLE CANYON

Stanley Glacier

SHADOW LAKE LODGE

PAINT POTS

Buttress Peak

Stanley Peak

Shadow Lake

Mount Drysdale

Numa Falls

BANFF SUNSHINE SUMMER GONDOLA

Isabelle Peak

The Rockwall

Vermilion River

SUNSHINE VILLAGE

Sunshine Meadows

Vermilion Range

Foster Peak

Floe Lake

Kootenay National Park

Mount Verendrye

Mount Shanks

Kootenay River

93

Mount Assiniboine Provincial Park

Columbia River

95

HECTOR LAKE VIEWPOINT

Mount Selkirk

Columbia Wetlands Wildlife Management Area

STEAMBOAT MOUNTAIN RD

WESTSIDE RD

Mount Crook

Mount Harkin

Mount Docking

Mount Kindersley

Kindersley Pass

VIEWPOINT

Cross River

SETTLERS RD

Sinclair Pass

93

Olive Lake

0   5 mi

0   5 km

★ **RADIUM HOT SPRINGS**

Radium Hot Springs

To U.S.-Canadian Border

© MOON.COM

Rentals and Sales

Each resort has ski and snowboard rental and sales facilities, but getting your gear down in town is often easier. Basic rental packages—skis, poles, and boots—are C$50-60 per day, while high-performance packages range C$70-100. Snowboards and boots rent for C$50-70 per day.

**ABOMINABLE SKI &
SPORTSWEAR**
229 Banff Ave., Banff; 403/762-2905; https://abominablesports.ca

MONOD SPORTS
129 Banff Ave., Banff; 403/762-4571; www.monodsports.com

RUDE BOYS
Snowboards only; 205 Caribou St., Banff; 403/762-8211; www.rudeboys.com

ICE-SKATING

Of all the ice-skating rinks in Canada, the one on frozen **Lake Louise,** in front of the chateau, is surely the most spectacular. Spotlights allow skating after dark. The rink is generally open mid-December-mid-April.

FOOD

Whether you're in search of an inexpensive snack for the family or silver service, you can find it in the town of Banff, which has more than 80 restaurants (more per capita than any other town or city across Canada). The quality of food and service varies greatly. Some restaurants revolve solely around the tourist trade, while others have reputations that attract diners from Calgary who have been known to stay overnight just to eat at their favorite haunt.

Around Lake Louise, there are good dining options serving all budgets.

STANDOUTS
Park
219 Banff Ave., Banff; 403/762-5114; www.parkdistillery.com; 11am-midnight daily; C$18-33

Park does a wonderful job of combining classic campfire cooking with modern dining trends—all within a massive space in the heart of downtown that perfectly reflects the food and the history of the park, with a massive stone fireplace and seating choices that include a balcony overlooking Banff Avenue and communal tables beside the open kitchen. Many of the dishes are cooked over a wood-fired grill or on a rotisserie, creating deliciously smoky campfire-like flavors: You could start with rotisserie chicken chowder or corn bread smothered in maple-rum butter, and then choose from mains such as pork-and-beans or AAA T-bone. Craft beers and house-distilled spirits round out this excellent choice.

Lookout Patio
Fairmont Banff Springs, 405 Spray Ave., Banff; 403/762-6860; www.fairmont.com/banff-springs; 11:30am-sunset daily summer; C$16-21

The Lookout Patio is an outdoor dining space that features magnificent views down the Bow Valley. The menu is Mexican-inspired, but you can also simply kick back with a cold drink and appetizer to share.

Lookout Patio (left); Cascade Ponds Day Use Area (right)

Cliffhouse Bistro
Mount Norquay Rd., 3.7 mi (6 km) from downtown Banff; 403/762-4421; https://banffnorquay.com; mid-June-early Oct. 11am-6:30pm daily; lunches C$14-18

For something completely unique, plan on riding the chairlift at Norquay to the Cliffhouse Bistro. Access is by chairlift (adult C$40, child C$25) to a 1950s stone building that has been creatively revamped to bring back its 1950s glory, complete with views across the Bow Valley and a log fireplace. You can enjoy the panorama over tea or coffee, or order lunches such as paninis, salads, and nachos to share.

Storm Mountain Lodge
Hwy. 93; 403/762-4155; https://stormmountainlodge.com/cuisine; 8am-10:30am, 11:30am-3pm, and 5pm-9pm daily May-mid-Oct., 5pm-9pm Fri.-Sun. early Dec.-Apr.; C$29-45

The food at Storm Mountain Lodge is excellent, but it's the ambience you'll remember—an intoxicating blend of historic appeal and rustic mountain charm. The chef uses mostly organic produce with seasonally available game and seafood—bison, venison, wild salmon, and the like—to create tasty and interesting dishes well suited to the I-must-be-in-the-Canadian-wilderness surroundings. Storm Mountain Lodge is a 25-minute drive northwest from Banff; take the Trans-Canada Highway toward Lake Louise and head west at the Castle Mountain interchange.

Baker Creek Bistro
Baker Creek Mountain Resort, Bow Valley Parkway, 6.2 mi (10 km) from Lake Louise; 403/522-3761; https://bakercreek.com/baker-creek-bistro; 7am-10pm daily; C$28-52

Dining is in a small room that characterizes the term "mountain hideaway," in an adjacent lounge bar, or out on a small deck decorated with pots of colorful flowers. The menu isn't large, but dishes feature lots of Canadian game and produce, with favorites such as beer-pork ribs, duck breast, and bison tenderloin.

Laggan's Mountain Bakery
Samson Mall, 101 Village Rd., Bldg. B, Lake Louise Village; 403/552-2017; www.laggans.com; 7am-7pm daily; lunches C$8-12

If you don't feel like a cooked breakfast, start your day off at Laggan's

BANFF NATIONAL PARK FOOD

NAME	LOCATION	TYPE
Nesters Market	town of Banff	grocery
Whitebark	Banff Aspen Lodge, town of Banff	café
Le Café	Banff Centre, town of Banff	sit-down restaurant
Melissa's	town of Banff	sit-down restaurant
★ Park	town of Banff	sit-down restaurant
Maple Leaf	town of Banff	sit-down restaurant
Balkan	town of Banff	sit-down restaurant
Ticino	High Country Inn, town of Banff	sit-down restaurant
Grizzly House	town of Banff	sit-down restaurant
Pad Thai	town of Banff	sit-down restaurant
Sushi House Banff	town of Banff	sit-down restaurant
★ Lookout Patio	Fairmont Banff Springs	sit-down restaurant
1888 Chop House	Fairmont Banff Springs	sit-down restaurant
Juniper Bistro	The Juniper	sit-down restaurant
★ Cliffhouse Bistro	Norquay	sit-down restaurant
★ Storm Mountain Lodge	Between Banff and Lake Louise	sit-down restaurant
★ Baker Creek Bistro	Baker Creek Mountain Resort, Bow Valley Parkway	sit-down restaurant
★ Laggan's Mountain Bakery	Samson Mall, Lake Louise Village	coffee shop
Bill Peyto's Café	HI-Lake Louise Alpine Centre, Lake Louise Village	sit-down restaurant

FOOD	PRICE	HOURS
groceries	budget	8am-11pm daily in summer, shorter hours the rest of the year
coffee and baked goods	budget	6:30am-7pm daily
casual North American	budget	10am-10pm daily
classic North American	moderate	7am-9:30pm daily
classic Canadian	moderate	11am-midnight daily
contemporary Canadian	moderate	10am-10pm daily
European	moderate	11:30am-9pm Sun.-Thurs., 11:30am-10pm Fri.-Sat.
European	moderate	5:30pm-10pm daily
fondue	splurge	11:30am-midnight daily
Thai	budget	noon-9pm daily
Japanese	moderate	11:30am-10pm daily
Mexican-inspired	moderate	11:30am-sunset daily
steakhouse	splurge	6pm-9:30pm daily
contemporary Canadian	moderate	7am-1:30pm and 5pm-10pm daily
tea, coffee, and lunches	budget	mid-June-early Oct. 11am-6:30pm daily
classic Canadian	moderate	8am-10:30am, 11:30am-3pm, and 5pm-9pm daily May-mid-Oct., 5pm-9pm Fri.-Sun. early Dec.-Apr.
Canadian	splurge	7am-10pm daily
coffee and baked goods	budget	7am-7pm daily
casual	moderate	7am-10pm daily

BANFF NATIONAL PARK FOOD

NAME	LOCATION	TYPE
Post Hotel	Lake Louise Village	sit-down restaurant
The Station Restaurant	Lake Louise Village	sit-down restaurant
Fairview Dining Room	Fairmont Chateau Lake Louise	sit-down restaurant
Num-ti-jah Lodge	Icefields Parkway	sit-down restaurant
The Crossing	Icefields Parkway	sit-down restaurant

Mountain Bakery, *the* place to hang out with a coffee and a freshly baked breakfast croissant, pastry, cake, or muffin. The chocolate brownie is delicious (order two slices to save having to line up twice). If the few tables are full, order takeout and enjoy your feast on the riverbank behind the mall.

BEST PICNIC SPOTS
Cascade Ponds Day Use Area
Lake Minnewanka Rd., 2.5 mi (4 km) north of downtown Banff

Picnic tables, many with fire pits (wood supplied), ring the shoreline at Cascade Ponds, but as the closest day use area to downtown Banff, it gets busy.

Two Jack Lake Day Use Area
Lake Minnewanka Rd., 5 mi (8 km) north of downtown Banff

This is another very popular day use area close to town, and tables here are in high demand on summer weekends, but the views across the lake to Mount Rundle are stunning.

Lake Minnewanka Day Use Area
Lake Minnewanka Rd., 4 mi (7 km) north of downtown Banff

One of Banff's largest picnic areas is along the rocky shoreline of Lake Minnewanka, although the farthest tables are a 10-minute walk from the parking lot. Fire grills and wood are supplied.

Johnson Lake Day Use Area
Lake Minnewanka Rd., 6 mi (10 km) north of downtown Banff

If you hear locals talk about going to the "beach," they are probably referring to Johnson Lake, with relatively warm water for swimming. If the picnic tables are full, there's room to spread out a blanket on the grassy slope.

Bow Lake Day Use Area
Icefields Parkway, 22 mi (35 km) north of Lake Louise

This small picnic area has easy access to one of Banff's most beautiful lakes. Spreading out a picnic on the pebbly shoreline is also an option.

FOOD	PRICE	HOURS
European	splurge	6:30pm-10pm daily
Canadian	splurge	11:30am-4pm and 5pm-9 daily
Canadian	splurge	5:30pm-9:30pm daily
Canadian	splurge	8am-10am and 6:30pm-9pm daily mid-June-Sept.
casual	moderate	7am-9pm daily early May-mid-Oct.

Coleman Creek Day Use Area
Icefields Parkway, 62 mi (100 km) north of Lake Louise

Riverside Coleman Creek is one of the few day use areas on the Banff side of the Icefields Parkway—but you'll need to plan ahead for a picnic as it's a long way from the nearest town.

CAMPING

Within Banff National Park, 13 campgrounds hold more than 2,400 sites. Although the town of Banff has five of these facilities with more than 1,500 sites in its immediate vicinity, you should make reservations well in advance. The three largest campgrounds are strung out over 0.9 mi (1.5 km) along Tunnel Mountain Road, with the nearest sites 1.6 mi (2.5 km) from town.

Open fires are permitted in designated areas throughout all campgrounds, but you must purchase a firewood permit (C$8.80 per site per night) to burn wood, which is provided at no cost. For general camping information, stop at the **Banff Visitor Centre** (224 Banff Ave.; 403/762-1550), or go online to Parks Canada (www.pc.gc.ca),and follow the links to Banff National Park.

Reservations
Sites at most campgrounds can be reserved through the **Parks Canada Campground Reservation Service** (877/737-3783; www.reservation.pc.gc.ca) starting in mid-January, and it's strongly recommended that you do reserve if you require electrical hookups or want to stay at one of the more popular campgrounds, such as Two Jack Lakeside (this campground is notorious for having every site booked for the entire season within minutes of the reservation system opening). Although a limited number of sites are set aside for those without reservations, they fill fast each day (especially in July and August).

Tips
The official checkout time is 11am, so if you don't have a reservation, plan

BANFF NATIONAL PARK CAMPGROUNDS

NAME	LOCATION	SEASON
Tunnel Mountain Village I Campground	east of downtown Banff	mid–May–early Oct.
Tunnel Mountain Village II Campground	east of downtown Banff	year-round
Tunnel Mountain Trailer Court	east of downtown Banff	mid–May–early Oct.
★ Two Jack Lakeside Campground	Lake Minnewanka Road	mid–May–early-Oct.
Two Jack Main Campground	Lake Minnewanka Road	late June–mid-Sept.
Johnston Canyon Campground	Bow Valley Parkway	late June–mid-Sept.
Castle Mountain Campground	Bow Valley Parkway	mid–May–Aug.
★ Lake Louise Campground	Lake Louise	serviced section year-round, unserviced section June-Sept.
Mosquito Creek Campground	Icefields Parkway	June–early Oct.
Silverhorn Creek Campground	Icefields Parkway	late June–mid-Sept.
★ Waterfowl Lakes Campground	Icefields Parkway	late June–mid-Sept.
Rampart Creek Campground	Icefields Parkway	June–early Oct.

SITES AND AMENITIES	RV LIMIT	PRICE	RESERVATIONS
618 tent sites, drinking water, flush toilets, showers, dump station	n/a	C$29	yes
209 tent and RV sites, drinking water, flush toilets, showers, dump station, electrical hookups	no limit	C$39	yes
322 tent and RV sites, drinking water, flush toilets, showers, dump station, electrical hookups	no limit	C$39	yes
74 tent sites, drinking water, flush toilets, showers	n/a	C$33	yes
380 tent and RV sites, drinking water, flush toilets, showers, dump station	RVs up to 27 ft (8 m)	C$23	yes
132 tent and RV sites, drinking water, flush toilets, showers, dump station	RVs up to 27 ft (8 m)	C$29	yes
43 tent and RV sites, drinking water, flush toilets	RVs up to 24 ft (7 m)	C$23	no
395 tent and RV sites, drinking water, flush toilets, showers, dump station, electrical hookups (serviced section)	no limit	C$39 serviced sites, C$35 tents	yes
32 tent and RV sites, drinking water, vault toilets	RVs up to 24 ft (7 m)	C$23	no
45 tent and RV sites, vault toilets	RVs up to 24 ft (7 m)	C$23	no
116 tent and RV sites, drinking water, flush and vault toilets, dump station	RVs up to 24 ft (7 m)	C$28	no
50 tent and RV sites, drinking water, vault toilets	RVs up to 24 ft (7 m)	C$23	yes

on arriving at your campground of choice earlier in the day than this to ensure getting a site. If there are no sites available, neighboring Kootenay and Yoho National Parks have campgrounds operating on a first-come, first-served basis.

STANDOUTS
Two Jack Lakeside Campground
June-mid-Sept.; C$33

Along Lake Minnewanka Road northeast of town are two campgrounds offering fewer services than the others, but with sites that offer more privacy. The pick of the two is Two Jack Lakeside Campground, for which you will need advance reservations. It features 80 sites tucked into trees at the south end of Two Jack Lake, an extension of Lake Minnewanka. Facilities include hot showers, kitchen shelters, drinking water, and flush toilets. It's just over 3.7 mi (6 km) from the Trans-Canada Highway underpass.

Lake Louise Campground
serviced section year-round, unserviced section June-September; C$39 serviced site, C$35 unserviced site

Exit the Trans-Canada Highway at the Lake Louise interchange, 35 mi (56 km) northwest of Banff, and take the first left beyond Samson Mall and under the railway bridge to reach Lake Louise Campground, within easy walking distance of the village. The campground is divided into two sections by the Bow River but is linked by the Bow River Loop hiking trail that leads into the village along either side of the river. Individual sites throughout are close together, but some privacy and shade are provided by towering lodgepole pines. Just under 200 serviced (powered) sites are grouped together at the end of the road. In addition to hookups, this section has showers and flush toilets. Across the river are 216 unserviced sites, each with a fire ring and picnic table. Other amenities include kitchen shelters and a modern bathroom complex complete with hot showers. A dump station is near the entrance to the campground (C$8 per use). An interpretive program runs throughout the summer, nightly at 9pm (except Tuesday) in the outdoor theater.

Waterfowl Lakes Campground
late June-mid-Sept.; C$28

Waterfowl Lakes Campground is 37 mi (60 km) north of Lake Louise along the Icefields Parkway. It features 116 sites between Upper and Lower Waterfowl Lakes, with a few sites in view of the lower lake. Facilities include drinking water, flush toilets, and kitchen shelters with wood-burning stoves. Rise early to watch the first rays of sun hit Mount Chephren from the shoreline of the lower lake, then plan on hiking the 2.5-mi (4-km) trail to **Chephren Lake**—you'll be among the first on the trail and back in time for a late breakfast.

Two Jack Lakeside Campground

LODGING

Finding a room in Banff National Park in summer is nearly as hard as trying to justify its price. By late afternoon, just about every room in the park will be occupied, and basic hotel rooms start at C$300. It is also worth noting that prices vary according to demand. The park's off-season is October-May, and hotels offer rate reductions during this period. Shop around, and you'll find many bargains.

In summer, accommodations at Lake Louise are even harder to come by than in Banff, so it's essential to make reservations well in advance.

North of Lake Louise, five hostels are spread along the Icefields Parkway, three in Banff National Park and two in Jasper National Park. Facilities at all five are limited, and beds should be reserved as far in advance as possible. For reservations, call 778/328-2220 or 866/762-4122, or book online (www.hihostels.ca).

All rates quoted are for a standard room in the high season (June-Sept.). Rooms have en suite bathrooms, unless otherwise indicated.

Reservations
In July and August and during the Christmas holidays, you should make reservations as far in advance as possible. Contact hotels directly for the best rates.

Tips
Hotel rooms in **Canmore,** a 20-minute drive east of Banff, are significantly less expensive than within the park.

STANDOUTS
Town of Banff
BREWSTER'S MOUNTAIN LODGE
208 Caribou St., Banff; 403/762-2900 or 888/762-2900; www.brewstermountainlodge.com; C$320-420 s or d

More than 100 years since Jim and Bill Brewster guided their first guests through the park, their descendants are still actively involved in the tourist industry, operating the central and very stylish Brewster's Mountain Lodge. The building features an eye-catching log exterior with an equally impressive lobby. The Western theme is continued in the 77 upstairs rooms. Standard rooms feature two queen-size beds, deluxe rooms offer a jetted tub and sitting area, and loft suites are designed for families. Packages provide good value here, while off-season rates are slashed up to 30 percent.

FAIRMONT BANFF SPRINGS
405 Spray Ave., Banff; 403/762-2211 or 800/257-7544; www.fairmont.com; starting at C$729 s or d
The 770-room Fairmont Banff Springs is Banff's best-known accommodation. Earlier this century, the hotel came under the ownership of Fairmont Hotels and Resorts, losing its century-old tag as a Canadian Pacific hotel and in the process its ties to the historic railway company that constructed the original hotel back in 1888. Even though the rooms have been modernized, many date to the 1920s, and as is common in older establishments, these accommodations are small. (Fairmont rooms are 155 square feet/14.4 square meters.)

BANFF NATIONAL PARK LODGING

NAME	LOCATION	SEASON
★ Brewster's Mountain Lodge	town of Banff	year-round
Banff Ptarmigan Inn	town of Banff	year-round
Moose Hotel & Suites	town of Banff	year-round
Banff Aspen Lodge	town of Banff	year-round
High Country Inn	town of Banff	year-round
Samesun Banff	town of Banff	year-round
Rundlestone Lodge	town of Banff	year-round
HI-Banff Alpine Centre	town of Banff	year-round
Douglas Fir Resort	town of Banff	year-round
★ Fairmont Banff Springs	town of Banff	year-round
Johnston Canyon Resort	Bow Valley Parkway	mid-May-early Oct.
Baker Creek Mountain Resort	Bow Valley Parkway	year-round
★ Storm Mountain Lodge	between Banff and Lake Louise	daily in summer, Thurs.-Mon. only the rest of the year
HI-Lake Louise Alpine Centre	Lake Louise Village	year-round
★ Post Hotel	Lake Louise Village	year-round
★ Paradise Lodge and Bungalows	Lake Louise	mid-May-early Oct.
Deer Lodge	Lake Louise	year-round
★ Fairmont Chateau Lake Louise	Lake Louise	year-round
Moraine Lake Lodge	Moraine Lake	June-Sept.

OPTIONS	PRICE
hotel rooms; loft suites	rooms starting at C$320
hotel rooms	rooms starting at C$375
one- and two-bedroom suites	suites starting at C$429
hotel rooms	rooms starting at C$429
hotel rooms	rooms starting at C$300
dormitory rooms (some women-only rooms)	dorm C$64-70
hotel rooms	rooms starting at C$340
two-, four-, and six-bed dormitory rooms; four-bed cabins	nonmember dorm C$60-66 nonmember private room starting at C$200
condo-style units	units starting at C$340
hotel rooms	rooms starting at C$729
cabins, some with kitchens	cabins starting at C$220
cabins with kitchens suites	suites starting at C$470-800
cabins	cabins starting at C$370
dormitory rooms with 4-5 beds; private rooms	nonmember dorm C$63 nonmember private room C$186
bungalow-style rooms, some with kitchens	rooms starting at C$510
cabins, some with kitchens; suites	cabins starting at C$300
hotel rooms	rooms starting at C$339-499
hotel rooms	rooms starting at C$799
hotel rooms	rooms starting at C$1,100

BANFF NATIONAL PARK LODGING

NAME	LOCATION	SEASON
★ Num-ti-jah Lodge	Icefields Parkway	late May-mid-Oct.
The Crossing	Icefields Parkway	mid-Apr.-mid-Oct.
HI-Mosquito Creek	Icefields Parkway	June-Mar.
HI-Rampart Creek	Icefields Parkway	May-Mar.

But room size is only a minor consideration when staying in this historic gem. With 12 eateries, four lounges, a luxurious spa facility, a huge indoor pool, elegant public spaces, a 27-hole golf course, tennis courts, horseback riding, and enough twisting, turning hallways, towers, and shops to warrant a detailed map, you'll not want to spend much time in your room. (Unless, of course, you are in the eight-room presidential suite.) During summer, rack rates for a regular Fairmont room are C$729, discounted to around C$400 or less the rest of the year. Many summer visitors stay as part of a package—the place to find these is on the website www.fairmont.com. Packages may simply include breakfast, while others will have you golfing, horseback riding, or relaxing in the spa.

Between Banff and Lake Louise
STORM MOUNTAIN LODGE
Hwy. 93; 403/762-4155; www.storm-mountainlodge.com; daily in summer, Thurs.-Mon. rest of year; C$370-500 s or d
Constructed by the Canadian Pacific Railway in 1922, Storm Mountain Lodge features 14 historic cabins restored to their former rustic glory. Each has its original log walls, along with a log bed, covered deck, a wood-burning fireplace, and bathroom with claw-foot tub. They don't have phones, Internet, or TVs, so there's little to distract you from the past. Off-season deals include a breakfast and dinner package (mid-Apr.-mid-June) for C$450 d. Outside, the wilderness beckons, with Storm Mountain as a backdrop. The lodge is at Vermilion Pass, a 25-minute drive from Banff or Lake Louise (head west from the Castle Mountain interchange).

Lake Louise
POST HOTEL
200 Pipestone Dr., Lake Louise Village; 403/522-3989 or 800/661-1586; www.posthotel.com; C$510-930 s or d
Originally called Lake Louise Ski Lodge, the Post Hotel is one of only a handful of Canadian accommodations that have been accepted into the prestigious Relais & Châteaux organization. Bordered to the east and south by the Pipestone River, it may lack views of Lake Louise, but it is as elegant—in a modern, woodsy way—as the château. Each bungalow-style room is furnished with

OPTIONS	PRICE
rooms with shared bathroom	rooms starting at C$375
hotel rooms	rooms starting at C$299
cabins with 4-6-beds	nonmembers C$40
cabins with 4-6-beds	nonmembers C$40

Canadian pine and has a balcony. Many rooms have whirlpools and fireplaces, while some have kitchens. Other facilities include the upscale Temple Mountain Spa, an indoor pool, a steam room, and a library. The hotel has 17 different room types, with 26 different rates depending on the view. Between the main lodge and the Pipestone River are four sought-after cabins, each with a wood-burning fireplace.

PARADISE LODGE AND BUNGALOWS

105 Lake Louise Dr., Lake Louise; 403/522-3595; www.paradiselodge. com; mid-May-early Oct.; starting at C$365 s or d

This family-operated lodge provides outstanding value in a wonderfully tranquil setting. Spread out around well-manicured gardens are 21 attractive cabins in four configurations. Each has a rustic yet warm and inviting interior, with comfortable beds, a separate sitting area, and an en suite bathroom. Each cabin has a small fridge, microwave, and coffeemaker, while the larger ones have full kitchens and separate bedrooms. Instead of television, children are kept happy with a playground that includes a sandbox and jungle gym. The least-expensive cabins, complete with a classic cast-iron stove/fireplace combo, are C$300 s or d, or pay C$325 for a cabin with a big deck and sweeping valley views. Twenty-four luxury suites, each with a fireplace, TV, one or two bedrooms, and fabulous mountain views, start at C$330, or C$365 with a kitchen. To get there from the valley floor, follow Lake Louise Drive toward the Fairmont Chateau Lake Louise for 1.9 mi (3 km); the lake itself is just 0.6 mi (1 km) farther up the hill.

FAIRMONT CHATEAU LAKE LOUISE

111 Lake Louise Dr., Lake Louise; 403/522-3511 or 866/540-4413; www. fairmont.com; starting at C$799

The famously fabulous Fairmont Chateau Lake Louise, a historic 500-room hotel on the shore of Lake Louise, has views equal to any mountain resort in the world. But all this historic charm and mountain scenery come at a price. Official rates drop as low as C$350 s or d outside of summer, with accommodation and ski pass packages sometimes advertised for around C$400 d. Children younger than 18 sharing with parents are free, but if you bring a pet, it'll be an extra C$40.

Fairmont Chateau Lake Louise (left); Num-ti-jah Lodge (right)

Along Icefields Parkway
NUM-TI-JAH LODGE
403/522-2167; www.num-ti-jah. com; late May-mid-Oct.; starting at C$375 s or d

Pioneer guide and outfitter Jimmy Simpson built Num-ti-jah Lodge on the north shore of Bow Lake, 25 mi (40 km) north of Lake Louise, as a base for his outfitting operation in 1920. The desire to build a large structure when only short timbers were available led to the unusual octagonal shape of the main lodge. With a rustic mountain ambience that has changed little since Simpson's day, Num-ti-jah provides a memorable overnight stay. Just don't expect the conveniences of a regular motel. Under the distinctively red, steep-pitched roof of the main lodge are 25 rooms, some that share bathrooms, and there's not a TV or phone in sight. Downstairs, guests soak up the warmth of a roaring log fire while mingling in a comfortable library filled with historical mountain literature. A dining room lined with memorabilia is open for breakfast and dinner daily (C$28-48).

Post Hotel

Fairmont Banff Springs

INFORMATION AND SERVICES

The town of **Banff** is a bustling commercial center within the boundaries of Banff National Park, where travelers can find services and supplies. The village of **Lake Louise** is another hub for services within the park. There are few services along Icefields Parkway, although gas is available at **Saskatchewan River Crossing** mid-April to mid-October.

Entrance Gate

The main fee station is located on the eastern approach to the park. Heading to Banff from Calgary, the Trans-Canada Highway passes through the town of Canmore, then enters the park, where toll booths are open 24 hours daily year-round

Visitor Centers

Banff Visitor Centre

224 Banff Ave.; 8am-8pm daily mid-May-Sept., 9am-5pm daily Oct.-mid-May

Many sources of information are available on the park and its commercial facilities. Once you've arrived, the best place to make your first stop is the Banff Visitor Centre. This central complex houses information desks for Parks Canada (403/762-1550) and the Banff Lake Louise Tourism Bureau (403/762-0270), as well as a retail outlet that stocks guidebooks, maps, and bear spray.

Lake Louise Visitor Centre

403/522-3833; 8am-8pm daily mid-June-Aug., 8am-6pm daily mid-May-mid-June and Sept., 9am-4pm daily rest of year

Lake Louise Visitor Centre is beside Samson Mall on Village Road in the heart of Lake Louise Village. This excellent Parks Canada facility has interpretive exhibits, slide and video displays, and staff on hand to answer questions, recommend hikes suited to your ability, and issue camping passes to those heading out into the backcountry.

TRANSPORTATION

Getting There

Air

Calgary International Airport (YYC), 80 mi (128 km) east, is the closest airport to Banff National Park. To get to the town of Banff, drive west on the Trans-Canada Highway; allow 90 minutes for the trip.

Another option is **Vancouver International Airport** (YVR), which is larger, but farther away. From Vancouver, the drive to Lake Louise is approximately 484 mi (784 km) east along the Trans-Canada Highway and takes about 10 hours.

From Glacier National Park

If you find yourself at **West Glacier,** on the park's west side, the quickest way to get to Banff is to head north on Highway 93 to the U.S.-Canada border, from where it's 267 mi (430 km) to Banff along Highway 93/95 via Cranbrook and Kootenay National Park. From West Glacier, allow six hours.

From **St. Mary,** on the east side of Glacier National Park, the most direct route to Banff National Park is to take Highway 2 north to Calgary (3 hours) and then to head west on the Trans-Canada Highway. The total distance between St. Mary and Banff is 260 mi (420 km); allow 4.5 hours.

From Jasper National Park

From Jasper in the north, the Icefields Parkway leads 143 mi (230 km) south to Lake Louise; allow around 3.5 hours for the drive. To get from Jasper to the town of Banff, the drive is 178 mi (286 km) total and takes at least four hours. Driving times can vary given the speed restrictions and often heavy traffic on this route.

Between Banff and Lake Louise

The village of Lake Louise is beside the Trans-Canada Highway 35 mi (56 km) northwest of Banff. The drive takes about 50 minutes.

Gas

Gas stations are scattered through the

town of Banff, including **Husky** (601 Banff Ave.; 24 hours daily) a little northeast of downtown. Lake Louise also has two gas stations, and along the Icefields Parkway, gas is available mid-April to mid-October at Saskatchewan River Crossing.

Parking

The downtown core of Banff is busy year-round, but especially so between late June and early September after 10am. If you're staying in a hotel along Banff Avenue or on Tunnel Mountain, don't drive into town—**walk** or catch a **Banff Transit bus** (ask at your accommodation for a schedule).

If you do drive into downtown, don't let not finding a parking spot on Banff Avenue ruin your holiday. Head to the **Fenlands Banff Recreation Centre** on Mount Norquay Road, the large parking lot on the east side of the Banff Railway Station, or the **parking garage** at the corner of Bear and Lynx Streets.

For travelers with **RVs** or **trailers,** finding a downtown parking spot can be a challenge. If you must bring your rig into town, try the RV-only parking spots on Railway Avenue opposite the railway station and at the corner of Lynx and Wolf Streets.

The website **www.banffparking.ca** is an excellent resource that includes real-time updates of various parking areas, including the number of empty stalls at parking lots through town.

Lake Louise and Moraine Lake are very busy during summer. My advice is simple: Arrive early to be assured a parking spot. Plan on arriving at **Lake Louise** before 8am—and preferably before 7am. For **Moraine Lake,** you will need to arrive even earlier—on many summer mornings the parking lot is full by 6am, at which point Moraine Lake Road is closed. When the parking lot at Lake Louise is full, visitors will be directed to the **Lake Louise Park & Ride,** 5 mi (8 km) south of the village along the Trans-Canada Highway, where **shuttle buses** are available. Visit the Parks Canada webpage (pc.gc.ca/banffnow) for shuttle reservations and up-to-date traffic and parking status throughout the park.

Buses and Shuttles

Parks Canada Shuttles

In summer and fall, Parks Canada operates buses from the **Lake Louise Park & Ride,** 5 mi (8 km) south of the village of Lake Louise along the Trans-Canada Highway, to Lake Louise and Moraine Lake. Shuttles operate continuously between 8am and 4pm, with earlier departures at the busiest times of year. The round-trip fare to either destination is adult C$10, senior or child C$5. For reservations and more information, visit www.pc.gc.ca/banffnow.

Roam Transit

403/760-8294; mid-May-Sept. twice an hour 7am-midnight; C$2-10 per sector

Roam Transit operates bus service along two routes through the town of Banff: one from the Banff Gondola north along Banff Avenue, the other from the Fairmont Banff Springs to the Tunnel Mountain campgrounds. Roam buses also run out to Lake Minnewanka and to Lake Louise.

Goats and Glaciers Lookout

JASPER NATIONAL PARK

VAST ICE FIELDS, BEAUTIFUL GLACIAL LAKES, SOOTHING HOT springs, thundering rivers, and the most extensive backcountry trail system of any Canadian national park make Jasper a stunning counterpart to its sister park, Banff.

Encompassing 4,208 square mi (10,900 sq km), Jasper is a haven for wildlife; much of its wilderness is traveled only by wolves and grizzlies.

The park's most spectacular natural landmarks can be admired from two major roads. The Yellowhead Highway runs east-west from Edmonton through the park to Mount Robson Provincial Park. The Icefields Parkway, regarded as one of the world's great mountain drives, runs north-south, connecting Jasper to Banff. At the junction of these two highways is the park's main service center—the town of Jasper. It has half the population of Banff, and its setting—at the confluence of the Athabasca and Miette Rivers, surrounded by rugged, snowcapped peaks—is a little less dramatic, though still beautiful. But the town is also less commercialized than Banff and its streets a little quieter—a major plus for those looking to get away from it all. Hiking is the number one attraction, but downhill skiing and rafting are also popular.

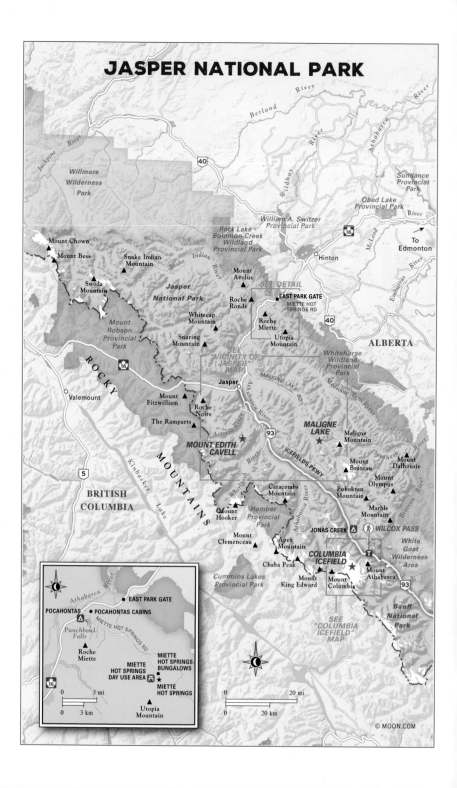

JASPER NATIONAL PARK

TOP 3

⭐ **1. COLUMBIA ICEFIELD:** Don't miss this glacial area at the southern end of Jasper National Park. Take the Ice Explorer tour to get a close-up view of this natural wonder (page 182).

⭐ **2. MOUNT EDITH CAVELL:** Although this peak is visible from various points within the park, no vantage point is as memorable as that from its base, reachable by road from Highway 93A. For a neck-straining view, take the Cavell Meadows Trail (page 185).

⭐ **3. MALIGNE LAKE:** This is the most famous body of water in Jasper National Park, and for good reason—it's simply stunning (page 190).

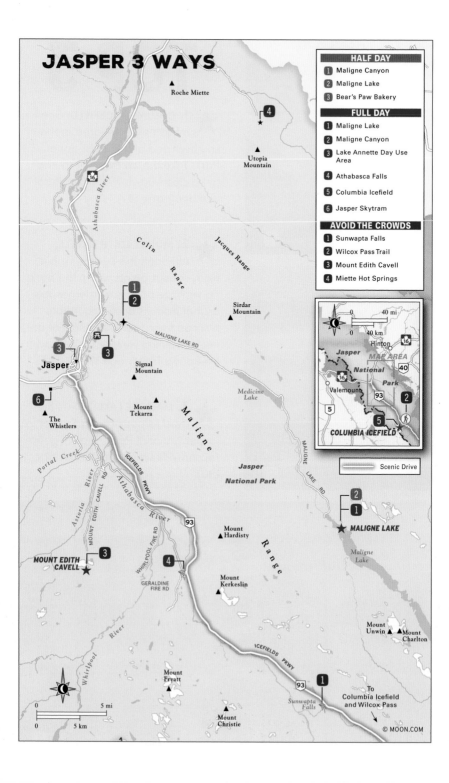

JASPER 3 WAYS

HALF DAY
1. Maligne Canyon
2. Maligne Lake
3. Bear's Paw Bakery

FULL DAY
1. Maligne Lake
2. Maligne Canyon
3. Lake Annette Day Use Area
4. Athabasca Falls
5. Columbia Icefield
6. Jasper Skytram

AVOID THE CROWDS
1. Sunwapta Falls
2. Wilcox Pass Trail
3. Mount Edith Cavell
4. Miette Hot Springs

Roche Miette

Utopia Mountain

Colin Range

Jacques Range

Sirdar Mountain

MALIGNE LAKE RD

Jasper

Signal Mountain

Medicine Lake

Mount Tekarra

Maligne

Jasper National Park

The Whistlers

Portal Creek

ICEFIELDS PKWY

MOUNT EDITH CAVELL RD

Astoria River

Athabasca River

93

Mount Hardisty

MALIGNE LAKE RD

MALIGNE LAKE

Maligne Lake

MOUNT EDITH CAVELL

WHIRLPOOL FIRE RD

GERALDINE FIRE RD

Mount Kerkeslin

Range

Whirlpool River

Mount Fryatt

Mount Christie

Mount Unwin

Mount Charlton

ICEFIELDS PKWY

93

Sunwapta Falls

To Columbia Icefield and Wilcox Pass

0   5 mi
0   5 km

Inset map
Hinton

Jasper
National   Park
16
Valemount
93
40
5
COLUMBIA ICEFIELD

0   40 mi
0   40 km

MAP AREA

Scenic Drive

© MOON.COM

JASPER NATIONAL PARK 3 WAYS

HALF DAY

1   Visit **Maligne Canyon** and walk the shorter loop option down and across this geological wonder.

2   Drive farther down Maligne Lake Road to **Maligne Lake** itself. Take a boat tour on the lake to Spirit Island.

3   Head back to the town of Jasper and wander along the downtown streets, which are lined with interesting stores. Grab lunch at the **Bear's Paw Bakery.**

FULL DAY

It's possible to hit the major highlights of Jasper in just one day, but it will be a full day, with around 186 mi (300 km) of driving, starting and ending in the town of Jasper.

1 Leave Jasper to arrive at **Maligne Lake** in time for the first tour boat departure at 9am.

2 On the way back into town, stop at **Maligne Canyon** and marvel at the forces of nature at work.

3 For lunch, have a picnic at the **Lake Annette Day Use Area.** Stroll around Lake Annette before or after you eat.

4 Drive down the Icefields Parkway, stopping en route to admire **Athabasca Falls.**

5 Keep heading south to the **Columbia Icefield,** the largest and most accessible glacial area along the Icefields Parkway.

6 Return to Jasper after a full day of driving, and ride the **Jasper Skytram** up to the summit, where the restaurant is an outstanding destination for dinner.

AVOID THE CROWDS

The best way to avoid the crowds in Jasper is to start your day early. As a bonus, early morning offers you the best chance of seeing wildlife—which is why heading down the Icefields Parkway at the beginning of your day is ideal.

1 Rise early and drive along the Icefields Parkway toward the Columbia Icefield. On the way, stop at **Sunwapta Falls,** where the Sunwapta River changes direction sharply and drops into a deep canyon. If you haven't had breakfast, take this opportunity to eat at Sunwapta Falls Rocky Mountain Lodge.

2 At the Columbia Icefield, hike the **Wilcox Pass Trail** to enjoy views over the Athabasca Glacier.

3 Returning to Jasper, detour to **Mount Edith Cavell** for up-close views of Jasper's most spectacular mountain peak.

4 Wind down after your day by taking a dip in the warm waters at **Miette Hot Springs.**

Wilcox Pass Trail

HIGHLIGHTS

★ COLUMBIA ICEFIELD

The largest and most accessible of 17 glacial areas along the Icefields Parkway is the 125-square-mi (325-sq-km) Columbia Icefield, beside the Icefields Parkway at the south end of the park, 65 mi (105 km) south of Jasper and 82 mi (132 km) north of Lake Louise. It's a remnant of the last major glaciation that covered most of Canada 20,000 years ago, and it has survived because of its elevation at 6,230-9,190 feet (1,900-2,800 m) above sea level, cold temperatures, and heavy snowfalls. From the main body of the ice cap, which sits astride the Continental Divide, six glaciers creep down three main valleys. Of these, **Athabasca Glacier** is the most accessible and can be seen from the Icefields Parkway; it is one of the world's few glaciers that you can drive right up to.

The ice field is made more spectacular by the impressive peaks that surround it. **Mount Athabasca** (11,450 ft/3,491 m) dominates the skyline, and three glaciers cling to its flanks. **Dome Glacier** is also visible from the highway; although part of the Columbia Icefield, it is not actually connected. Instead, it is made of ice that breaks off the ice field 980 feet (300 m) above, supplemented by large quantities of snow each winter.

Icefield Centre

July-Aug. daily 9am-10pm, reduced hours May-June, Sept.-mid-Oct., closed mid-Oct.-Apr.

The magnificent Icefield Centre is nestled at the base of Mount Wilcox,

overlooking the Athabasca Glacier. The center is the staging point for Ice Explorer tours of the glacier, but before heading out onto the ice field, don't miss the **Glacier Gallery** on the lower floor. This large display area details all aspects of the frozen world, including the story of glacier formation and movement. The centerpiece is a scaled-down fiberglass model of the Athabasca Glacier, which is surrounded by hands-on displays and audiovisual presentations.

On the main floor of the center, you'll find a **Parks Canada desk**

Mount Edith Cavell (top); Athabasca Glacier (bottom left); Toe of the Glacier Trail (bottom right)

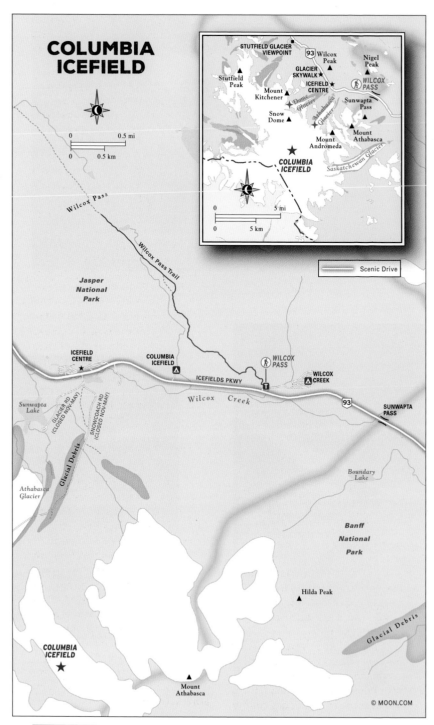

COLUMBIA ICEFIELD

0   0.5 mi

0   0.5 km

STUTFIELD GLACIER VIEWPOINT

93 Wilcox Peak ★

Nigel Peak ▲

Stutfield Peak ▲

GLACIER SKYWALK ★

ICEFIELD CENTRE ★

Mount Kitchener ▲

Dome Glacier

Athabasca Glacier

WILCOX PASS

Sunwapta Pass

Snow Dome ▲

Mount Andromeda ▲

Mount Athabasca ▲

Saskatchewan Glacier

COLUMBIA ICEFIELD ★

0   5 mi

0   5 km

Scenic Drive

Wilcox Pass

Wilcox Pass Trail

Jasper National Park

ICEFIELD CENTRE

COLUMBIA ICEFIELD ⛺

WILCOX PASS

WILCOX CREEK ⛺

ICEFIELDS PKWY

GLACIER RD (CLOSED NOV-MAY)

SNOWCOACH RD (CLOSED NOV-MAY)

Sunwapta Lake

Glacial Debris

Wilcox Creek

93

SUNWAPTA PASS

Athabasca Glacier

Boundary Lake

Banff National Park

Hilda Peak ▲

Glacial Debris

COLUMBIA ICEFIELD ★

Mount Athabasca ▲

© MOON.COM

(780/852-6288; 10am-5pm daily early May-late Sept.)—a good source of information for northbound visitors—the Ice Explorer ticketing desk, restrooms, and the obligatory gift shop. Upstairs, you'll find food options with indoor and outdoor seating. The outside tables offering unparalleled glacier views.

Athabasca Glacier

Athabasca Glacier is an impressive 1,480 acres (600 ha) in area and up to 330 feet (100 m) deep. The speed at which glaciers advance and retreat varies with the long-term climate. Athabasca Glacier has retreated to its current position from across the highway, a distance of more than 1 mi (1.6 km) in a little more than 100 years. Currently it retreats up to 6 feet (2 m) per year. The rubble between the toe of Athabasca Glacier and the highway is a mixture of rock, sand, and gravel known as **till,** deposited by the glacier as it retreats.

From the Icefields Parkway, an unpaved road leads down through piles of till to a parking area beside Sunwapta Lake. An interesting alternative is to leave your vehicle beside the highway and take the 1-mi (1.6-km) hiking trail through the lunarlike landscape to the parking area. From this point, a short path leads up to the toe of the glacier. (Along the access road, look for the small markers showing how far the toe of the glacier reached in years past; the farthest marker is across the highway beside the stairs leading up to the Icefield Centre.)

The ice field can be dangerous for unprepared visitors. Like that of all glaciers, the broken surface of the Athabasca is especially hazardous because snow bridges can hide its deep crevasses. The crevasses are uncovered as the winter snows melt.

GLACIER TOUR
Pursuit; 403/762-6700 or 866/606-6700; www.banffjaspercollection. com; May-mid-Oct. daily 9am-6pm; adult C$114, child C$57; reserve online

Operated by Pursuit, Ice Explorers are specially developed vehicles with balloon tires that can travel over the crevassed surface and allow visitors to experience the glacier firsthand. The 90-minute tour of Athabasca Glacier, which begins with a bus ride from the Icefield Centre, includes time spent walking on the surface of the glacier. Try to reserve your tour for before 10am or after 3pm, after the tour buses have departed for the day. Early in the season, the glacier is still covered in a layer of snow and is therefore not as spectacular as during the summer. Full-day trips to the Columbia Icefield, which last nine hours and include the Ice Explorer excursion, are also available.

★ MOUNT EDITH CAVELL

This 11,033-foot (3,363-m) peak is the most distinctive and impressive in the park. Known to indigenous people as the "White Ghost" for its snowcapped summit, the mountain was given its official name in honor of a British nurse who was executed for helping prisoners of war escape German-occupied Belgium during World War I. The peak was first climbed that same year; today the most popular route to the summit is up the east ridge (to the left of the summit). The imposing north face (facing the parking lot) has been climbed but is rated as an extremely difficult climb.

Cavell Road

The most impressive place to marvel at the mountain is from directly below the north face, at the end of Cavell Road. Located off Highway 93A, 8 mi (13 km) south from the town of Jasper, this steep, narrow road ascends 980 feet (300 m) in 9 mi (14.5 km). Due to the many switchbacks, trailers must be left in the designated area at the bottom.

From the parking lot at the end of Cavell Road, you must strain your neck to take in the magnificent sight of the mountain's 4,920-foot (1,500-m) north face and **Angel Glacier,** which lies in a saddle on the mountain's lower slopes. On warm days, those who are patient may be lucky enough to witness an avalanche tumbling from the glacier, creating a roar that echoes across the valley. From the parking area, a short interpretive trail, **Path of the Glacier Trail** (0.75 mi/1.2 km; 1 hour round-trip), traverses barren moraines deposited by the receding Angel Glacier and leads to some great viewpoints. The trail also leads to the longer **Cavell Meadows Trail** (page 198).

TOWN OF JASPER
Jasper-Yellowhead Museum and Archives

400 Bonhomme St.; 780/852-3013; 10am-5pm daily mid-May-Oct.; adult C$7, senior and child C$6

At the back of the town of Jasper is the excellent Jasper-Yellowhead Museum and Archives, as unstuffy as any museum could possibly be and well worth a visit even for non-museum types. The main gallery features colorful, modern picture boards with exhibits that take visitors along a timeline of Jasper's human history through the fur trade, the coming of the railway, and the creation of the park. Documentaries are shown on demand in a small television room. The museum also features extensive archives, including hundreds of historical photos, manuscripts, documents, maps, and videos.

Jasper Skytram

780/852-3093; 8am-9pm daily in summer, shorter hours late Mar.-June and Sept.-Oct., closed the rest of the year; adult C$52, child 6-15 C$27.50

Jasper Skytram

The Jasper Skytram climbs more than 3,280 vertical feet (1,000 vertical m) up the steep north face of **The Whistlers,** named for the hoary marmots that live on the summit. Jasper Skytram operates two 30-passenger cars that take seven minutes to reach the upper terminal, during which time the conductor gives a lecture about the mountain and its environment. From the upper terminal, a 0.9-mi (1.4-km) trail leads to the 8,104-foot (2,470-m) true summit. The view is breathtaking; to the south is the Columbia Icefield, and on a clear day you can see Mount Robson (12,970 ft/3,954 m)—the highest peak in the Canadian Rockies—to the northwest. Free two-hour guided hikes leave the upper terminal for the true summit at 10am, 11am, 2pm, and 3pm daily. You should allow two hours on top and, on a clear summer's day, two more hours in line at the bottom. Jasper Skytram is 1.9 mi (3 km) south of town on Highway 93 (Icefields Parkway), and then a similar distance up Whistlers Road.

MALIGNE VALLEY

Maligne Lake, one of the world's most photographed lakes, lies 30 mi (48 km) southeast of Jasper. It's the source of the **Maligne River,** which flows northward to **Medicine Lake** and then disappears underground, eventually emerging downstream of Maligne Canyon. The river was known to the indigenous people as Chaba Imne (River of the Great Beaver), but the name by which we know it today was coined by a missionary. After his horses were swept away by its swift-flowing waters in 1846, he described the river as being *"la traverse maligne,"* (wicked crossing). Driving up the Maligne River Valley to the lake is a lesson in 600

million years of geology that can be appreciated by anyone.

To get to Maligne Valley, head northeast from Jasper along Highway 16 for 2.5 mi (4 km) and turn south (right) on Maligne Lake Road. The access road to Maligne Canyon veers left off Maligne Lake Road 6.8 mi (11 km) from Jasper. Maligne Lake is at the end of Maligne Lake Road, 30 mi (48 km) from Jasper.

Maligne Canyon

As the Maligne River drops into the Athabasca River Valley, its gradient is particularly steep. The fast-flowing water has eroded a deep canyon out of the easily dissolved limestone bedrock. The canyon is up to 165 feet (50 m) deep, yet so narrow that squirrels often jump across.

An interpretive trail winds down from the parking lot at the upper end of the canyon, crossing the canyon six times. The most spectacular sections of the canyon can be seen from the first two bridges, at the upper end of the trail. In summer, a **teahouse** operates at the top of the canyon. Opposite the teahouse, you'll see large potholes in the riverbed. These potholes are created when rocks and pebbles become trapped in what begins as a shallow depression; under the force of the rushing water, they carve jug-shaped hollows into the soft bedrock.

To avoid the crowds at the upper end of the canyon, an alternative would be to park at **Sixth Bridge,** near the confluence of the Maligne and Athabasca Rivers, and walk *up* the canyon.

By late December, the torrent that is the Maligne River has frozen solid. Where it cascades down through Maligne Canyon, the river is temporarily stalled for the winter, creating

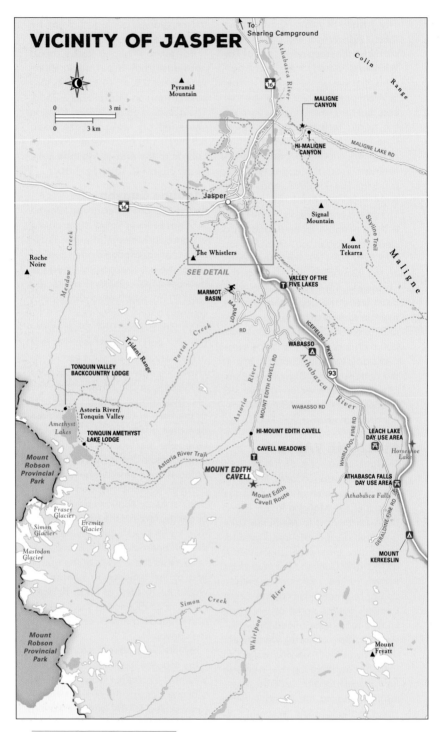

VICINITY OF JASPER

To Snaring Campground

Colin Range

Pyramid Mountain

Athabasca River

16

MALIGNE CANYON

HI-MALIGNE CANYON

MALIGNE LAKE RD

0   3 mi
0   3 km

16

Jasper

Signal Mountain

Skyline Trail

Maligne

Roche Noire

Meadow Creek

The Whistlers

Mount Tekarra

SEE DETAIL

VALLEY OF THE FIVE LAKES

MARMOT BASIN

Trident Range

Portal Creek

MARMOT RD

ICEFIELDS PKWY

WABASSO

Athabasca River

TONQUIN VALLEY BACKCOUNTRY LODGE

Astoria River/ Tonquin Valley

MOUNT EDITH CAVELL RD

93

WABASSO RD

Amethyst Lakes

TONQUIN AMETHYST LAKE LODGE

Astoria River

HI-MOUNT EDITH CAVELL

CAVELL MEADOWS

WHIRLPOOL FIRE RD

LEACH LAKE DAY USE AREA

Horseshoe Lake

Astoria River Trail

Mount Robson Provincial Park

MOUNT EDITH CAVELL

ATHABASCA FALLS DAY USE AREA

Athabasca Falls

Fraser Glacier

Mount Edith Cavell Route

Simon Glacier

Eremite Glacier

GERALDINE FIRE RD

Mastodon Glacier

MOUNT KERKESLIN

Mount Robson Provincial Park

Simon Creek

Whirlpool River

Mount Fryatt

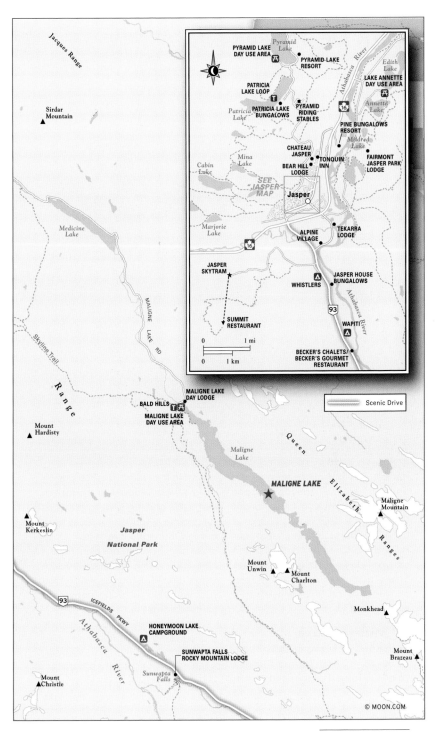

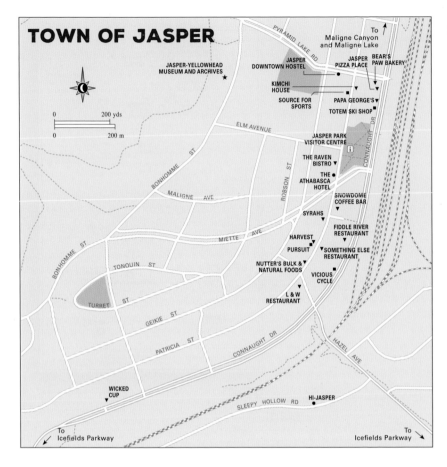

TOWN OF JASPER

0   200 yds
0   200 m

remarkable formations through the deep limestone canyon. **Jasper Adventure Centre** (414 Connaught Dr.; 780/852-4056; adult C$69, child C$34.50) offers intriguing three-hour guided tours into the depths of the canyon daily throughout winter. These guided tours of the frozen canyon are an experience you'll never forget.

★ Maligne Lake

At the end of Maligne Lake Road, 30 mi (48 km) from town, is Maligne Lake, the largest glacier-fed lake in the Canadian Rockies and second

largest in the world. The first paying visitors were brought to the lake in the 1920s, and it has been a mecca for camera-toting tourists from around the world ever since. Once at the lake, activities are plentiful. But other than taking in the spectacular vistas, the only thing you won't need your wallet for is hiking one of the numerous trails in the area.

The most popular tourist activity at the lake is a 90-minute narrated **cruise** (10am-5pm daily in summer; adult C$75-110, child C$37.50-55, reservations recommended) on a glass-enclosed boat up the lake to oft-photographed **Spirit Island.** Rowboats, double kayaks, and canoes can be rented at the **Boat House** (9am-5pm daily June-mid-Sept.), a provincial historic site dating to 1929, for C$75 per hour or C$200 per day. The lake also has excellent trout fishing; guided fishing tours are available.

All commercial operations to and around the lake are operated by **Pursuit** (616 Patricia St.; 403/762-6700 or 866/606-6700; www.banffjaspercollection.com; 8am-6pm daily), with a ticket office in downtown Jasper. At the lake itself, in addition to the cruises and boat rentals, Pursuit operates Maligne Lake Lodge, a day-use facility that includes a souvenir shop and a couple restaurants with lake views.

MIETTE HOT SPRINGS
780/866-3939; 10:30am-9pm daily mid-May-mid-Oct., extended to 8:30am-10:30pm daily in summer; day pass adult C$10, seniors and children C$8.25

Miette Hot Springs Road branches south from Highway 27 mi (16 km) east of Jasper. After curving, swerving, rising, and falling many times, Miette Hot Springs Road ends 11 mi (18 km) from Highway 16 at the warmest springs in the Canadian Rockies, Miette Hot Springs. In the early 1900s, these springs were one of the park's biggest attractions. In 1910, a packhorse trail was built up the valley, and the government constructed a bathhouse. The original hand-hewn log structure was replaced in the 1930s with pools that remained in use until new facilities were built in 1985. Water that flows

into the pools is artificially cooled from 128°F (54°C) to a soothing 100°F (39°C). A newer addition to the complex is a smaller, cool plunge pool.

Many hiking trails begin from the hot springs complex; the shortest is from the picnic area to the source of the springs (allow five minutes each way). Overlooking the pools is a café, while lodging is just down the hill.

Spirit Island on Maligne Lake (top); Maligne Canyon (bottom)

Maligne Lake

SCENIC DRIVES

ICEFIELDS PARKWAY (JASPER)

DRIVING DISTANCE: 67 mi (108 km) one-way
DRIVING TIME: 2 hours one-way
START: Sunwapta Pass
END: Town of Jasper

Sunwapta Pass (6,690 ft/2,040 m), 2.5 mi (4 km) south of the Columbia Icefield, marks the boundary between Banff and Jasper National Parks.

No gas is available along this stretch of the Icefields Parkway. The nearest gas stations are at Saskatchewan River Crossing (Banff National Park) and in the town of Jasper, 93 mi (150 km) apart, so keep your tank topped up to be safe.

The following sights along the Icefields Parkway are detailed from south to north, from the Icefield Centre to the town of Jasper, a distance of 65 mi (105 km). The scenery along this stretch of road is no less spectacular than the other half through Banff National Park, and it's easy to spend at least a full day en route.

Columbia Icefield

The Columbia Icefield is beside the Icefields Parkway at the south end of the park, 65 mi (105 km) south of Jasper and 82 mi (132 km) north of Lake Louise. Don't miss **Athabasca Glacier,** the Columbia Icefield's most accessible, which can be seen from the Icefields Parkway, and you can drive right up to. Overlooking Athabasca Glacier is the **Icefield Centre,** which provides a good overview of glaciers, as well as information for visitors.

Along the Sunwapta River

Sunwapta Lake, at the toe of the Athabasca Glacier, is the source of the Sunwapta River, which the Icefields Parkway follows for 30 mi (48 km) to Sunwapta Falls.

Immediately north of Icefield Centre is an unheralded pullout where few travelers stop, but which allows for an excellent panorama of the area away from the crowds. Across the glacial-green Sunwapta River is a wasteland of till and a distinctive terminal moraine left behind by the retreating **Dome Glacier.**

Icefields Parkway (top); Sunwapta Falls
(bottom left); Goats and Glaciers Lookout
(bottom right)

Between the Dome and Athabasca Glaciers is 11,350-foot (3,459-m) **Snow Dome.**

The architecturally impressive **Columbia Icefield Skywalk** (403/762-6700 or 866/606-6700; www.banffjaspercollection.com; 9am-6pm daily May-mid-Oct.; adult C$34, child C$17) projects out into the Sunwapta Canyon 918 feet (280 m) above the valley floor around 3.7 mi (6 km) north of the Icefield Centre. Access is by shuttle bus from the Icefield Centre (no passenger vehicles are allowed to stop at the skywalk itself). A short interpretive trail leads along the canyon edge and then out onto the glass-floored skywalk. Looking upstream from the skywalk, you can see the massive, ice-draped slopes of **Mount Athabasca** (11,450 ft/3,491 m) framed by the walls of the valley—a truly inspiring view of this great mountain. Directly across the valley is the ice-capped east face of **Mount Kitchener.**

From the skywalk, northbound travelers lose 980 feet (300 m) of elevation over the next 2.5 mi (4 km), descending to the floor of the Sunwapta Valley. The first worthwhile stop is **Tangle Falls;** the waterfall is on the east side (on the right for northbound drivers) but parking is on the west side of the road, so be very careful when crossing over, both to park and when walking back across to view the falls. The waterfall is picturesque year-round, but extra special in winter when it is frozen solid.

Less than 1.2 mi (2 km) farther north, the road continues its descent to a viewpoint for **Stutfield Glacier.** Most of the glacier is hidden from view by a densely wooded ridge, but the valley floor below its toe is littered with till left by the glacier's retreat. The main body of the Columbia Icefield can be seen along the cliff top high above, and south of the glacier you can see Mount Kitchener.

About 3.7 mi (6 km) farther down the road is **Tangle Ridge,** a grayish-brown wall of limestone over which Beauty Creek cascades. At this point the Icefields Parkway runs alongside the Sunwapta River, following its braided course through the **Endless Range,** the eastern wall of a classic glacier-carved valley.

Sunwapta Falls

A farther 25 mi (41 km) along the road, a 0.3-mi (500-m) spur at Sunwapta Falls Rocky Mountain Lodge leads to Sunwapta Falls. Here the Sunwapta River changes direction sharply and drops into a deep canyon. The best viewpoint is from the bridge across the river, but it's also worth following the path on the parking lot side of the river downstream along the rim of the canyon. About 1.2 mi (2 km) downstream, the river flows into the much wider Athabasca Valley at Lower Sunwapta Falls.

Goats and Glaciers Lookout

After following the Athabasca River for 11 mi (17 km), the road ascends to a lookout with picnic tables offering panoramic river views. Below the lookout is a steep bank of exposed, glacially ground material containing natural deposits of salt. The local mountain goats spend most of their time on the steep slopes of Mount Kerkeslin, to the northeast, but occasionally cross the road and can be seen searching for the salt licks along the roadside or riverbank, trying to replenish lost nutrients.

Athabasca Falls

Approximately 5.6 mi (9 km) beyond Goats and Glaciers Lookout and

20 mi (32 km) south of Jasper, the Icefields Parkway divides when an old stretch of highway (Highway 93A) crosses the Athabasca River and continues along its west side for 15.5 mi (25 km) before rejoining the parkway 4.3 mi (7 km) south of the town. At the southern end of this loop, the Athabasca River is forced through a narrow gorge and over a cliff into a cauldron of roaring water below. As the river slowly erodes the center of the riverbed, the falls will move upstream. Trails lead from a day-use area to various viewpoints above and below the falls. The trail branching under Highway 93A follows an abandoned river channel before emerging at the bottom of the canyon. Facilities at Athabasca Falls include picnic tables and restrooms.

North to Jasper

Take Wabasso Road (Highway 93A) beyond Athabasca Falls to reach Mount Edith Cavell, or continue north along the Icefields Parkway to access the following sights. The first worthwhile stop along this route is **Horseshoe Lake,** reached along a 0.2-mi (350-m) trail from a parking lot 1.9 mi (3 km) north of Athabasca Falls. The southern end of this delightful little body of water is ringed by a band of cliffs popular with locals in summer as a cliff-diving spot but worth visiting for its scenery alone.

About 1.2 mi (2 km) north of the Horseshoe Lake parking lot are a couple of lookouts with sweeping views across the Athabasca River to **Athabasca Pass,** used by David Thompson on his historic expedition across the continent. To the north of the pass lies Mount Edith Cavell. From this lookout it is 16 mi (26 km) to the town of Jasper.

ATHABASCA RIVER (HIGHWAY 16)

DRIVING DISTANCE: 31 mi (50 km) one-way
DRIVING TIME: 1 hour one-way
START: Jasper
END: East Park Gate

From Jasper, it's 31 mi (50 km) to the

Jasper Lake, Highway 16

park's eastern boundary along Highway 16, following the Athabasca River the entire way. Beyond the turnoff to **Maligne Lake,** Highway 16 enters a wide valley flanked to the west by The Palisade ridge and to the east by the Colin Range. The valley is a classic montane environment, with open meadows and forests of Douglas fir and lodgepole pine. After crossing the Athabasca River, 12.4 mi (20 km) from Jasper, the highway parallels **Jasper Lake,** which is lined by sand dunes along its southern edge. At the highway, a plaque marks the site of **Jasper House** (the actual site is on the opposite side of the river). The next worthwhile stop is **Disaster Point,** 2.5 mi (4 km) farther north. This is a great spot for viewing bighorn sheep, which gather at a mineral lick, an area of exposed mineral salts. Disaster Point is on the lower slopes of **Roche Miette,** a distinctive 7,600-foot-high (2,316-m-high) peak that juts out into the Athabasca River Valley. Across the highway, the braided Athabasca River is flanked by wetlands alive with migrating birds in the spring and fall.

The junction with Miette Hot Springs Road (27 mi/43 km east of Jasper) marks the site of **Pocahontas,** a coal-mining town in existence between 1910 and 1921. The mine itself was high above the township, with coal transported to the valley floor by cable car. Most buildings have long since been removed, but a short interpretive walk leads through the remaining foundations. About 0.6 mi (1 km) along Miette Hot Springs Road, a short trail leads to photogenic **Punchbowl Falls.** Here Mountain Creek cascades through a narrow crevice in a cliff to a pool of turbulent water. From Pocahontas, the **East Park Gate** of Jasper National Park is 4.3 mi (7 km) away.

BEST HIKES

BALD HILLS
DISTANCE: 3.2 mi (5.2 km) one-way
DURATION: 2 hours one-way
ELEVATION GAIN: 1,620 feet (495 m)
EFFORT: moderate-strenuous
TRAIL SURFACE: unpaved
TRAILHEAD: picnic area at the end of Maligne Lake Road

This trail follows an old road for its entire distance to the site of a fire lookout that has long since been removed. It is well worth continuing on a network of trails through alpine meadows to higher elevations, where sweeping views take in the jade-green waters of Maligne Lake, the Queen Elizabeth Ranges, and the twin peaks of Mount Unwin and Mount Charlton. The Bald Hills extend for 4.3 mi (7 km), their highest summit not exceeding 8,530 feet (2,600 m). On the return journey, make the short detour to **Moose Lake.**

CAVELL MEADOWS
DISTANCE: 3.8 mi (6 km) round-trip
DURATION: 2 hours round-trip
ELEVATION GAIN: 1,250 feet (380 m)
EFFORT: moderate
TRAIL SURFACE: unpaved
TRAILHEAD: parking lot at the end of Cavell Road, 17 mi (27.5 km) south of town

This trail, beginning from the parking lot beneath Mount Edith Cavell,

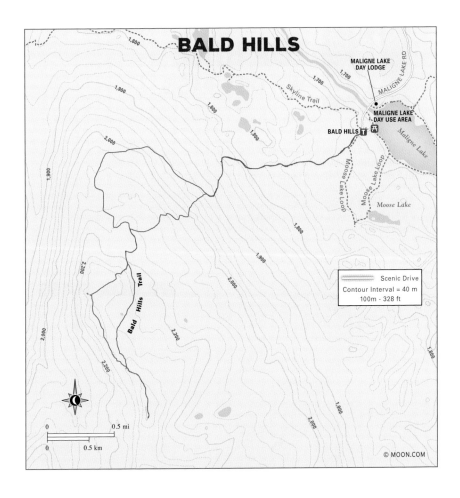

BALD HILLS

MALIGNE LAKE
DAY LODGE

MALIGNE LAKE RD

MALIGNE LAKE
DAY USE AREA

BALD HILLS

Skyline Trail

Maligne Lake

Moose Lake Loop

Moose Lake

Bald Hills Trail

Scenic Drive
Contour Interval = 40 m
100m - 328 ft

0   0.5 mi

0   0.5 km

© MOON.COM

provides access to an alpine meadow and panoramic views of Angel Glacier. The trail begins by following the paved Path of the Glacier Trail, then branches left, climbing steadily along a rocky ridge and then through a subalpine forest of Engelmann spruce and then stunted subalpine fir to emerge facing the northeast face of Mount Edith Cavell and Angel Glacier. The view of the glacier from this point is nothing less than awesome, as the ice spills out of a cirque, clinging to a 984-foot-high (300-m-high) cliff face. The trail continues to higher viewpoints and

an alpine meadow that, by mid-July, is filled with wildflowers.

PATRICIA LAKE LOOP

DISTANCE: 3.1 mi (5 km) round-trip
DURATION: 1.5 hours round-trip
ELEVATION GAIN: minimal
EFFORT: easy
TRAIL SURFACE: unpaved
TRAILHEAD: 1.2 mi (2 km) along Pyramid Lake Road

This trail begins across the road from the riding stables on Pyramid Lake Road. It traverses a mixed forest of aspen and lodgepole pine—prime

TOP HIKE
WILCOX PASS

DISTANCE: 2.5 mi (4 km) one-way
DURATION: 1.5 hours one-way
ELEVATION GAIN: 1,115 feet (340 m)
EFFORT: moderate
TRAIL SURFACE: unpaved
TRAILHEAD: Wilcox Creek Campground, 1.9 mi (3 km) south of the Icefield Centre

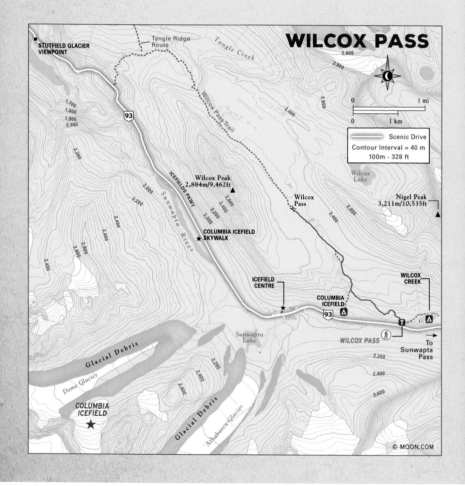

Views of the **Columbia Icefield** from the Icefields Parkway pale in comparison with those achieved along this trail, on the same side of the valley as the Icefield Centre. This trail was once used by northbound outfitters because, 120 years ago, the Athabasca Glacier covered the valley floor and had to be bypassed. Beginning from the Wilcox Creek Campground access road, the trail climbs through a stunted forest of Engelmann spruce and subalpine fir to a ridge with panoramic views of the valley, **Mount Athabasca,** and the **Athabasca Glacier.** Ascending gradually from there, the trail enters a fragile environment of alpine meadows. From these meadows and the pass, most hikers return along the same trail (the distance quoted), although it is possible to continue north, descending to the Icefields Parkway at **Tangle Ridge,** 7.1 mi (11.5 km) along the road from the trailhead.

Valley of the Five Lakes

habitat for larger mammals such as elk, deer, and moose. The second half of the trail skirts **Cottonwood Slough,** where you'll see several beaver ponds. Unlike the name suggests, this trail doesn't encircle Patricia Lake but instead just passes along a portion of its southern shoreline.

VALLEY OF THE FIVE LAKES

DISTANCE: 2.9 mi (4.6 km) round-trip
DURATION: 1.5 hours round-trip
ELEVATION GAIN: minimal
EFFORT: easy
TRAIL SURFACE: unpaved

TRAILHEAD: 6.2 mi (10 km) south along the Icefields Parkway of the town of Jasper

These shallow, turquoise lakes, nestled in an open valley, are small but make a worthwhile destination. From the trailhead and large parking lot, the trail passes through a forest of lodgepole pine, crosses a stream, and climbs a low ridge from where you'll have a panoramic view of surrounding peaks. As the trail descends to the lakes, turn right at the first intersection to loop past the southernmost lake, then veer north to loop around the remaining lakes.

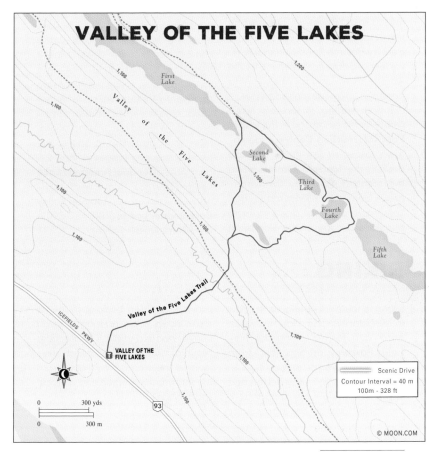

BACKPACKING

With 745 mi (1,200 km) of hiking trails, Jasper National Park has an extensive system of interconnecting backcountry trails that, for experienced hikers, can provide a wilderness adventure rivaled by few areas on the face of the earth. The most popular trails for extended backcountry trips are the **Skyline Trail** (27.6 mi/44.5 km; 3 days each way), between Maligne Lake and Maligne Lake Road; the **Athabasca Pass Trail** (31 mi/50 km; 3 days each way), which was used by fur traders for 40 years as the main route across the Canadian Rockies; and the **South Boundary Trail** (100 mi/160 km; 10 days each way), which traverses a remote section of the front ranges into Banff National Park. For less of a time commitment, try the Astoria River/Tonquin Valley trail to Amethyst Lakes, described below.

Before setting off on any hikes, whatever the length, go to the **Jasper Park Information Centre** in downtown Jasper or the Parks Canada desk in the **Icefield Centre** along the Icefields Parkway for waterproof Gem Trek hiking maps, trail conditions, and trail closures, or to purchase a copy of the *Canadian Rockies Trail Guide* by Brian Patton and Bart Robinson.

ASTORIA RIVER/ TONQUIN VALLEY

11.8 mi (19 km) one-way

For experienced backpackers only, this overnight trail starts opposite the hostel on Cavell Road and descends through a forest on the north side of Mount Edith Cavell for 3.1 mi (5 km), then crosses the Astoria River and begins a long ascent into spectacular Tonquin Valley. Amethyst Lakes and the 3,280-foot (1,000-m) cliffs of the Ramparts first come into view after 8 mi (13 km). At the 10.5-mi (17-km) mark, the trail divides. To the left it climbs into Eremite Valley, where there is a campground. The right fork continues, following the Astoria River to Tonquin Valley, Amethyst Lakes, and a choice of four campgrounds. With advance reservations, hikers can also stay at one of the two backcountry lodges in the Tonquin Valley: **Tonquin Amethyst Lake Lodge** (780/852-1188; www.tonquinadventures.com) or **Tonquin Valley Backcountry Lodge** (780/852-3909; www.tonquinvalley.com).

BIKING

Biking in the park continues to grow in popularity. The ride between Banff and Jasper, along the **Icefields Parkway,** attracts riders from around the world. In addition to the paved roads, many designated unpaved bicycle trails radiate from the town. Cyclists are particularly prone to sudden bear encounters; make noise when passing through heavily wooded areas. The brochure *Mountain Biking Trail Guide* lists designated trails and is available from the information center and all local sport shops.

ATHABASCA RIVER TRAIL

One of the most popular biking routes is the Athabasca River Trail. It begins at the base of **Old Fort Point,** a distinctive knoll above the Athabasca River to the south of town, and follows the river to a point below Maligne Canyon, for a distance of 5 mi (8 km) one-way.

RENTALS

Expect bike rentals to run C$20-35 per hour or C$40-80 for any 24-hour period.

SOURCE FOR SPORTS
406 Patricia St., Jasper; 780/852-3654; 9am-9pm daily

VICIOUS CYCLE
630 Connaught Dr., Jasper; 780/852-1111; 9am-6pm Sun.-Thurs., 9am-7pm Fri.-Sat.

RAFTING

Within the park, the Athabasca and Sunwapta Rivers are run by a half-dozen outfitters.

ATHABASCA RIVER

On the Athabasca River, the **Mile 5 Run** is an easy two-hour float that appeals to all ages. Farther upstream, some operators offer a trip that begins from below **Athabasca Falls,** on a stretch of the river that passes through a narrow canyon; this run takes three hours.

SUNWAPTA RIVER

The boulder-strewn rapids of the Sunwapta River offer more thrills and spills—these trips are for the more adventurous and last 3-4 hours.

OUTFITTERS

Most companies offer a choice of rivers and provide transportation to and from downtown hotels. Expect to pay C$80-90 for trips on the Athabasca and C$85-100 for the Sunwapta. The following companies run on at least one of the rivers mid-May-September.

MALIGNE RAFTING
780/852-3331 or 844/808-7177; www.raftjasper.com

JASPER RAFT TOURS
780/852-2665 or 888/553-5628; www.jasperrafttours.com

JASPER'S WHITEWATER RAFTING
780/852-7238 or 800/557-7238; www.whitewaterraftingjasper.com

WINTER SPORTS

Winter is certainly a quiet time in the park, but that doesn't mean there's a lack of things to do. Marmot Basin offers world-class alpine skiing, and many snow-covered hiking trails are groomed for cross-country skiing.

DOWNHILL SKIING
Marmot Basin
780/852-3816 or 866/952-3816; www.skimarmot.com; Dec.-Apr.; lift tickets adult C$105, senior and youth C$85

rafting on the Athabasca River

The skiing at Marmot Basin is highly underrated. The resort has nine lifts servicing 1,675 acres (680 ha) of terrain with a vertical rise of 2,940 feet (900 m). The longest run is 3.5 mi (5.6 km). A huge injection of cash in recent years has improved the facilities, and the resort's Canadian Rockies Express is the longest detachable quad in Alberta. Lifts take skiers and boarders into Charlie's Basin, a massive powder-filled bowl, and to the summit of Eagle Ridge, which accesses open bowls and lightly treed glades of two other mountain faces. Marmot doesn't get the crowds of the three alpine resorts in Banff National Park, so lift lines are uncommon. The season runs early December-late April.

CROSS-COUNTRY SKIING

For many people, traveling Jasper's hiking trails on skis is just as exhilarating as traversing them on foot. An extensive network of 185 mi (300 km) of summer hiking trails is designated for skiers, with around 62 mi (100 km) groomed.

The four main areas of trails are along **Pyramid Lake Road,** around **Maligne Lake,** in the **Athabasca Falls** area, and at Whistlers Campground. A booklet available at the park information center details each trail and its difficulty. Weather forecasts and avalanche-hazard reports are also posted here.

RENTALS

SOURCE FOR SPORTS
406 Patricia St., Jasper; 780/852-3654; 9am-9pm daily

TOTEM SKI SHOP
408 Connaught Dr., Jasper; 780/852-3078; 9am-10pm daily

FOOD

It's easy to get a good, or even great, meal in Jasper. Connaught Drive and Patricia Street are lined with cafés and restaurants. Considering this is a national park, menus are reasonably well priced. You should expect hearty fare, with lots of beef, game, and a surprisingly good selection of seafood.

STANDOUTS
Icefields Parkway
BECKER'S GOURMET RESTAURANT
780/852-3535; 8am-11am, 5:30pm-9pm daily May-mid-Oct.; C$34-49

One of Jasper's best restaurants, Becker's Gourmet Restaurant is 3.7 mi (6 km) out of town to the south along the Icefields Parkway, but well worth the short drive. From this cozy dining room, where the atmosphere is intimate, or the adjacent enclosed conservatory, the views of Mount Kerkeslin and the Athabasca River are inspiring. This restaurant is a throwback to days gone by, with an ever-changing menu of seasonal game and produce that includes a wild game platter. A menu staple is the pesto-crusted rack of lamb. For dessert, the strawberry shortcake is a delight. At just C$18 per person, the breakfast buffet is one of the best dining deals in the park, and certainly worth the drive out from town.

Town of Jasper
WICKED CUP
Maligne Lodge, 912 Connaught Dr.; 780/852-1942; 7am-7pm daily; lunches C$9-12

Well worth searching out is Wicked Cup, on the west side of downtown. Seating is inside or out on a heated deck, and the café is far enough from downtown that it is usually crowd-free. The selection of coffee drinks and teas is extensive, and the food made to order and delicious, including lots of healthy breakfast choices.

HARVEST
616 Patricia St.; 780/852-9676; 9am-9pm daily; breakfasts C$14-18

Harvest is a casual, contemporary restaurant that serves up excellent food at reasonable prices. Breakfasts include mashed avocado on toast, Belgian waffles, and a delicious kale and potato hash topped with a poached egg and hollandaise sauce. The dinner menu is loaded with tapas-style choices designed for sharing—think a cheese board, fish tacos, cauliflower bravas, and fondue. Ingredients are fresh and simply prepared, making for a tasty dining experience.

GREAT HALL GASTROPUB
Fairmont Jasper Park Lodge, 1 Old Lodge Rd.; 780/852-3301; 7am-11pm daily; C$22-70

The elegantly rustic Great Hall Gastropub is a good place to enjoy delicious breakfasts, ranging from a continental buffet to chocolate chip waffles. The rest of the day, the highlight is traditional Canadian fare, such as elk pie, whiskey-flamed arctic char, or a chargrilled Albertan rib-eye steak. Be sure to leave room for dessert—the chocolate fudge cake is incredible. Across from the reception area in the Fairmont Jasper Park Lodge is a dedicated dining reservation desk for the restaurant, staffed 11am-8pm daily in summer. Children five and under eat free.

JASPER NATIONAL PARK FOOD

NAME	LOCATION	TYPE
★ Becker's Gourmet Restaurant	Icefields Parkway	sit-down restaurant
Tekarra Lodge	Icefields Parkway	sit-down restaurant
Summit Restaurant	Jasper Skytram	sit-down restaurant
Bear's Paw Bakery	town of Jasper	café
SnowDome Coffee Bar	town of Jasper	café
★ Wicked Cup	Maligne Lodge, town of Jasper	café
Nutter's	town of Jasper	groceries
L&W Restaurant	town of Jasper	sit-down restaurant
Jasper Pizza Place	town of Jasper	sit-down restaurant
Papa George's	Astoria Hotel, town of Jasper	sit-down restaurant
★ Harvest	town of Jasper	sit-down restaurant
Fiddle River Restaurant	town of Jasper	sit-down restaurant
Something Else Restaurant	town of Jasper	sit-down restaurant
Raven Bistro	town of Jasper	sit-down restaurant
Syrahs	town of Jasper	sit-down restaurant
Kimchi House	town of Jasper	sit-down and takeout
Orso Trattoria	Fairmont Jasper Park Lodge	sit-down restaurant
Oka Sushi	Fairmont Jasper Park Lodge	sit-down restaurant
Emerald Lounge	Fairmont Jasper Park Lodge	sit-down restaurant
★ Great Hall Gastropub	Fairmont Jasper Park Lodge	sit-down restaurant
Maligne Canyon Wilderness Kitchen	Maligne Lake Road	sit-down restaurant

FOOD	PRICE	HOURS
Canadian	splurge	8am-11am, 5:30pm-9pm daily May-mid-Oct.
Canadian	splurge	8am-11am and 5:30pm-9:30pm daily mid-May-early Oct.
Canadian	moderate	10am-5pm daily late Apr.-June and Sept.-mid-Oct., 9am-8pm daily July-Aug.
coffee and baked goods	budget	6am-6pm daily
coffee and baked goods	budget	7am-8pm daily
coffee and baked goods	budget	7am-7pm daily
bulk foods	budget	9am-8pm daily in summer, shorter hours the rest of the year
Mediterranean	moderate	11am-11pm daily
pizza	moderate	11am-11pm daily
casual Canadian	moderate	7:30am-2pm and 5pm-10pm daily
casual Canadian	moderate	9am-9pm daily
seafood	moderate	5pm-9:30pm daily
European	moderate	11am-11pm daily
European	moderate	5pm-10pm Mon.-Fri., 9am-1pm and 5pm-10pm Sat.-Sun.
European	moderate	5:30pm-9pm daily
Asian	budget	10am-10pm daily
Italian	splurge	7am-11am and 5pm-10pm daily
Asian	moderate	6pm-9pm Mon.-Sat.
Canadian	moderate	11:30am-midnight daily
Canadian	splurge	5:30pm-10pm daily
contemporary Canadian	moderate	11am-9pm daily summer, Fri.-Sun. only rest of year

BEST PICNIC SPOTS

Pyramid Lake Day Use Area

Pyramid Lake Rd., 3.8 mi (6 km) north of the town of Jasper

With good paddling and swimming, the picnic areas along the west shore of Pyramid Lake are the perfect place to base yourself on a warm summer's day.

Lake Annette Day Use Area

Off Maligne Lake Rd., 4.3 mi (7 km) northeast of the town of Jasper

Picnic tables are spread through a forested area between Lakes Annette and Edith, providing easy access to two lakes, a playground, and change rooms.

Maligne Lake Day Use Area

Maligne Lake Rd., 30 mi (48 km) north then southeast of the town of Jasper

At the very end of Maligne Lake Road, picnic tables are spread along the shore of Jasper's largest lake—the perfect place to relax after hiking up into the adjacent Bald Hills.

Miette Hot Springs Day Use Area

Miette Hot Springs Rd., 39 mi (62 km) north of the town of Jasper

Best known for hot springs, the end of Miette Hot Springs Road also has picnic tables with raised fire grills.

Athabasca Falls Day Use Area

Icefields Parkway, 19 mi (31 km) south of the town of Jasper

Most visitors stop at Athabasca Falls to view the waterfall, but tables spread along the riverfront are the perfect place for a picnic.

Leach Lake Day Use Area

Highway 93A, 14 mi (22 km) south of the town of Jasper

There's only a couple of picnic tables at Leach Lake, but it's a quiet spot with mountain views and a lake with dock.

CAMPING

Most campgrounds in Jasper begin opening in mid-June, and all but Wapiti are closed by mid-October. All campsites have a picnic table and fire ring, with a fire permit costing C$9 (includes firewood).

Unlike neighboring Banff National Park, Jasper's 10 campgrounds can handle all but the busiest summer nights. And on the rare occasion all campsites fill, campers are directed to overflow areas. These are glorified parking lots with no designated sites, but fees are reduced (C$12 per unit).

Reservations

Sites in the most popular campgrounds—**Whistlers, Wapiti, Wabasso,** and **Pocahontas**—can be reserved through the **Parks Canada Campground Reservation Service** (877/737-3783; www.reservation. pc.gc.ca) for C$12.

Tips

If you're traveling in June through September and know which dates you'll be in Jasper, it is strongly advised to take advantage of the reservation service above. Whistlers,

Columbia Icefield Campground (left); Wabasso Campground (right)

Wapiti, and Wabasso are the only three campgrounds in the park with powered sites, and therefore they're in great demand.

STANDOUTS
Wabasso Campground
mid-June-early Sept.; C$22.50-33.30
Sites, some powered, at Wabasso Campground, along Wabasso Road approximately 10 mi (16 km) south of Jasper, are set among stands of spruce and aspen, with easy access to the Athabasca River. Facilities include heated bathrooms with flush toilets and hot and cold water.

Wapiti Campground
mid-May-mid-Sept.; C$28.40-33.30
About 1.2 mi (2 km) farther south of Whistlers Campground along the Icefields Parkway is Wapiti Campground, where 86 of the 362 sites have power hookups. Some sites are close to the Athabasca River; facilities include heated bathrooms and showers. Wapiti is also open throughout winter (mid-Oct.-early May) with fewer sites and no dump station.

Whistlers Campground
May-mid-Oct.; C$23.50-39.20
Whistlers Campground, 1.9 mi (3 km) south of Jasper, has 781 sites, making it the largest campground in either Banff or Jasper National Parks. It is divided into four sections, and prices vary with the services available: walk-in tent sites C$23.50, unserviced sites C$28.40, powered sites C$33.30, full hookups C$39.20. Washrooms and streetlights are spread throughout, while each section has showers, playgrounds, and a nightly interpretive program.

JASPER NATIONAL PARK CAMPGROUNDS

NAME	LOCATION	SEASON
Wilcox Creek Campground	Icefields Parkway	early June-late Sept.
Columbia Icefield Campground	Icefields Parkway	June-mid-Oct.
Jonas Creek Campground	Icefields Parkway	mid-June-early Sept.
Honeymoon Lake Campground	Icefields Parkway	mid-June-early Sept.
Mount Kerkeslin Campground	Icefields Parkway	mid-June-early Sept.
★ Wabasso Campground	Icefields Parkway	mid-June-early Sept.
★ Wapiti Campground	Icefields Parkway	mid-May-mid-Sept.
★ Whistlers Campground	Icefields Parkway	May-mid-Oct.
Snaring River Campground	Highway 16	mid-May-mid-Sept.
Pocahontas Campground	Highway 16	mid-May-mid-Sept.

LODGING

In summer, motel and hotel rooms here are expensive. Most of the motels and lodges are within walking distance of the town of Jasper and have indoor pools and restaurants. Luckily, alternatives to staying in C$400-plus hotel rooms do exist. The best of these are the lodges scattered around the edge of town, where rates are mostly similar, but the experience more authentic. Open in summer only, each offers a rustic

SITES AND AMENITIES	RV LIMIT	PRICE	RESERVATIONS
46 tent and RV sites, pit toilets, dump station	27 ft (8 m)	C$17	no
33 tent-only sites, pit toilets	n/a	C$17	no
25 tent and RV sites, drinking water, pit toilets	25 ft (7.5 m)	C$17	no
35 tent and RV sites, drinking water, pit toilets	25 ft (7.5 m)	C$17	no
42 tent and RV sites, drinking water, pit toilets	25 ft (7.5 m)	C$17	no
231 tent and RV sites, drinking water, flush toilets, dump station, electrical hookups	35 ft (10 m)	C$22.50-33.30	yes
362 tent and RV sites, drinking water, flush toilets, showers, dump station, electrical hookups	no limit	C$28.40-33.30	yes
781 tent and RV sites, drinking water, flush toilets, showers, dump station, electrical hookups	no limit	C$23.50-39.20	yes
62 tent and RV sites, drinking water, pit toilets	27 ft (8 m)	C$16.50	no
140 tent and RV sites, drinking water, flush toilets	27 ft (8 m)	C$22.50	yes

yet distinct style of accommodation in keeping with the theme of staying in a national park. Additionally, many private residences have rooms for rent in summer, and three hostels are close to town.

Rates quoted are for a standard room in summer. Outside the busy June-September period, most lodgings reduce rates drastically (ask also about ski packages during winter). Rooms have en suite bathrooms, unless otherwise indicated.

Two accommodations east of the town of Jasper—but still within the park boundary—are open in summer only.

JASPER NATIONAL PARK LODGING

NAME	LOCATION	SEASON
★ Sunwapta Falls Rocky Mountain Lodge	Icefields Parkway	May-mid-Oct.
★ Becker's Chalets	Icefields Parkway	May-mid-Oct.
Jasper House Bungalows	Icefields Parkway	mid-May-mid-Oct.
★ Alpine Village	Icefields Parkway	late Apr.-mid-Oct.
HI-Mount Edith Cavell	Cavell Road	mid-June-mid-Oct.
Jasper Downtown Hostel	town of Jasper	year-round
HI-Jasper	town of Jasper	year-round
Athabasca Hotel	town of Jasper	year-round
★ Bear Hill Lodge	town of Jasper	year-round
Tonquin Inn	town of Jasper	year-round
Chateau Jasper	town of Jasper	year-round
Pine Bungalows	town of Jasper	May-mid-Oct.
Patricia Lake Bungalows	town of Jasper	May-mid-Oct.
Tekarra Lodge	town of Jasper	mid-May-early Oct.
Pyramid Lake Resort	town of Jasper	year-round
★ Fairmont Jasper Park Lodge	town of Jasper	year-round
HI-Maligne Canyon	Maligne Lake Road	June-Sept.
Pocahontas Cabins	Miette Hot Springs Road	May-Sept.
Miette Hot Springs Bungalows	Miette Hot Springs Road	May-Sept.

OPTIONS	PRICE
motel rooms	rooms starting at C$269
hotel rooms; chalets with kitchenette; duplexes that sleep up to 8	rooms starting at C$170
cabins; motel-style units	motel-style units starting at C$230
cabins; suites	cabins starting at C$230
dormitory rooms (no showers and only pit toilets)	nonmembers C$40
dormitory rooms with 2-8 beds; private rooms with en suite bathrooms	dorm beds C$45-50 private rooms starting at C$160
dormitory rooms with 1-4 beds (some women-only rooms); private rooms with en suite bathroom	nonmember dorm C$52 private rooms starting at C$166
hotel rooms, some with shared bathrooms	from C$139 s or d
cabins; suites with kitchens	cabins starting at C$280
hotel rooms	rooms starting at C$310
hotel rooms	rooms starting at C$320
cabins with kitchens	cabins starting at C$250
cottages with kitchens; suite-style units	cottages starting at C$285
cabins with kitchenettes	cabins starting at C$322
motel rooms	rooms starting at C$305
hotel rooms; suites; historic cabins starting from C$1,500 per night	rooms starting at C$699 cabins starting at C$1,500
dormitory beds in two cabins	nonmembers C$40
cabins, some with kitchenette or full kitchen	cabins starting at C$185
motel units; bungalows cabins	motel units starting at C$125 d

Sunwapta Falls Rocky Mountain Lodge

Reservations

Book as far in advance as possible, especially in July and August. Contact non-branded properties directly.

Tips

If you are looking to save money, consider renting a room in a private residence. Unlike traditional bed and breakfasts, many of these properties are offering room-only, often with a private entrance. For listings, check out the Jasper Home Accommodation Association website (http://stayinjasper.com).

STANDOUTS
Sunwapta Falls Rocky Mountain Lodge
780/852-4852 or 888/922-9222; www.sunwapta.com; May-mid-Oct.; C$269-319 s or d

Historic Sunwapta Falls Rocky Mountain Lodge is 34 mi (55 km) south of the town of Jasper and within walking distance of the picturesque waterfall for which it is named. It features

52 comfortable motel-like units, with either two queen beds or one queen bed and a fireplace; some have balconies. In the main lodge is a lunchtime self-serve restaurant popular with passing travelers. In the evening this same room is transformed into a restaurant featuring simply prepared Canadian game and seafood in the C$25-43 range.

Becker's Chalets
780/852-3779; www.beckerschalets. com; May-mid-Oct.; C$170-480 s or d

Becker's Chalets is spread along a picturesque bend of the Athabasca River, 3.7 mi (6 km) south of town. This historic lodging took its first guests more than 50 years ago and continues to be a park favorite for many guests who make staying here an annual ritual. Moderately priced chalets, each with a kitchenette, gas fireplace, and double bed, are an excellent deal (C$210, or C$235 for those on the riverfront). Deluxe log duplexes featuring all the modern conveniences, including color TV, start at a reasonable C$215 s or d and go up to C$480 for a unit that sleeps eight. Also available are a few one-bed sleeping rooms (C$170). Becker's also boasts one of the park's finest restaurants.

Alpine Village
780/852-3285; www.alpinevillage-jasper.com; late Apr.-mid-Oct.; C$230-510 s or d

At the junction of Highway 93A and the Icefields Parkway 1.9 mi (3 km) south of town, is Alpine Village. This resort is laid out across well-manicured lawns, and all buildings are surrounded by colorful gardens of geraniums and petunias. After a day exploring the park, guests can soak away their cares in the outdoor hot pool or kick back on a row of Adirondack chairs scattered along the Athabasca River, directly opposite the resort. The older sleeping cabins have been renovated (C$230 s or d, C$280 with a kitchen and fireplace), while the Deluxe Bedroom Suites feature open plans, stone fireplaces, luxurious bathrooms, and decks with private forested views. The Deluxe Family Cabins sleep up to five, with two beds in an upstairs loft, a fireplace, and a full kitchen. The Whistler cabins, with vaulted ceilings, full kitchens, and king beds, are my lodging of choice here.

Bear Hill Lodge
100 Bonhomme St.; 780/852-3209; www.bearhilllodge.com; starting at C$280 s or d

With a variety of cabin layouts and a central location, Bear Hill Lodge makes a great base camp for travelers who want the cabin experience within walking distance of downtown services. The original cabins are

The Fairmont Jasper Park Lodge overlooks Lac Beauvert.

basic, but each has a TV, bathroom, gas fireplace, and coffee-making facilities. Chalet Rooms are larger and more modern, and each has a wood-burning fireplace but no kitchen. The three Homestead suites are more spacious still; each sleeps up to eight adults in private bedrooms and a full kitchen. Breakfasts (summer only; C$14 per person) feature a wide selection of freshly baked items, fruit, and cereals. Other amenities include a sauna, a barbecue area, laundry facilities, and Internet access.

Fairmont Jasper Park Lodge
1 Old Lodge Rd.; 780/852-3301 or 800/257-7544; www.fairmont.com; starting at C$699 s or d

The Fairmont Jasper Park Lodge lies along the shore of **Lac Beauvert** across the Athabasca River from downtown.

This is the park's original resort and its most famous. It's a sprawling

INFORMATION AND SERVICES

The town of **Jasper** is the service center of Jasper National Park, and despite being within a national park, it has all the facilities of a regular town.

Entrance Gate

The East Park Gate is a toll booth 31 mi (50 km) east of the town of Jasper. It is open 24 hours daily year-round to collect the entrance fee. Approaching Jasper from the south along the Icefields Parkway, the park boundary is marked by a sign at Sunwapta Pass, but there is no toll booth.

Visitor Centers

Jasper Park Visitor Centre

Connaught Dr., Jasper; 780/852-6176; www.pc.gc.ca; 9am-7pm daily mid-May-mid-Sept., 10am-5pm Wed.-Sun. the rest of the year, closed Nov.

The residence of Jasper's first superintendent, this beautiful old stone building dating to 1913 is now used by Parks Canada as the Jasper Park Visitor Centre. The staff provides general information on the park and property offering plenty of activities. The best known of these is the golf course, but guests also enjoy walking trails, horseback riding, canoeing, tennis, and swimming in an outdoor heated pool that remains open year-round. The main lodge features stone floors, carved wooden pillars, and a high ceiling. This building contains multiple restaurants and lounges, an activity booking desk, a fitness room, a game room, and Jasper's only covered shopping arcade. The 441 rooms vary in configuration and are linked can direct you to hikes in the immediate vicinity. Also within the same building is the **Parks Canada Trail Office** (780/852-6177), which has trail reports and handles other questions for hikers heading into the backcountry. **Tourism Jasper** (780/852-6236; www.jasper.travel) also has a desk in the building, and the friendly staff never seem to tire of explaining that all the rooms in town are full. As well as providing general information on the town, they have a large collection of brochures on activities, shopping, and restaurants. Also in the building is the **Friends of Jasper National Park** outlet (780/852-4767), selling maps, books, bear spray, and thoughtful souvenirs. Look for notices posted out front with the day's interpretive programs.

Icefields Centre Information Desk

780/852-6288; 10am-5pm daily early May-late Sept.

At the Icefields Centre, opposite the Columbia Icefield along the Icefields Parkway, Parks Canada operates an information desk where you can learn about trail conditions in the immediate area.

by paths and green space. All have coffeemakers, TVs, telephones, and Internet access. Starting from C$1,500 per night, the various historic cabins provide the Fairmont Jasper Park Lodge's premier accommodations and are among the most exclusive guest rooms in all of Canada, having hosted Queen Elizabeth and Marilyn Monroe, among others. Outside of summer, the Fairmont Jasper Park Lodge becomes a bargain, with rooms with lake views (remember, it'll be frozen in winter) for less than C$350.

TRANSPORTATION
Getting There
Jasper is linked to the outside world by road and rail. Alberta's capital, Edmonton, is 226 mi (364 km) to the east along the wide, mostly twinned Highway 16. Heading south along the Icefields Parkway and east on the Trans-Canada Highway, Banff is 178 mi (287 km; 4 hours) and Calgary is 252 mi (406 km; 5 hours). From Vancouver, Jasper is 486 mi (781 km) to the northeast via Highways 1, 5, and 16; allow at least nine hours.

Air
The closest airport handling domestic and international flights is at Edmonton, a four-hour drive to the east. Edmonton International Airport is south of the provincial capital. From the airport, head north on Highway 2 and take Anthony Henday Drive to bypass downtown Edmonton. From the west side of the city, it's easy driving on a divided Highway 16 to Hinton and the park's east entrance.

From Banff National Park
To get from the town of Banff to Jasper, it's a minimum four-hour drive (176 mi/286 km) west along the Trans-Canada Highway to Lake Louise and then north along the Icefields Parkway. Driving times can vary given the speed restrictions and often heavy traffic on this route; allow five or six hours for the drive in mid-summer.

Parking
Public parking lots are spread out in the town of Jasper between the rail line and Connaught Drive as they loop around the edge of downtown. RV parking is allowed along this stretch, or in the designated RV parking lot across the railway line on Hazel Avenue.

Shuttles
Pursuit (403/762-6700 or 866/606-6700; www.banffjaspercollection.com) provides a complimentary shuttle between downtown Jasper and Maligne Lake for those who have tour boat reservations.

elk

WILDLIFE-WATCHING

ONE OF THE BIGGEST ATTRACTIONS OF GLACIER, BANFF, AND Jasper National Parks is the abundance of wildlife, especially large mammals such as elk, moose, bighorn sheep, and bears, which are all widespread. Glacier National Park has even been designated a Biosphere Reserve by UNESCO due to its breadth of indigenous wildlife. Be sure to bring binoculars in order to appreciate these creatures from a distance.

BEARS

Two bear species roam the mountains in Glacier, Banff, and Jasper: **black bears** and **grizzly bears.** They can be differentiated by size and shape. The second largest of eight recognized species of bears worldwide (only polar bears are larger), grizzlies are larger than black bears and have a flatter, dish-shaped face and a distinctive hump of muscle behind their neck. Color is not a reliable way to tell them apart. Black bears are not always black. They can be brown or cinnamon, causing them to be confused with the brown-colored grizzly. If you spot a bear feeding beside the road, chances are it's a black bear. Grizzlies are only occasionally seen by casual observers; most sightings occur in alpine and subalpine zones, although sightings at lower elevations are not unusual, especially when snow falls early or late.

Omnivores and opportunistic feeders, bears will eat anything that is easy pickings. Intent on gaining 100-150 pounds (45-68 kg) before winter, bears feed on a diet heavy in plant matter: bulbs, roots, berries, shoots, and flowers. Ants, insects, carrion, and ground squirrels fill in proteins. Contrary to popular opinion, humans are not on their menu of favorite foods.

Bears don't actually hibernate, as their respiration and pulse remain close to normal. Instead, they enter a deep sleep in which the body temperature drops slightly. Bears emerge in the spring ravenously hungry, heading straight for avalanche chutes to rummage for snow-buried carcasses.

Safety

Food is the biggest bear attractant. Proper use, storage, and handling of food and garbage prevents bears from being conditioned and turning aggressive. Pick up any food you drop and pack out all your garbage. All national parks have strict food and garbage rules, which have minimized aggressive bear encounters, attacks, and both human and bear deaths.

Camp Safely: Use low-odor foods, keep food and cooking gear out of sleeping sites in the backcountry, and store them inside your vehicle in front-country campgrounds. Check

black bear cub (top); grizzly sow and two cubs in Many Glacier (bottom left); a black bear, a common sight along the Icefields Parkway (bottom right)

park websites (www.nps.gov/glac, www.pc.gc.ca/banff, www.pc.gc.ca/jasper) for useful information on camping in bear country.

Hike Safely: Making noise, especially human voices, best prevents surprising a bear, so talk, sing, hoot, and holler. You may feel silly at first, but everyone does it.

Most hikers carry **pepper spray.** Its capsicum derivative deters bear attacks without injuring the bears or humans. Unlike insect repellents, do not use bear sprays on your body, in tents, or on gear; it is to be sprayed directly into a bear's face, aiming for the eyes and nose. Wind and rain may reduce its effectiveness. Small purse-size pepper sprays are too small to deter bears; buy an 8-ounce (237-ml) can. Practice how to use it, but still make noise on the trail. Carry it on the front of your pack where it is easily reached. Pepper spray is not allowed on airplanes unless it's in checked luggage, and only brands with U.S. Environmental Protection Agency labels can be carried into Canada.

Where to See Them (From a Distance)
GLACIER NATIONAL PARK
- Many Glacier (page 66)
- Granite Park Chalet (page 101)

BANFF NATIONAL PARK
- Bow Valley Parkway (page 135)
- Lake Louise Sightseeing Gondola (page 132)
- Icefields Parkway (page 136)

JASPER NATIONAL PARK
- Icefields Parkway (page 194)
- Maligne Valley (page 187)

WOLVES
Wolves weigh up to 132 pounds (60 kg), stand up to 3 ft (1 m) high at the shoulder, and resemble large huskies or German shepherds. Their color ranges from snow white to brown or black, but in this region, it's most often shades of gray. They usually form packs of up to eight members, traveling, hunting, and resting together, and adhering to a hierarchical social order. As individuals, they are complex and intriguing, capable of expressing happiness, humor, and loneliness.

Where to See Them
GLACIER NATIONAL PARK
- Lower Lake McDonald area (page 59)
- North Fork (page 74)

BANFF NATIONAL PARK
- Bow Valley Parkway (page 135)
- Vermilion Lakes (page 122)

MOOSE
The giant of the deer family is the moose, an awkward-looking mammal that appears to have been designed by a cartoonist. It has the largest antlers of any animal in the world, stands up to 6 ft (1.8 m) at the shoulder, and weighs up to 1,100 pounds (500 kg). Its body is dark brown, and it has a prominent nose, long spindly legs, small eyes, big ears, and an odd flap of skin called a bell dangling beneath its chin. Each spring, the bull begins to grow palm-shaped antlers that by August will be fully grown. Moose are solitary animals preferring marshy areas and weedy lakes, but they are known to wander to higher elevations searching out open spaces

in summer. They forage in and around ponds, streambeds, and lakes on willows, aspens, birches, grasses, and all aquatic vegetation. Although they may appear docile, moose will attack humans if they feel threatened.

Moose thrive in Glacier's high and low country, but they are not particularly common in Banff and Jasper.

Where to See Them
GLACIER NATIONAL PARK
- Many Glacier Road (page 68)
- Many Glacier Boat Tour (page 69)
- Grinnell Lake (page 84)

BANFF NATIONAL PARK
- Vermilion Lakes (page 122)
- Upper Waterfowl Lake (page 139)

JASPER NATIONAL PARK
- Patricia Lake (page 199)
- Moose Lake (page 198)

ELK
The elk has a tan body with a dark-brown neck, dark-brown legs, and a white rump. This second-largest member of the deer family weighs 550-1,000 pounds (250-450 kg) and stands 5 ft (1.5 m) at the shoulder. Beginning each spring, bulls grow an impressive set of antlers, covered in what is known as velvet. The velvet contains nutrients that stimulate antler growth. By fall, the antlers have reached their full size and the velvet is shed. Rutting season takes place between August and October; listen for the shrill bugles of the bulls serenading the females. During the rut, randy males will challenge anything with

wolf

their antlers and can be dangerous. The bulls shed their antlers each spring, but don't relax too much: Also in spring, females protecting their young can be equally dangerous.

In Glacier, elk live throughout the park. Large herds of elk also live in and around the towns of Banff and Jasper, often nonchalantly wandering along streets and feeding on tasty plants in residential gardens.

Where to See Them
GLACIER NATIONAL PARK
- Many Glacier (page 66)
- Two Dog Flats (page 64)

BANFF NATIONAL PARK
- Town of Banff (page 118)
- Lake Minnewanka (page 123)
- Bow Valley Parkway (page 135)

JASPER NATIONAL PARK
- Town of Jasper (page 186)
- Highway 16 (page 197)

DEER
Mule deer and white-tailed deer are similar in size and appearance. Their color varies with the season, but is generally light brown in summer, turning dirty gray in winter. While both species are considerably smaller than elk, the mule deer is a little stockier than the white-tailed deer. The mule deer has a white rump, a white tail with a dark tip, and large mulelike ears. The white-tailed deer's tail is dark on top, but when the animal runs, it holds its tail erect, revealing an all-white underside. Both inhabit open forests along valley floors.

Where to See Them
GLACIER NATIONAL PARK
- Lake McDonald (page 59)
- Two Medicine (page 70)

BANFF NATIONAL PARK
- Town of Banff (page 118)
- Bow Valley Parkway (page 135)

JASPER NATIONAL PARK
- Town of Jasper (page 186)
- Patricia Lake (page 199)
- North end of Icefields Parkway (page 194)

moose (top); elk (bottom left); mule deer
(bottom right)

MOUNTAIN GOATS

The remarkable rock-climbing ability of these nimble-footed creatures allows them to live on rocky ledges or near-vertical slopes, safe from predators. The goats stand 3 ft (1 m) at the shoulder and weigh 140-290 pounds (65-130 kg). Both sexes possess a peculiar beard, or rather, goatee, and have horns. It is possible to determine the sex by the shape of the horns; those of the female grow straight up before curling slightly backward, whereas those of the male curl back in a single arch. The goats shed their thick coats each summer, making them look ragged, but by fall they regrow a fine, new white woolen coat.

Where to See Them
GLACIER NATIONAL PARK

- Logan Pass (page 61)

- Hidden Lake Overlook Trail (page 75)

- Highline Trail (page 76)

JASPER NATIONAL PARK

- Goats and Glaciers Lookout, Icefields Parkway (page 196)

BIGHORN SHEEP

Bighorn sheep are some of the most distinctive mammals seen in these parks. Easily recognized by their impressive horns, they are often spotted grazing on grassy mountain slopes or at salt licks beside the road. The color of their coat varies with the season; in summer, it's a brownish-gray with a cream-colored belly and rump, turning lighter in winter. Fully grown males can weigh up to 270 pounds (120 kg), while females generally weigh around 180 pounds (80 kg).

Both sexes possess horns, rather than antlers like members of the deer family. Unlike antlers, horns are not shed each year and can grow to astounding sizes. The horns of rams are larger than those of ewes and curve up to 360 degrees. The spiraled horns of an older ram can measure longer than 3 ft (1 m) and weigh as much as 33 pounds (15 kg). During the fall mating season, a hierarchy is established among the rams for the right to breed ewes. As the males face off against each other to establish dominance, their horns act as both a weapon and a buffer against the head butting of other rams. The skull structure of the bighorn, rams in particular, has become adapted to these head-butting clashes, keeping the animals from being knocked unconscious.

Bighorn sheep are particularly tolerant of humans and often approach parked vehicles; although they are not especially dangerous, as with all mammals, you should not approach or feed them.

Where to See Them
GLACIER NATIONAL PARK

- Logan Pass (page 61)

- Hidden Lake Overlook Trail (page 75)

- Dawson-Pitamakin Loop (page 87)

BANFF NATIONAL PARK

- Banff Gondola (page 122)

- Lake Minnewanka (page 123)

JASPER NATIONAL PARK

- Disaster Point, Highway 16 (page 198)

mountain goats

bighorn males facing off against each other to establish dominance

- Near Tangle Falls, Icefields Parkway (page 196)

MARMOT

High in the mountains, above the tree line, hoary marmots are often seen sunning themselves on boulders in rocky areas or meadows. They are stocky creatures, weighing 9-19 pounds (4-9 kg) and resembling fat housecat-size fur balls. When danger approaches, these large rodents emit a shrill whistle to warn their colony. Marmots are active for only a few months each summer, spending up to nine months a year in hibernation.

Where to See Them
GLACIER NATIONAL PARK
- Cobalt Lake (page 86)
- Highline Trail (page 76)

BANFF NATIONAL PARK
- Helen Lake, Icefields Parkway (page 144)
- Bow Summit, Icefields Parkway (page 139)

JASPER NATIONAL PARK
- Jasper SkyTram (page 186)
- Bald Hills (page 198)

PIKAS

In subalpine country, a chorus of eeks, screams, and squeaks bounce through rockfalls. The noisemakers are pikas, which look like tailless mice. However, pikas are not rodents but rather lagomorphs (members of the rabbit family), which are distinguished by a double set of incisors in the upper jaw. The small, grayish pika is a neighbor to the marmot, living among the rubble and boulders of scree slopes above timberline.

Where to See Them
GLACIER NATIONAL PARK
- Piegan Pass Trail (page 79)

BANFF NATIONAL PARK
- Bourgeau Lake (page 141)

hoary marmot (left); pika (right)

SAFETY AROUND WILDLIFE

Grizzly bears often cause traffic jams.

Spotting wildlife is one of the thrills of visiting these three parks. In order to maintain the health and safety of animals and humans alike, obey park rules and use common sense.

- **Keep your distance.** Although it's tempting to get close to wildlife for a better look or a photograph, it disturbs the animal and, in many cases, can be dangerous. Instead, use binoculars to get close-up views, and use telephoto or zoom lenses for photographing wildlife. Do not attempt to take selfies with wildlife. Stay at least 100 yards (100 m) from bears and wolves and 25 yards (30 m) from other large animals, such as deer, elk, moose, mountain goats, and bighorn sheep.

- **Do not feed the animals.** Many animals may seem tame, but feeding them endangers yourself, the animal, and other visitors, as animals become aggressive when looking for handouts (even the smallest critters, such as squirrels).

- **Store food safely.** When camping, keep food out of reach of animals, such as in your vehicle or in approved storage containers. Just leaving it in a cooler isn't good enough.

- **Drive carefully.** The most common cause of premature death for larger mammals is being hit by vehicles.

wildflowers along Many Glacier Road, Glacier

WILDFLOWERS

GLACIER, BANFF, AND JASPER NATIONAL PARK ARE ALL RICH IN floral diversity. Glacier is even a UNESCO Biosphere Reserve for its variety of wildflower niches. Forests, prairies, and peaks have different vegetation specific to elevation, habitat, and weather. The season for wildflower blooms is short—most reach their peak during varying points in July and early August.

VEGETATION ZONES

Botanists divide the mountains of Glacier, Banff, and Jasper into three distinct vegetation zones (also called biomes): montane, subalpine, and alpine. The boundaries of these zones are determined by several factors, the most important being elevation. Latitude and exposure are also factors, but less so. Typically, within any 4,920 feet (1,500 m) of elevation change, you'll pass through each of the three zones.

The **montane** zone occurs at low to mid-elevations, below about 4,920 feet (1,500 m). Next is the **subalpine** zone, which is generally 4,920-7,220 feet (1,500-2,200 m) above sea level. The upper limit of the subalpine zone is the tree line.

The **alpine** zone extends from the tree line to mountain summits. Here, the land appears to be barren rock, but a host of miniature plants adapt to the harsh conditions of high winds, drying altitude, short summers, cold temperatures, and rocky soil that lacks organic matter. Hugging the ground, large areas of alpine meadows burst with color for a short period each summer.

LILIES

In Glacier's subalpine zone, early July brings on fields of **yellow glacier lilies** as they force their blooms through the snow. Recognize their flowers by their posture hanging downward but with their six petals curving upward. Later in the summer, grizzly bears dig up their bulbs to eat, leaving swaths of meadows looking like they've been rototilled. In Banff and Jasper National Parks, **wood lilies** flower in late spring at lower elevations, while up in the alpine meadows of Banff, glacier and **avalanche lilies** bloom.

Where to See Them
GLACIER NATIONAL PARK
- Logan Pass (page 61)
- Granite Park Chalet (page 101)

BANFF NATIONAL PARK
- Sunshine Meadows (page 123)
- Johnson Lake (page 158)

JASPER NATIONAL PARK
- Patricia Lake (page 199)

MOSS CAMPION

Mats of moss campion are among the plants that fling their energy into tiny flowers amid the harsh alpine tundra. Their tiny pink flowers are about the size of your littlest fingertip. To survive the harsh winds and arid conditions, they hug the ground in green mats or cushions that often look mossy, hence the name. Some mats can be around 100 years old.

Where to See Them
GLACIER NATIONAL PARK
- Scenic Point Trail (page 85)
- Siyeh Pass Trail (page 79)

BANFF NATIONAL PARK
- Bow Glacier Falls (page 145)

JASPER NATIONAL PARK
- Bald Hills (page 198)

LUPINE

In mountain meadows, lupine blooms in shades of blue to purple with a hint of white on long showy stalks towering above palm-like leaf clusters. At lower elevations, they grow taller than at upper elevations. You can recognize the spent plant as a member of the pea family due to its pods. In Glacier, lupine thrive in aspen parklands of the montane zone on the east side of the park in July and early August. You may also see a much shorter variety in the alpine tundra zones. In Banff and Jasper, lupine are among the wildflowers that bloom in alpine meadows for a short period each summer.

Where to See Them
GLACIER NATIONAL PARK
- Many Glacier Road (page 68)
- Going-to-the-Sun Road (page 60)

BANFF NATIONAL PARK
- Bow Lake (page 138)

JASPER NATIONAL PARK
- Tonquin Valley (page 204)

COW PARSNIP
At lower elevations, the large white heads of cow parsnip bloom alongside roads in late June and early July before continuing into higher elevations as summer progresses. Sometimes their bloom clusters are so big that they appear like inverted dinner plates. These plants, members of the celery family, are an important food source for grizzly bears. A few people have allergic reactions to cow parsnip with blistering, so you may want to avoid touching them.

Where to See Them
GLACIER NATIONAL PARK
- Lower elevations of Going-to-the-Sun Road (page 60)

BEAR GRASS
Between tree islands in the subalpine zone, lush mountain meadows bloom with a colorful array of plants, including bear grass. Some

glacier lily (top); moss campion (middle); lupine (bottom)

bear grass in Glacier

years, bear grass stalks bloom so thickly in July that subalpine hillsides look snow-covered. Their sturdy, stiff evergreen leaves form a low mound, while their stalks shoot up to 3 feet tall (almost a meter). The creamy star-like flowers bloom in a large cluster at the head of the stalk and are a favorite food for deer and elk.

Where to See Them
GLACIER NATIONAL PARK
- Highline Trail (page 76)
- Iceberg Lake Trail (page 84)

PAINTBRUSH

Paintbrush spew across the subalpine mountain meadows of Glacier National Park and the montane zone of Banff and Jasper in fields of yellow, red, fuchsia, white, salmon, scarlet, and orange. You can recognize paintrbush because it looks like an upended brush dipped in paint. At lower elevations, they often bloom in early July. In subalpine meadows, blooming peaks mid-July-mid-August.

Where to See Them
GLACIER NATIONAL PARK
- Logan Pass and Hidden Lake Overlook (page 61)
- Piegan Pass Trail (page 79)
- Going-to-the-Sun Road (page 60)

BANFF NATIONAL PARK
- Bow Valley Parkway (page 135)
- Icefields Parkway (page 136)
- Helen Lake (page 144)

JASPER NATIONAL PARK
- Cavell Meadows (page 198)
- Maligne Valley (page 187)

red paintbrush (top); shooting stars (middle); blue camas (bottom)

SHOOTING STARS

Late May-early June brings tiny shooting stars to montane meadows and along lakeshores as far north as Saskatchewan River Crossing in Banff. The subalpine meadows won't bloom with them until July. The pink to lavender flowers with yellow centers and black stamens look as though the petals have been blown backward to form a rocket. They grow on short fragile stalks singly or with several flowers.

Where to See Them
GLACIER NATIONAL PARK

- Hidden Lake Overlook Trail (page 75)

- Many Glacier Road (page 68)

BANFF NATIONAL PARK

- Johnson Lake (page 158)

CAMAS

In Glacier, camas are among the flowers that thrive in open meadows. **Blue camas** grows on a long stalk in damp montane meadows. The bulbs of the plant provided food for early Indigenous people. The **mountain death camas,** a cluster of cream-colored flowers, covers a wider range from montane meadows to subalpine meadows. Contrary to the blue camas, all parts of the plant are poisonous to humans if ingested.

Where to See Them
GLACIER NATIONAL PARK

- Mountain death camas: Highline Trail (page 76)

- Blue camas: Two Medicine Road (page 70)

COLUMBINE

Yellow columbine bloom between tree islands in the subalpine zone. This delicate flower blooms atop a spindly tall stalk with five conical petals surrounded by lighter sepals. Find it in July and early August. In the harsh alpine tundra, **Jones' columbine** grow low to the ground in early July. Their deep blue-purple flowers have the traditional columbine cone shapes, but on tiny stalks for protection.

Where to See Them
GLACIER NATIONAL PARK

- Yellow columbine: Grinnell Glacier Trail (page 81)

- Jones' columbine: Siyeh Pass Trail (page 79)

BANFF NATIONAL PARK

- Sunshine Meadows (page 123)

- Helen Lake (page 144)

JASPER NATIONAL PARK

- Cavell Meadows (page 198)

columbine

BALSAMROOT

In Glacier's drier eastside montane meadows between groves of aspen trees, arrowleaf balsamroot grows in more arid locales favored by the sunflower family. Recognize them by their big showy yellow flowers and large dusty green arrowhead-shaped leaves. These are early summer flowers, often seen in June and early July. Indigenous people used all parts of the plant for food, and deer munch on the flowers or leaves.

Where to See Them
GLACIER NATIONAL PARK

- Two Dog Flats (page 64)

- Many Glacier Road (page 68)

MONKEYFLOWER

In midsummer, wet streambeds line with monkeyflower in subalpine meadows. The fuchsia monkeyflower has tiny yellow spots and grows on long leafy stalks. On the contrary, the short yellow monkeyflower hugs the ground around water. Recognize the flower by its streamside locale and tubular shape; it acquired its name because of the monkey-like face in the flower.

Where to See Them
GLACIER NATIONAL PARK

- Hidden Lake Overlook
  Trail (page 75)

- Cobalt Lake Trail (page 86)

MOUNTAIN AVENS

Mountain avens are low-to-the-ground white wildflowers that bloom in meadows and rocky areas above the tree line for a short period each summer. They often grow in areas where glaciers have recently receded, gaining a foothold as a dense mat among the barren rocky till. Their white flowers face the sun as it moves, and they dry into fuzzy tufts in late summer.

Where to See Them
GLACIER NATIONAL PARK

- Scenic Point Trail (page 85)

- Siyeh Pass Trail (page 79)

BANFF NATIONAL PARK

- Sunshine Meadows (page 123)

- Parker's Ridge (page 145)

balsamroots (top); pink monkeyflower along a stream (bottom left); mountain avens (bottom right)

JASPER NATIONAL PARK

- Cavell Meadows (page 198)
- Wilcox Pass Trail (page 200)

ALPINE FORGET-ME-NOTS

Growing in seemingly barren mountain tundra and in alpine meadows throughout the region, these small but distinctive flowers are yellow- or pink-centered with blue petals. To survive, they limit their growth, staying low to the ground to escape drying winds.

Where to See Them
GLACIER NATIONAL PARK

- Scenic Point Trail (page 85)
- Dawson-Pitamakin Loop (page 87)

BANFF NATIONAL PARK

- Sunshine Meadows (page 123)
- Parker's Ridge (page 145)

JASPER NATIONAL PARK

- Cavell Meadows (page 198)

HEATHER

Heather with tiny pink bell-like flowers blooms in Glacier's sub-alpine meadows during late July. In addition to pink heather, white and yellow heather grows in alpine meadows of Banff and Jasper, flowering between mid-July and mid-August.

Where to See Them
GLACIER NATIONAL PARK

- Hidden Lake Overlook Trail (page 75)
- Iceberg Lake Trail (page 84)

BANFF NATIONAL PARK

- Sunshine Meadows (page 123)
- Parker's Ridge (page 145)

JASPER NATIONAL PARK

- Cavell Meadows (page 198)

WILD ROSES

This large pink flower is common throughout montane forests in Banff and Jasper between late May and July.

---

alpine forget-me-nots (left); heather (right)

Where to See Them
BANFF NATIONAL PARK
- Bow Valley Parkway (page 135)

- Johnston Canyon (page 129)

JASPER NATIONAL PARK
- Cottonwood Slough (page 203)

- Maligne Valley (page 187)

FIREWEED

Tall and showy, these pink flowers thrive along roadsides and in areas where wildfire has swept through.

Where to See Them
GLACIER NATIONAL PARK
- North Fork (page 74)

BANFF NATIONAL PARK
- Bow Valley Parkway (page 135)

- Saskatchewan River Crossing (page 139)

JASPER NATIONAL PARK
- Medicine Lake (page 187)

wild rose (top); fireweed (bottom)

Bow Lake, Icefields Parkway

ESSENTIALS

GETTING THERE

AIR

Located closest to Banff, Calgary International Airport is the best airport for visiting all three parks. There are also closer airports to Glacier and Jasper.

Calgary International Airport

YYC; 403/735-1200; www.calgaryairport.com
DRIVING TIME TO GLACIER: 4 hours to Many Glacier and St. Mary (border crossing at Carway-Piegan open 7am-11pm daily year-round)
DRIVING TIME TO BANFF: 90 minutes to the town of Banff
DRIVING TIME TO JASPER: 5 hours to the town of Jasper

Glacier National Park

GLACIER PARK INTERNATIONAL AIRPORT
FCA; Kalispell, Montana; www.iflyglacier.com
DRIVING TIME TO GLACIER: 35 minutes to West Glacier Entrance; 2.5-3 hours to St. Mary and Many Glacier

GREAT FALLS INTERNATIONAL AIRPORT
GTF; 406/727-3404; www.gtfairport.com
DRIVING TIME TO GLACIER: 2.5 hours to Two Medicine; 3 hours to St. Mary and Many Glacier

LETHBRIDGE AIRPORT
YQL; 417 Stubb Ross Rd.; www.lethbridgeairport.ca; Westjet (www.westjet.com) only
DRIVING TIME TO GLACIER: 2 hours to St. Mary and Many Glacier

Jasper National Park

EDMONTON INTERNATIONAL AIRPORT
YEG; 1000 Airport Rd. NW, Edmonton; https://flyeia.com

DRIVING TIME TO JASPER: 4 hours to the town of Jasper

CAR

Most visitors to Glacier, Banff, and Jasper arrive by car after landing at one of the area airports. Driving to the parks from other metropolitan areas can take 8 hours or more.

Driving Times

All driving times are for dry roads in summer.

VANCOUVER, BRITISH COLUMBIA

- **Driving Time to Glacier:** 11.5 hours
- **Driving Time to Banff:** 9 hours
- **Driving Time to Jasper:** 8 hours

SEATTLE, WASHINGTON

- **Driving Time to Glacier:** 9 hours

- **Driving Time to Banff:** 10 hours
- **Driving Time to Jasper:** 9 hours

SALT LAKE CITY, UTAH

- **Driving Time to Glacier:** 10 hours
- **Driving Time to Banff:** 14 hours
- **Driving Time to Jasper:** 17 hours

Road Rules
UNITED STATES

Driver's licenses from other countries are valid in Montana for 12 months as long as you have an International Driver Permit. Proof of insurance is also required (bring paperwork or insurance card). Drivers and passengers are required to wear seat belts. Highway signs post distances in **miles** and speeds in **miles per hour** (mph). The speed limit on most highways surrounding Glacier is 65 mph during the day or 60 mph at night.

CANADA

Driver's licenses from all countries are valid in Canada for up to three months. You should also carry vehicle registration papers or rental contracts. Proof of insurance must also be carried, and you must wear seat belts. All highway signs in Canada give distances in **kilometers** and speeds in **kilometers per hour** (kph). Within Canadian national parks, the speed limit is 90 kph (56 mph), reduced even further on some roads, such as the Bow Valley Parkway.

Border Crossing

Driving between Glacier and Banff or Jasper involves crossing the U.S.-Canada border. Most drivers will pass through the border at **Rooseville** (BC 93/US 93; 24 hours daily year-round) or **Carway-Piegan** (AB 2/US 89; 7am-11pm daily year-round). There is also a seasonal (mid-May-Sept.) port of entry at the **Chief Mountain border crossing** (Chief Mountain International Highway; 7am-10pm daily June-Labor Day, 9am-6pm daily May and Sept. after Labor Day).

ENTERING CANADA

International travelers entering Canada must have passports. The one exception is travelers from the United States and Western Hemisphere Travel Initiative countries, who may use U.S. passport cards, enhanced driver's licenses, or NEXUS cards instead. Visas are not required for visitors from about 50 countries, including the United States. All others must apply for visas. Find the list of visa-exempt countries and visa requirements at www.cic.gc.ca.

ENTERING THE UNITED STATES

International travelers entering the United States must have passports. One exception applies to travelers from Canada and countries in the Western Hemisphere Travel Initiative, who may use a U.S. passport card, enhanced driver's license, or NEXUS card instead. Visas may also be required for some countries; check www.state.travel.gov for countries with visa waivers and visa applications. Except most Canadians, international travelers entering the United States via a land border must have a current I-94 form ($6).

CUSTOMS

In general, Canada and the United States have similar customs laws: no plants, drugs, firewood, or live bait can cross the border. Some fresh meats, poultry products, fruits, and vegetables are restricted, as are firearms in Canada. Pets are permitted to cross the border with a certificate of rabies vaccination dated within 30 days prior to crossing. Bear sprays are considered firearms in Canada; they must have a U.S. Environmental Protection Agency-approved label to go across the border. For clarification, call the **Roosville Canadian customs office** (250/887-3413).

TRAIN
Glacier National Park
AMTRAK *EMPIRE BUILDER*
800/872-7245; www.amtrak.com

In the United States, Glacier is one of the rare national parks serviced by train. Traveling east from Seattle or Portland and west from Chicago, Amtrak's daily **Empire Builder** stops at West Glacier year-round and also at East Glacier in the summer. Seattle/Portland to West Glacier takes a little more than 15 hours; Chicago to East Glacier takes 30 hours or more.

Banff and Jasper National Parks

VIA RAIL CANADIAN
416/366-8411 or 888/842-7245;
www.viarail.ca

Government-run **VIA Rail** provides passenger-train service right across Canada. The **Canadian** is a service between Toronto and Vancouver with stops at Edmonton and Jasper. If you're traveling anywhere in western Canada from the eastern provinces, the least expensive way to travel is on a **Canada Pass,** which allows unlimited trips anywhere on the VIA Rail system for 30 days (C$1,300) or 60 days (C$1,520).

ROCKY MOUNTAINEER VACATIONS

604/606-7245 or 877/460-3200;
www.rockymountaineer.com; starting at C$1,499 per person d

This luxurious rail trip runs between Vancouver and Banff or Jasper and passes through the spectacular interior mountain ranges of British Columbia. Travel is during daylight hours only, so you don't miss anything. Trains depart in either direction in the morning (every second or third day throughout summer), overnighting at Kamloops.

GETTING AROUND
DRIVING
Glacier National Park

To get around Glacier, most visitors opt to drive themselves, allowing for more freedom in scheduling, although some parking lots fill early in the morning.

Driving in Glacier National Park is not easy. Narrow roads built for cars in the 1930s barely fit today's SUVs, much less RVs and trailers. With no shoulders and sharp curves, roads require reduced speeds and shifting into second gear on extended descents to avoid burning brakes. Check the park's Recreational Access Display (www.nps.gov/applications/glac/dashboard) for real-time information on roads, weather, parking lots, and campgrounds. Smaller cars are easier to drive because of the narrow roads, and you do not need a 4WD.

Two roads go west-east across the Continental Divide: Going-to-the-Sun Road bisects the park, while U.S. 2 hugs Glacier's southern border. Both are two-lane roads; however, the seasonal Going-to-the-Sun Road (mid-June–mid-Oct.) is the more difficult drive, climbing 1,500 feet (457 m) higher on a skinnier, snakier road than year-round U.S. 2. The Sun Road does not permit RVs or trailer-combos over 21 feet (6.4 m) long.

No paved roads run north-south through the park. One super rough dirt road (Inside North Fork Rd.) runs partially down Glacier's west side going to limited destinations, but it does not connect to any park hub.

Paved two-lane roads also lead to Two Medicine, St. Mary, Many Glacier, and Waterton, but just because roads are paved doesn't mean that they are smooth. Potholed and washboard dirt roads reach several remote campgrounds up the North Fork and in Cut Bank.

Gas up before you head into the park, and make sure your car is in good condition. There are no gas stations inside the park. Find gas in the towns of West Glacier, East Glacier, St. Mary, Babb, and Waterton, but few of the stations can repair severely broken-down vehicles.

Banff and Jasper National Parks

For most of the year, driving in Banff and Jasper National Parks is easy and enjoyable. All roads are paved, and aside from snow in winter, there are no major concerns. In summer, roads into major attractions get very busy and occasionally close when parking lots are full. This includes parking lots around the Lake Minnewanka loop, Johnston Canyon, Lake Louise, and Moraine Lake. These destinations are manned by traffic control personal on the busiest days. The best advice is to arrive early—in the case of Moraine Lake, the lot is often full and the road closed by 6am (plan on arriving by 5am to be sure of a parking spot). Gas is available year-round in Banff, Lake Louise, and Jasper. Between mid-April and mid-October, gas is also available along the Icefields Parkway at Saskatchewan River Crossing.

TRAVELING BY RV

RVing is a great way to travel, but in Glacier it has its limitations. Roads are narrow, curvy, and shoulderless, and many inside-park campsites cannot fit larger RVs and do not have hookups. Most of all, RVs are restricted on Going-to-the-Sun Road to under 21 feet (6.4 m) long. RVs over 21 ft (6.4 m) and all trailers are prohibited on the Inside North Fork Road. Six campgrounds inside Glacier have disposal stations: Apgar, Fish Creek, Many Glacier, Rising Sun, St. Mary, and Two Medicine.

Conversely, camper vans, recreational vehicles, and travel trailers are a great way to get around Banff and Jasper. The only road with any restriction is Cavell Road in Jasper, where RVs and trailers are not allowed. The most difficult places to navigate larger vehicles are the towns of Banff and Jasper, but both have designated RV parking lots. For Banff, check https://banffparking.ca for information on where to park. At least one campground near the towns of Banff and Jasper and the village of Lake Louise have sites suitable for the longest RVs, with hookups and dump stations, although you will need reservations well in advance.

BUSES AND SHUTTLES
Glacier National Park
BUS

Inside Glacier, the National Park Service runs **free Going-to-the-Sun Road shuttles** July-Labor Day and more limited in September. These are shuttles, not guided tours. Between Apgar and St. Mary, they stop at lodges, trailheads, campgrounds, and Logan Pass. Get on or off at any of the stops denoted by interpretive signs. No tickets are needed, and no reservations are taken. Departing every 15-30 minutes, these extremely popular shuttles enable point-to-point hiking on some of Glacier's most spectacular trails. Check schedules and routes online (www.nps.gov/glac).

Two companies operate fee-based shuttles on Glacier's east side. For hikers and backpackers, these aid in doing point-to-point trails, and for travelers without vehicles, they help connect with the Sun Road shuttles. Pursuit Glacier Park Collection (844/868-7474; www.glacierparkcollection.com) runs van service daily early June-late September north-south between East Glacier, Two Medicine, and St. Mary. Xanterra (855/733-4522; www.glaciernationalparklodges.com) operates daily shuttles July-Labor Day from Many Glacier to St. Mary.

BOAT

Hikers and backpackers also use tour boats as shuttles to reduce foot miles. In Glacier, **Glacier Park Boat Company** (406/257-2426; https://glacierparkboats.com; June-Sept.) carts hikers across Two Medicine Lake and in Many Glacier across Swiftcurrent Lake and Lake Josephine. Both add early morning Hiker Express shuttles in July-August. Get advance reservations for round-trip shuttles only. No reservations are necessary to catch a return boat; pay cash for a half-price fare upon boarding. Return shuttles run until all hikers are accommodated.

Banff National Park
BUS
In summer and fall, Parks Canada operates buses from the **Lake Louise Park & Ride** (www.pc.gc.ca/banffnow; round-trip adult C$10, senior or child C$5), 5 mi (8 km) south of the village of Lake Louise along the Trans-Canada Highway, to Lake Louise and Moraine Lake. Shuttles operate continuously 8am-4pm, with earlier departures at the busiest times of year.

Roam Transit (403/760-8294; mid-May-Sept. twice an hour 7am-midnight; C$2-10 per sector) operates bus service along two routes through the town of Banff: one from the Banff Gondola north along Banff Avenue, the other from the Fairmont Banff Springs to the Tunnel Mountain campgrounds. Roam buses also run to Canmore and Lake Louise.

Jasper National Park
BUS
Pursuit (403/762-6700 or 866/606-6700; www.banffjaspercollection.com) provides a complimentary shuttle between downtown Jasper and Maligne Lake for those who have tour boat reservations.

NEARBY TOWNS
NEAR GLACIER NATIONAL PARK
Flathead Valley, a year-round recreation hub about 35 minutes outside the West Entrance of Glacier National Park, offers the most options for food and lodging near the park and is where the closest airport to the park is located. Kalispell, Whitefish, and Columbia Falls are all located in Flathead Valley. The small towns of St. Mary and Babb are located near the St. Mary and Many Glacier Entrances on the eastern side of the park. East Glacier is a small town located outside the southeastern corner of the park, near the Two Medicine Entrance.

Kalispell
Built at highway crossroads, Kalispell is Flathead Valley's largest town. Most of the hotels and restaurants are located 15 minutes south of Glacier Park International Airport (on U.S. 2), the opposite direction from Glacier National Park, and almost 1 hour from West Glacier.

FOOD
Kalispell has common national chain restaurants along U.S. 93, but in the downtown area, Kalispell also has many large grocery markets for those wanting to get supplies.

LODGING
Kalispell has several chain hotels sprawled on the outskirts of downtown, including hotels around the mall and strip mall areas. You can find them online (https://kalispellchamber.com). Other than chain hotels, the pickings are slim. Rates will be highest in summer, with lower prices in fall, winter, and spring.

INFORMATION
The **Flathead Valley Convention and Visitors Bureau** (406/756-9091 or 800/543-3105; www.fcvb.org) and **Kalispell Chamber of Commerce** (406/758-2800; kalispellchamber.com) provide mostly online information.

Whitefish
Whitefish is a resort town loaded with lodging and restaurants. It is 15-20 minutes west of U.S. 2 and Glacier Park International Airport (on U.S. 2) and 45 minutes west of Glacier National Park. It garners the most visitors in the Flathead. Whitefish boasts shops, boutiques, restaurants, bars, art galleries, and theaters. In the summer, downtown streets crowd with shopping tourists, especially during the Tuesday evening farmers market. In winter, its ski town heritage emerges in early February with the Winter Carnival. The town also serves as a springboard for boating, paddling, golfing, hiking, mountain biking, and skiing. One of its biggest summer

attractions is the scenic chairlift ride at Whitefish Mountain Resort (406-862-2900; www.skiwhitefish.com) to see the panorama of Glacier's peaks.

FOOD

As a resort town, Whitefish is overloaded with outstanding restaurants, from casual to fine dining. Because of the crowds, make reservations to avoid long waits in summer or winter. In spring and fall, a few restaurants alter their hours.

LODGING

Whitefish is the only town Flathead Valley town that offers luxury lodging, but it also has a myriad of less-pricey options, including chains and independent hotels. Find a full listing at https://explorewhitefish.com. You can also locate vacation homes and cabins to rent through **Lakeshore Rentals** (406/863-9337 or 877/817-3012; www.lakeshorerentals.us). Reservations in town are mandatory in summer, but when town books out, rooms are usually still available at Whitefish Mountain Resort. In town, summer has the highest rates, with the second-highest rates in winter.

INFORMATION

The **Flathead Valley Convention and Visitors Bureau** (406-756-9091 or 800/543-3105; www.fcvb.org) and **Whitefish Convention and Visitors Bureau** (877/862-3548; https://explorewhitefish.com) provide mostly online information.

Columbia Falls

Sprawling along the highway, Columbia Falls is the closest Flathead Valley town to Glacier and Glacier Park International Airport. The town is 18 minutes from West Glacier and 12 minutes from the airport.

The gateway to Glacier, Columbia Falls never had a waterfall of its own until the town built one. A recent boom in restaurants has upgraded the quality of dining. In summer, it has a public outdoor swimming pool, Big Sky Waterpark, and a Thursday night farmers market with music, food, and family fun.

FOOD

Columbia Falls hadn't been known as a dining mecca until recently. New restaurateurs have ushered in fresh tastes, catapulting the cuisine beyond the fast-food enterprises along the highway.

LODGING

The town has a lodge and a couple of small independent motels located on U.S. 2 for those on a budget. Surrounding Columbia Falls, cabins and vacation homes are scattered in the woods and along the Flathead River. Locate properties rented by their owners via **VRBO** (www.vrbo.com) and **Airbnb** (www.airbnb.com). Summer rates are highest, but you can find lower rates and deals during the rest of the year. Contrary to Glacier, Wi-Fi is common in Columbia Falls lodging.

INFORMATION

The **Flathead Valley Convention and Visitors Bureau** (406-756-9091 or 800/543-3105; www.fcvb.org) and **Columbia Falls Chamber of Commerce** (406/892-2072; www.columbiafallschamber.org) provide mostly online information.

West Glacier, Montana

Located only 2 mi (3.2 km) from Lake McDonald, West Glacier sits just outside the park's West Entrance and makes a good base. It's convenient for hopping on the train, going river rafting or fishing, and heading off on guided backpacking trips. During midsummer, most West Glacier lodging fills nightly; reservations are advised. Lower rates are available in spring and fall. Additional food and accommodations options are also available in Coram, 5 mi (8 km) west of West Glacier.

FOOD

West Glacier offers a range of dining options, to supplement the limited dining inside the park. Seasonal restaurants cater to summer visitors; hours can shorten in spring or fall, and only a few remain open in winter. There are also two seasonal stores (May-Sept.) that carry convenience foods, beer, wine, camping items, ice, and firewood.

LODGING

The limited inside-park lodging at Apgar is extremely popular, so West Glacier options often serve as backup for both hotels and campgrounds. During mid-summer, most West Glacier lodging fills nightly; reservations are advised. Lower rates are available in spring and fall.

INFORMATION

Two visitor centers offer information on things to do surrounding Glacier. Located in Belton Train Depot, the **West Glacier Visitor Information Center** (junction of Going-to-the-Sun Rd. and Hwy. 2; 406/892-3250; http://glacier.org; 9am-5pm daily summer) has the main Glacier Conservancy bookstore and information for Flathead Valley. The **Crown of the Continent Discovery Center** (12000 U.S. 2 E.; 406/387-4405; www.crowndiscoverycenter.com; 10am-7pm daily early May-mid-Oct.) has regional planning information, hands-on displays, and brochures on geotourism activities that includes national parks, national forests, World Heritage Sites, and wilderness areas in Montana and Canada.

St. Mary, Montana

St. Mary is the eastern portal to Going-to-the-Sun Road, located 21 mi (34 km) southeast of Many Glacier. At the junction of the Sun Road and the Blackfeet Highway (U.S. 89), the town clusters at the park boundary along the highway. Only the visitor center and St. Mary Campground are within the park; the town, restaurants, grocery stores, lodging, and commercial campgrounds are on the Blackfeet Reservation. St. Mary is convenient for exploring Going-to-the-Sun Road, and it works as a home base for day trips to Waterton, Many

Glacier, and Two Medicine, plus it's a good place to stay if you're heading up to Banff. It is a seasonal town with most services open mid-May-September, but otherwise everything closes.

FOOD

St. Mary has several eateries, which include options at the lodge in St. Mary Village and family-run cafés. There are also two summer-only (daily June-Sept.) grocery stores on U.S. 89. Restaurants and grocery stores in St. Mary do not serve alcohol during North American Indian Days, a reservation-wide four-day celebration beginning the second Thursday in July. Alcohol sales are also prohibited on other selected days, such as graduation in June.

LODGING

Amenities at St. Mary accommodations are limited, especially internet access. In most locations, Wi-Fi is slow and usually only available in lobbies. The St. Mary Village complex has several different options ranging from value rooms to upscale accommodations. Other properties in St. Mary offer cabin accommodations.

INFORMATION

Located at the St. Mary entrance to Glacier National Park, the **St. Mary Visitor Center** (406/888-7800; www.nps.gov/glac; 8am-5pm daily late May-early Oct., open until 6pm July-mid-Aug.) provides information on the park but not on the town of St. Mary.

East Glacier, Montana

Outside the park boundary on the Blackfeet Reservation, East Glacier caters to tourists with multiple restaurants, motels, cabins, a lodge, and hostels. East Glacier sits about 7 mi (11 km) from the Two Medicine park entrance

FOOD

Most visitors hit East Glacier to dine out. The casual eateries include cafés, bakeries, and a Mexican food restaurant. During special days on the Blackfeet

Reservation, such as graduation and North American Indian Days, none of the restaurants, groceries, or bars serves alcohol, including East Glacier. The four-day celebration is usually scheduled beginning the second Thursday in July. Given the small size of the town, you'll be able to walk to most of the restaurants from your accommodation.

LODGING

On the west side of the railroad tracks, historic Glacier Park Lodge is on MT 49 along with a compact strip of motels—think very rustic, not a highway megastrip. On the east side of the tracks along U.S. 2, East Glacier has several motels within a few blocks of restaurants. All fill completely in midsummer, so reservations are strongly advised. There is also an RV park with hookups.

Great Falls

Straddling the mighty Missouri River, Great Falls, Montana, is an east-side gateway to Glacier with an airport. The drive from Great Falls to East Glacier is about 2.5 hours.

FOOD AND LODGING

Great Falls has hotels and motels ranging from low-end to moderately priced accommodations, but nothing upscale. Most national hotel chains are down-town. Check listings with **Great Falls Convention and Visitors Bureau** (800/735-8535; www.genuinemon-tana.com). Food options range from fast-food and chain restaurants to inde-pendent steakhouses.

INFORMATION

For information on Great Falls and accommodations, check with the **Great Falls Convention and Visitors Bureau** (800/735-8535; www.genu-inemontana.com).

NEAR BANFF NATIONAL PARK

The town of Banff, which is located within the national park, is a commercial center in its own right, with a range of restaurants, accommodations, and ser-vices available. Canmore and Calgary are two larger population centers near the park.

Canmore

Canmore lies in the Bow Valley, 17 mi (28 km) southeast of Banff and just a 20-minute drive to the park. With a range of excellent restaurants and a choice of comparatively well-priced accommodations, the town can make a good base for your trip to Banff.

FOOD

Canmore offers a range of food options. You can get inexpensive meals at the many cafés; other choices run the gamut, from the lively atmosphere of dining in the front yard of a converted residence to top-notch Alberta beef.

LODGING

Most of Canmore's newer lodgings are on Bow Valley Trail (Highway 1A). Although hotel pricing in Canmore may be high, it is definitely cheaper than nearby Banff, so much of the local busi-ness is overflow from the adjacent park. As with all resort towns in the Canadian Rockies, reservations should be made as far in advance as possible in summer.

More than 40 bed-and-breakfasts operate in Canmore. They are all small, family-run affairs with only one or two rooms (a local town bylaw limits the number of guest rooms in private homes to just two). For a full list of B&Bs, check the website of the Canmore/Bow Valley Bed and Breakfast Association (www.bbcanmore.com) for one that suits your needs.

INFORMATION

The best source of pre-trip information is **Tourism Canmore Kananaskis** (www.explorecanmore.ca). A **Travel Alberta Information Centre** (2801 Bow Valley Trail; 403/678-5277; 8am-8pm daily May-Sept., 9am-6pm daily Oct.), just off the Trans-Canada High-way on the west side of town, provides plenty of information about Canmore—and other destinations throughout the province.

Calgary

Located 90 minutes east of Banff and with an international airport, Calgary is the entry point for the vast majority of those arriving by air to visit these parks. A city of more than one million residents, Calgary is a major center for the oil and gas industry. Calgary is also the closest large city to Glacier National Park; it's a 4-hour drive to the east-side entrances of Many Glacier and St. Mary.

FOOD

Calgary has many reasonably priced restaurants, as well as a wide variety of choices. The area southwest of downtown, along 17th Avenue and 4th Street, has become a focal point for Calgary's restaurant scene, with cuisine to suit all tastes. Familiar North American fast-food restaurants line Macleod Trail south of the city center.

LODGING

Accommodations in Calgary vary from campgrounds, a hostel, and budget motels to a broad selection of high-quality hotels catering to top-end travelers and business conventions. Most downtown hotels offer reduced rates on weekends—Friday and Saturday nights might be half the regular room rate. During Stampede Week, a 10-day early July celebration of everything cowboy, prices are higher than the rest of the year, and accommodations are booked months in advance.

INFORMATION

Tourism Calgary (403/263-8510 or 800/661-1678; www.visitcalgary.com) operates a Visitor Information Centre at Calgary International Airport (403/735-1234; 6am-11pm daily) that greets visitors arriving by air across from Carousel 4. They also man a kiosk at street level of the Calgary Tower (101 9th Ave. SW) 9am-4pm daily mid-May-September.

NEAR JASPER NATIONAL PARK

Jasper is relatively remote, but it has all the services needed for visitors. The closest town outside the park boundary is Hinton to the east.

Hinton

On the south bank of the Athabasca River and surrounded in total wilderness, Hinton is just outside the Jasper National Park boundary 50 mi (80 km) east of the town of Jasper. Although mostly a forestry town, it is a gateway to interesting parks north and south of town, and the motels and restaurants have prices you'll appreciate after pricing out Jasper.

FOOD

The main strip through Hinton has all the usual fast-food and family restaurants, but you can also find local cafês and an array of Asian restaurants dotted through town. If Hinton is your last stop before Jasper, it's a good place to stock up on groceries at reasonable prices.

LODGING

Highway 16 through Hinton is lined with mid-priced motels, including many in the Wyndham and Choice chains, a Holiday Inn, and a few lower-priced independents. Hotel rates vary greatly with demand; in summer, expect to pay upward of C$200 per night, but the rest of the year, many rooms are under C$100.

INFORMATION

The **Hinton Visitor Information Centre** (309 Gregg Ave.; 780/865-7000; https://explorehinton.org; 9am-5pm daily) is on the main highway through town. Here you can purchase park and attraction passes for Jasper, take advantage of free coffee and Wi-Fi, and find out about opportunities to explore the surrounding region.

RECREATION
HIKING
Glacier National Park
Conditions on Glacier's trails vary significantly depending on the season, elevation, recent severe weather, and bear closures. Swinging and plank bridges across rivers and creeks are installed in late May-June. Some years, bridges are installed and then removed a few weeks later to wait for rivers swollen with runoff to subside. Most years, higher passes are snowbound until mid-July. Steep snowfields often inhibit hiking on the Highline Trail until mid-July or so. Ptarmigan Tunnel's doors are usually open mid-July-early October. Several backcountry campsites are snowbound until August. To find out about trail conditions before hiking, stop at ranger stations or visitor centers for updates, or consult trail status reports June-September on the park's website (www.nps.gov/glac). Bear or fire closures are also listed online.

Banff National Park
Banff National Park holds a great variety of trails. Here you can find anything from short interpretive trails with little elevation gain to strenuous slogs up to high alpine passes. Trailheads for some of the best hikes are accessible on foot from the town of Banff. Those farther north begin at higher elevations, from which access to the tree line is less arduous. Although lower elevation trails begin opening in May, the main hiking season July-September. The park's website (www.pc.gc.ca/banff) lists all trail conditions, including closures.

Jasper National Park
The trails in Jasper National Park are oriented more toward the experienced backpacker, offering plentiful routes for long backcountry trips. Locals often hit the trails around the town of Jasper as early as April, but the main hiking season is July-September. This is also the busiest time of year in the park, so plan on heading out early in the day to avoid crowds. For trail reports, check the park's website (www.pc.gc.ca/banff), which lists trail conditions and closures.

BACKPACKING
Glacier National Park
Find backpacking information, permit applications, advance reservations, trail status reports, and backcountry campsite availability online (www.nps.gov/glac). Pick up **permits** (adults $7 pp/night) for backpacking trips 24 hours in advance in person at the **Apgar Backcountry Permit Office** (406/888-7859 May-Oct., 406/888-7800 Nov.-Apr.), **St. Mary Visitor Center** (406/888-7800; late May-late Sept.), or **Many Glacier Ranger Station** (406/888-7800; late May-late Sept.). For advance reservations, apply online starting in mid-March (www.nps.gov/glac; $40). To speak with someone in person regarding conditions and routes, call the permit offices.

Each backcountry campground has 2-7 sites, with four people allowed per site. All backcountry campgrounds have pit toilets (some with great views), community cook sites, and separate tent sites. No food, garbage, toiletries, or cookware should be kept in the tent sites. There will be a bear pole, hanging bar, or bear-proof food storage boxes in or near every cooking site. Many backcountry campsites do not allow fires; carry a lightweight stove for cooking. Take low-odor foods to avoid attracting bears, and practice Leave No Trace principles religiously.

Banff and Jasper National Parks
Staying overnight in the backcountry of Banff or Jasper offers many rewards. Some effort is involved in preparing for a backcountry trip, such as gathering the necessary gear, but you'll be traveling through country inaccessible to the casual day hiker, well away from the crowds and far from any road. Banff and Jasper National Parks also have backcountry lodges. Another option

for backcountry accommodations is offered by the **Alpine Club of Canada** (403/678-3200; www.alpineclubofcanada.ca). The club maintains a series of huts, each generally a full-day hike from the nearest road, in these parks.

Gear

Bring backpacking gear (tent, sleeping bag, pad, clothing, rain gear, topographic maps, compass or GPS device, first-aid kit, insect repellent, sunscreen, fuel, cooking gear, and stove) plus a 25-ft (7.6-m) rope for hanging food, a small screen or strainer for sifting food particles out of gray water, a one-micron or smaller filter for purifying water (tablets and boiling can also do the job), and a small trowel for emergency human waste disposal when a pit toilet is unavailable.

BIKING

Glacier National Park is a tough place to cycle. There are no shoulders, roads are narrow and curvy, and drivers gawk at scenery instead of the road, all putting cyclists in precarious positions. Spring, when roads are closed to cars for plowing, is a good season for biking. All manner of bikes (roadies, mountain bikes, kiddie trailers, tagalongs, tot striders, and even tricycles) hit the roads on sunny spring days, especially on Going-to-the-Sun Road. Riding starts in mid-April and goes until the roads open to cars, which can be May-mid-July. You can ride as far as plowing operations and avalanche conditions permit.

Banff and Jasper National Parks are perfect for both road biking and mountain biking. On-road cyclists will appreciate the wide shoulders on all main highways. Mountain biking is allowed on designated trails throughout the national parks. Park information centers hand out brochures detailing these trails and giving them ratings.

PADDLING AND RAFTING

Glacier National Park has instituted strict boating and paddling guidelines in order to protect its pristine waters from aquatic invasive species. The lakes are only open in summer and only available by permit to boaters and paddlers who have passed an inspection. Permitting requirements make bringing a powerboat from home impractical for most short-term visitors. River rafting is a big activity outside the park in West Glacier, which is near two rivers that run along the park boundaries.

In Banff and Jasper, canoeing and stand-up paddleboarding are great ways to explore the waterways of the mountains that are otherwise inaccessible—such as Vermilion Lakes in Banff National Park, where a great variety of birds can be appreciated from water level. In Jasper, river rafting offers a chance to get out on the water. To help stop the spread of aquatic invasive species, watercraft inspection stations are set up along major highways leading out of the Canadian Rockies.

WINTER SPORTS

In Glacier National Park, some roads and trails in the park make for nice cross-country skiing and snowshoeing routes. For route descriptions, pick up *Skiing and Snowshoeing* in the visitor centers or online (www.nps.gov/glac). Skiers and snowshoers should be well equipped and versed in winter travel safety before venturing out.

Although cross-country skiing and snowshoeing can be done in Banff National Park, it's well known as a world-class downhill skiing destination, with three winter resorts, including Lake Louise, the second largest in all of Canada. Jasper has one downhill skiing resort, as well as 185 mi (300 km) of cross-country skiing trails. Most resorts open in early December and close in May.

DARK SKIES

GLACIER NATIONAL PARK

Glacier is certified as an International Dark Sky Park. That means it has minimal light pollution, offering outstanding nighttime stargazing. Rangers offer free astronomy programs at Apgar and St. Mary Visitor Centers, and Logan Pass star parties (tickets required) happen 3-4 times per summer. To see the Milky Way, opt for nights that have a quarter moon or less. In spring and fall, you can sometimes catch the northern lights shimmering in the sky.

the Milky Way, visible at Logan Pass

Skywatching Spots

- Logan Pass

- Two Medicine Campground

- St. Mary Observatory

BANFF NATIONAL PARK

Once you leave the bright lights of the town of Banff behind, the wonders of the night sky can be appreciated from many places.

Skywatching Spots

- Vermilion Lakes

- Lake Minnewanka

- Bow Lake

JASPER NATIONAL PARK

Jasper is officially a Dark Sky Park (https://jasperdarksky.travel), which is celebrated with a festival in mid-October.

Skywatching Spots

- Old Fort Point

- Maligne Lake

- Columbia Icefield

INTERPRETIVE PROGRAMS

GLACIER NATIONAL PARK

Ranger programs in Glacier National Park include guided walks, astronomy programs, and even amphitheater presentations. Find program schedules at park visitor centers.

Evening Programs

Rangers also lead free 45-minute park naturalist evening programs on wildlife, fires, and natural phenomena at the following locations in summer.

- Lake McDonald Lodge
- Fish Creek Campground Amphitheater
- Apgar Campground Amphitheater
- Rising Sun Amphitheater
- Many Glacier Hotel
- Many Glacier Campground Amphitheater
- St. Mary Campground Amphitheater
- St. Mary Visitor Center
- Two Medicine Campground Amphitheater

Native America Speaks

For more than three decades, Glacier's naturalist programs have included the acclaimed Native America Speaks program in summer. Look for shows in park lodges, St. Mary Visitor Center, and at campground amphitheaters, including Chewing Blackbones outside Babb. Free 45-minute evening campground amphitheater shows feature members of the Blackfeet, Salish, and Kootenai people who use storytelling, humor, and music to share their culture and heritage. Check the park newspaper for the current schedules and location of presentations.

Two specialty programs occur throughout the summer. Jack Gladstone, a Grammy-nominated Blackfeet musician, presents Triple Divide: Heritage and Legacy (www.jackgladstone.com), which blends storytelling and music into a one-hour multimedia walk through Glacier's history from the Blackfeet perspective. At the St. Mary Visitor Center's auditorium, the Two Medicine Lake Singers and Dancers draw standing-room-only crowds for demonstrating Blackfeet dances in full traditional regalia. Tickets (adults $5, kids 12 and under free) go on sale the Monday before a performance for the 90-minute show, and they sell out quickly.

Kid-Friendly Programs

Kids can earn a Junior Ranger badge by completing self-guided activities in the *Junior Ranger Activity Guide,* available at all visitor centers. Most activities target ages 6-12 and coincide with a trip over Going-to-the-Sun Road. When kids return the completed newspaper to a visitor center, they are sworn in as Junior Rangers and receive Glacier National Park badges. Waterton has a comparable program with the Parks Canada Xplorers Program.

BANFF AND JASPER NATIONAL PARKS

Parks Canada offers a number of different interpretive programs, including guided walks, campground presentations, and wildlife talks. Program schedules are posted at visitor centers and campgrounds.

CELL SERVICE AND INTERNET

Glacier has very limited cell service reception and public Wi-Fi. Plan to download apps, maps, podcasts, and PDFs you will need for your travels before you arrive. Limited public Wi-Fi is available at two visitor centers and for guests in lodge lobbies. Cell and Internet service is available in towns surrounding Glacier, but is limited in St. Mary and East Glacier.

Cell service and Internet access is available in and around the towns of Banff and Jasper, as well as in the village of Lake Louise. Beyond these population centers, there is no access, including along the entire length of the Icefields Parkway.

ACCESSIBILITY

The website www.wheelchairtraveling.com offers a wide range of tips on accessible travel, as well as first-hand stories of travel. The Society for Accessible Travel and Hospitality (212/447-7284; www.sath.org) supplies information on tour operators, vehicle rentals, specific destinations, and companion services. For frequent travelers, the membership fee ($49 per year) is well worth it. *Emerging Horizons* (www.emerginghorizons.com) is an online magazine dedicated to travelers with special needs.

GLACIER NATIONAL PARK

Information about Glacier's options for visitors with special needs, including mobility, hearing, and vision disabilities, is available online (www.nps.gov/glac/planyourvisit/accessibility.htm). The park's *Accessible Facilities and Services* brochure, which contains the same information, is available at visitor centers. The **Disabled Traveler's Companion** (www.tdtcompanion.com) also gives comprehensive information for traveling in Glacier.

Blind or permanently disabled U.S. citizens or permanent residents can get a free lifetime National Parks and Federal Recreational Lands Access Pass for access to all national parks and other federal sites. The pass admits the pass holder plus three other adults in the same vehicle; children under age 16 are free. Pass holders also get 50 percent discounts on federally run tours and campgrounds. Get these passes in person at entrance stations with proof of medical disability or eligibility for receiving federal benefits.

Five campgrounds in Glacier reserve a couple of sites each for wheelchair needs: Apgar, Fish Creek, Rising Sun, Sprague Creek, and Two Medicine. Picnic areas at Apgar, Rising Sun, and Sun Point also have wheelchair access, as do all lodges within the park boundaries, although they have a limited number of guest rooms that conform to Americans with Disabilities Act accessibility guidelines. Most parking lots offer designated parking. Shuttles on the Sun Road have wheelchair ramps or lifts for accessibility.

While pet dogs are not permitted on Glacier's backcountry trails, service dogs are allowed. But due to bears, they are discouraged. With service dogs, be safe by sticking to well-traveled trails during midday.

BANFF AND JASPER NATIONAL PARKS

The best source for pre-trip planning information for visitors with disabilities is the Banff Lake Louise Tourism website (www.bannflakelouise.com/accessibility). Throughout both parks, some trails are paved and wheelchair accessible, shuttles have wheelchair ramps, and all but the most remote accommodations are accessible. Both commercial hot springs have water-accessible wheelchairs.

TRAVELING WITH PETS

If traveling with your pet to all three parks, which requires crossing the U.S.-Canada border, you will need to have a certificate of rabies vaccination dated within 30 days prior to crossing the border.

GLACIER NATIONAL PARK

Pets are allowed in Glacier National Park, but only in limited areas: campgrounds, parking lots, and roadsides. They are not allowed on trails, beaches, off-trail in the backcountry, or at any park lodges or motor inns. Protection of fragile vegetation and prevention of conflicts with wildlife are two main reasons pets are not allowed on Glacier National Park trails. For pooch-walking purposes, you can head to the paved Apgar Bike Trail (2 mi/3.2 km), which allows pedestrians as well as pets (on leashes). Contrary to Glacier, Waterton permits dogs on leashes on its trails.

When outside a vehicle or in a campground, pets must be on a leash or caged. Be kind enough to avoid leaving them unattended in a car anywhere. Be considerate of wildlife and other visitors by keeping your pet under control and disposing of waste in garbage cans.

BANFF AND JASPER NATIONAL PARKS

Pets are permitted in both national parks but must be on leash and under control at all times (the exception is off-leash parks in the towns of Banff and Jasper). Some hotels are pet-friendly, and all campgrounds allow pets. Although dogs are allowed on hiking trails, there may be restrictions if wildlife is present.

HEALTH AND SAFETY

For traveling in the United States, you should have health insurance, as the health care needs are up to individuals to cover financially. Be sure your health insurance plan will cover doctors, emergency clinics, and hospitals in the United States.

It's a good idea to have health insurance or some form of coverage before heading to Canada; check that your plan covers foreign services. Some hospitals impose a surcharge for nonresidents.

EMERGENCY SERVICES

Glacier National Park

For emergencies inside the park, call 406/888-7800. For emergencies outside the park, call 911. All hospitals are located outside the park.

- **Logan Medical Center Medical Center:** 310 Sunny View Ln., Kalispell; 406/752-5111; 35 minutes from West Glacier

- **North Valley Hospital:** 1600 Hospital Way, Whitefish; 406/863-3500; 35 minutes from West Glacier

- **Blackfeet Community Hospital:** 760 Blackweasel Rd., Browning; 406/338-6100; 1 hour from St. Mary

Banff and Jasper National Parks

Call 911 for all emergencies within the two parks. There are hospitals inside the parks, each in their respective towns.

- **Mineral Springs Hospital:** 301 Lynx St., Banff; 403/762-2222

- **Seton-Jasper Healthcare Centre:** 518 Robson St., Jasper; 780/852-3344

WATER HAZARDS

Be extremely cautious around lakes, fast-moving streams, and waterfalls, where slick moss and algae cover the rocks.

GIARDIA

Lakes and streams can carry parasites like *Giardia lamblia*. If ingested, it causes cramping, nausea, and severe diarrhea for up to six weeks. Avoid giardia by boiling water (for one minute, plus one minute for each 1,000 ft/305 m of elevation above sea level) or using a one-micron filter. Bleach also works (add two drops per quart and wait 30 minutes). Tap water in campgrounds, hotels, and picnic areas has been treated.

DEHYDRATION

Many first-time hikers to these parks are surprised to find they drink more water than at home. Wind, altitude, and lower humidity can add up to a fast case of dehydration. It manifests first as a headache. While hiking, drink lots of water, even more than you normally would. With children, monitor their fluid intake.

ALTITUDE

Some visitors from lower elevations feel the effects of altitude at high elevations like Logan Pass. Watch for lightheadedness, headaches, or shortness of breath. To acclimatize, slow down the pace of hiking and drink lots of fluids. If symptoms spike, descend in elevation as soon as possible. Altitude also increases UV radiation exposure: To prevent sunburn, use a strong sunscreen and wear sunglasses and a hat.

ICE AND SNOW

While glacial ice often looks solid to step on, it harbors unseen caverns beneath. Buried crevasses (large vertical cracks) are difficult to see, and snow bridges can collapse as a person crosses. Be safe by staying off the ice; even tiny ice fields have caused fatalities. Steep-angled snowfields also pose a danger from falling. Use an ice ax and caution, or stay off them.

HYPOTHERMIA

Insidious and subtle, exhausted and physically unprepared hikers are at risk for hypothermia. The body's inner core loses heat, reducing mental and physical functions. Watch for uncontrolled shivering, incoherence, poor judgment, fumbling, mumbling, and slurred speech. Avoid becoming hypothermic by staying dry. Don rain gear and warm moisture-wicking layers, rather than cottons that won't dry and fail to retain heat. Get hypothermic hikers into dry clothing and shelter. Give warm nonalcoholic and noncaffeinated liquids. If the victim cannot regain body heat, get into a sleeping bag with the victim, both stripped for skin-to-skin contact.

HANTAVIRUS

Hantavirus infection, with flu-like symptoms, is contracted by inhaling dust from deer mice droppings. Avoid burrows and woodpiles thick with rodents. Store all food in rodent-proof containers. If you find rodent dust in your gear, disinfect it with water and bleach (1.5 cups bleach to 1 gallon water). If you contract the virus, get immediate medical attention.

MOSQUITOES AND TICKS

Bugs can carry diseases such as West Nile virus and Rocky Mountain spotted fever. Protect yourself by wearing long sleeves and pants as well as using insect repellent in spring-summer, when mosquitoes and ticks are common. If you are bitten by a tick, remove it, disinfect the bite, and see a doctor if lesions or a rash appears.

RESOURCES
GLACIER
Glacier National Park
www.nps.gov/glac
The official website for Glacier National Park. It provides information on park conditions, roads, campsites, trails, history, and more. Six webcams are updated every few minutes. In addition to trip planning information, the site includes downloadable maps, publications, and backcountry permit information as well as a Going-to-the-Sun Road status report, updated daily.

Glacier National Park Conservancy
https://glacier.org
The best resource for books, maps, posters, and cards on Glacier Park. Proceeds from book sales are donated to the park to support education, preservation, and research.

The Glacier Institute
www.glacierinstitute.org
An educational nonprofit park partner, the Glacier Institute presents programs for kids and adults in field settings

CORONAVIRUS IN GLACIER, BANFF & JASPER

At the time of writing in February 2021, travel was significantly impacted by the effects of the coronavirus, but the situation is constantly evolving. **Discretionary travel between the United States and Canada was restricted.** Visitors were required to wear face masks in public indoor spaces, as well as outdoors where mandated. Now more than ever, Moon encourages its readers to be courteous and ethical in their travel. We ask travelers to be respectful to residents and mindful of the evolving situation in their chosen destination when planning their trip.

BEFORE YOU GO

- Check local websites for local **restrictions** and the overall **health status** of the destination.

- If you are planning to cross the U.S.-Canada border, check **entry and re-entry requirements** for both countries.

- If you plan to fly, check with your airline and the destination's health authority for updated **travel requirements.**

- Check the website of any venues, activities, and tours you wish to patronize to confirm that they're open, if their hours have been adjusted, and to learn about any specific visitation requirements, such as **mandatory reservations** or **limited occupancy.**

- Pack **hand sanitizer,** a **thermometer,** and plenty of **face masks.** Consider packing **snacks,** a **refillable water bottle,** and even a **cooler** to limit the number of businesses you need to visit.

- **Assess the risk** of entering crowded spaces, joining tours, and taking public transit.

- Expect **general disruptions.** Visitors should be aware that park services may be limited. **Entrances** may be closed, **restaurants** may be offering takeout-only options or other modified services, and **transportation** and **tour services** may be suspended altogether.

- In Glacier, sections of **Going-to-the-Sun Road, campgrounds,** and **some trails** may be closed, and **activities** like boating and paddling may be restricted to certain areas. Additionally, the **Blackfeet Nation reservation** bordering Glacier National Park and adjacent park entrances may be closed to non-tribal members and nonresidents. Masks are required inside all U.S. National Park buildings and outside on trails where social distancing can't be maintained.

RESOURCES

- **U.S. Border Crossing:** https://travel.state.gov/content/travel/en/traveladvisories/ea/covid-19-information.html

- **Canada Border Crossing:** www.cbsa-asfc.gc.ca/services/covid

- **Glacier National Park Status Update** (www.nps.gov/glac/planyourvisit/statusupdate.htm): This page lists the current status for Glacier's entrances, roads, activities, lodges, restaurants, and campgrounds.

- **Montana COVID-19 status:** The Covid-19 Montana Response (https://montana.maps.arcgis.com/home/index.html) has a map where you can find out the current number of vaccinations and COVID cases, hospitalizations, and deaths for the state and for the counties of Flathead and Glacier, which surround Glacier National Park.

- **Banff National Park** (https://banff.ca/COVID): Information on this page includes current COVID numbers, up-to-date closures, and links to visitor resources.

- **Jasper National Park** (www.jasper-alberta.com/covid): This page details everything COVID-related for the town of Jasper.

- **Nearby areas:** Find information about current regulations for the **Blackfeet Nation** (https://blackfeetnation.com/covid19), **Flathead County** (https://flatheadhealth.org/novel-coronavirus-covid-19), **Whitefish** (www.whitefishcovidcares.com), **Hinton** (www.hinton.ca/covid), and elsewhere in **Alberta** (www.alberta.ca/covid)

taught by expert instructors. Field classes take place in Glacier as well as surrounding ecosystems.

Glacier National Park Volunteer Associates
https://gnpva.org
This nonprofit assists with historic preservation, education, and trail work. The organization looks for volunteers to help on projects ranging from a few days to summer-long.

National Park Service Reservation Center
www.recreation.gov
Fish Creek, Many Glacier, and St. Mary Campgrounds take reservations using this service.

Xanterra
www.glaciernationalparklodges.com
This park concessionaire operates Many Glacier Hotel, Lake McDonald Lodge, Rising Sun Motor Inn, Swiftcurrent Motor Inn, and Apgar Village Inn, as well as tours and shuttles.

Pursuit Glacier Park Collection
www.glacierparkcollection.com
Pursuit operates Apgar Village Lodge and Motel Lake McDonald, as well as a shuttle on the east side of the park.

BANFF AND JASPER
Alberta Parks and BC Parks
https://albertaparks.ca
https://bcparks.ca
These departments oversee management of the provincial parks in Alberta and British Columbia. The websites detail facilities, fees, and seasonal openings of the parks.

Parks Canada
www.pc.gc.ca
Official website of the agency that manages Canada's national parks and national historic sites. The website has information on each park and historic site, including fees, camping, and wildlife.

Parks Canada Campground Reservation Service
www.pccamping.ca
Online reservation service for national park campgrounds.

Citizenship and Immigration Canada
www.cic.gc.ca
Check this government website for anything related to entry into Canada.

Fairmont Hotels and Resorts
www.fairmont.com
Lodging chain that owns famous mountain resorts such as the Banff Springs, Chateau Lake Louise, and Jasper Park Lodge.

Pursuit
www.banffjaspercollection.com
Banff-based operator offering attractions, tours, airport shuttles, and accommodations in both parks.

INDEX

LIST OF MAPS

PHOTO CREDITS

Title page photo © Andrew Hempstead; page 4 © Becky Lomax (top, middle, bottom); page 5 © Becky Lomax (top, middle, bottom); pages 6-7 © Becky Lomax; pages 8-9 © Carla Chidiac | Dreamstime.com; page 10 © NPS / Tim Rains; page 11 © Becky Lomax (top, bottom), page 12 © Becky Lomax (top), NPS / Tim Rains (bottom); page 13 © Becky Lomax; page 14 © Andrew Hempstead; page 15 © Andrew Hempstead; page 16 © Andrew Hempstead; page 17 © Fallsview | Dreamstime.com; pages 18-19 © Andrew Hempstead; pages 20-21 © Helena Bilkina | Dreamstime.com; page 22 © Kelly Vandellen | Dreamstime.com; page 23 © Py2000 | Dreamstime.com; page 24 © Andrew Hempstead; page 25 © Andrew Hempstead; page 26 © Becky Lomax; page 28 © Becky Lomax (top), Evatschoppe | Dreamstime.com (bottom); page 31 © Andrew Hempstead; pages 32-33 © Andrew Hempstead; page 34 © Becky Lomax; page 35 © Andrew Hempstead; pages 37-36 © Andrew Hempstead; page 38 © Vorasate Ariyarattnahirun | Dreamstime.com; page 39 © Andrew Hempstead (top, bottom); page 41 © Andrew Hempstead; page 43 © Bornin54 | Dreamstime.com; page 44 © Andrew Hempstead; page 47 © Andrew Hempstead; pages 48-49 © Becky Lomax; page 52 © Becky Lomax; page 53 © NPS / Jacob W. Frank (top), NPS / Tim Rains (middle), Becky Lomax (bottom), page 55 © Becky Lomax (bottom left and right), page 57 © Becky Lomax (top left and right), NPS / Jacob W. Frank (bottom); page 58 © Becky Lomax (bottom left and right); page 59 © NPS / David Restivo (bottom left), Becky Lomax (bottom right); page 61 © Becky Lomax (top), NPS / Tim Rains (middle), Becky Lomax (bottom); page 64 © Becky Lomax (bottom left and right); page 67 © Becky Lomax; page 69 © Becky Lomax (top, middle), NPS / Tim Rains (bottom), page 70 © Becky Lomax; page 74 © Tomas Nevesely | Dreamstime.com; page 76 © NPS / Glacier National Park; page 78 © Becky Lomax; page 80 © NPS / Tim Rains (top, middle), Becky Lomax (bottom), pages 82-82 © Becky Lomax; page 85 © Becky Lomax; page 87 © Becky Lomax (bottom left and right); page 88 © Becky Lomax; page 91 © Becky Lomax; page 92 © Becky Lomax; page 93 © Becky Lomax; page 98 © Becky Lomax; page 102 © Becky Lomax; page 106 © NPS; page 107 © NPS; pages 108-109 © Andrew Hempstead; page 111 © Andrew Hempstead (top and bottom), Luckyphotographer | Dreamstime.com (middle); page 113 © Andrew Hempstead (bottom left and right); page 115 © Andrew Hempstead (top left, right and bottom); page 116 © Andrew Hempstead (left), Helena Bilkova | Dreamstime.com (right); page 117 © Andrew Hempstead; page 119 © Andrew Hempstead; page 122 © Andrew Hempstead; page 123 © Andrew Hempstead; page 129 © Andrew Hempstead; pages 130-131 © Andrew Hempstead; page 134 © Andrew Hempstead; page 138 © Andrew Hempstead; page 141 © Andrew Hempstead; page 144 © Andrew Hempstead; page 145 © Andrew Hempstead; page 147 © Andrew Hempstead; page 148 © Andrew Hempstead; page 150 © Andrew Hempstead; page 151 © Sburel | Dreamstime.com; page 153 © Andrew Hempstead; page 155 © Andrew Hempstead; page 162 © Andrew Hempstead; page 168 © Andrew Hempstead; page 169 © Andrew Hempstead; pages 171-172 © Andrew Hempstead; page 175 © Riekefoto | Dreamstime.com (top), Andrew Hempstead (middle, bottom); page © 173 Andrew Hempstead (left), Lyndonwiens | Dreamstime.com (right); page 179 © Andrew Hempstead; page 180 © Andrew Hempstead; page 181 © Andrew Hempstead; page 183 © Andrew Hempstead; page 184 © Andrew Hempstead; page 186 © Jacek Sopotnicki | Dreamstime.com; page 191 © Andrew Hempstead;

Get inspired for your next adventure

Follow **@moonguides** on Instagram or subscribe to our newsletter at **moon.com**

#TravelWithMoon

MAP SYMBOLS

═══════ Highway	○ City/Town	🅿 Parking Area	🏕 Small Park
═══════ Primary Road	◉ State Capital	🅣 Trailhead	▲ Mountain Peak
═══════ Secondary Road	⊛ National Capital	🅑 Bike Trailhead	✦ Unique Natural Feature
······· Unpaved Road	★ Top 3 Sight	🅐 Camping	
---------- Trail	🚶 Top Hike	🅟 Picnic Area	✦ Unique Hydro Feature
━━━━━━ Paved Trail	★ Highlight/Sight	Ⓜ Mass Transit	🗻 Waterfall
·········· Pedestrian Walkway	• Accommodation	✈ Airport	🎿 Ski Area
············ Ferry	▼ Restaurant/Bar	✗ Airfield	◯ Glacier
------- Railroad	■ Other Site	🛆 Place of Worship	

CONVERSION TABLES

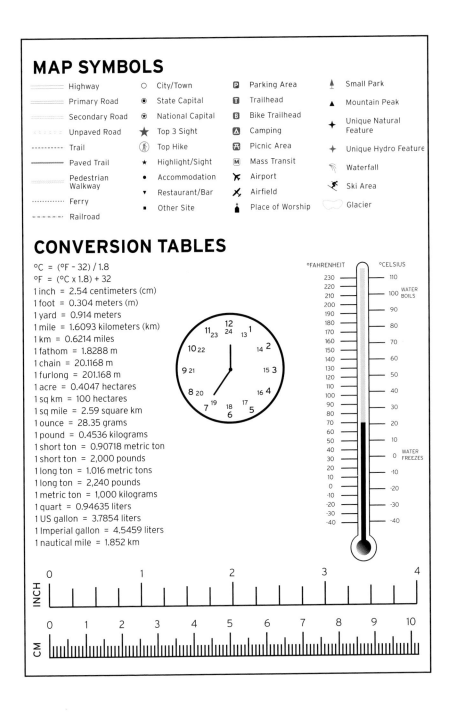

°C = (°F - 32) / 1.8
°F = (°C x 1.8) + 32
1 inch = 2.54 centimeters (cm)
1 foot = 0.304 meters (m)
1 yard = 0.914 meters
1 mile = 1.6093 kilometers (km)
1 km = 0.6214 miles
1 fathom = 1.8288 m
1 chain = 20.1168 m
1 furlong = 201.168 m
1 acre = 0.4047 hectares
1 sq km = 100 hectares
1 sq mile = 2.59 square km
1 ounce = 28.35 grams
1 pound = 0.4536 kilograms
1 short ton = 0.90718 metric ton
1 short ton = 2,000 pounds
1 long ton = 1.016 metric tons
1 long ton = 2,240 pounds
1 metric ton = 1,000 kilograms
1 quart = 0.94635 liters
1 US gallon = 3.7854 liters
1 Imperial gallon = 4.5459 liters
1 nautical mile = 1.852 km

°FAHRENHEIT · °CELSIUS

230 / 110
220
210 / 100 WATER BOILS
200
190 / 90
180 / 80
170
160 / 70
150
140 / 60
130
120 / 50
110
100 / 40
90 / 30
80
70 / 20
60
50 / 10
40
30 / 0 WATER FREEZES
20 / -10
10
0 / -20
-10
-20 / -30
-30
-40 / -40

MOON BEST OF GLACIER, BANFF & JASPER

Avalon Travel
Hachette Book Group
1700 Fourth Street
Berkeley, CA 94710, USA
www.moon.com

Editor: Grace Fujimoto
Managing Editor: Hannah Brezack
Copy Editor: Kathryn Roque
Production and Graphics Coordinator:
  Suzanne Albertson
Cover Design: Marcie Lawrence
Interior Design: Tabitha Lahr
Moon Logo: Tim McGrath
Map Editor: Albert Angulo
Cartographers: Karin Dahl and
  John Culp

ISBN-13: 978-1-64049-545-6

Printing History
1st Edition — July 2021
5 4 3 2 1

Front cover photo: © YinYang/Getty Images. Sunrise at Many Glacier in the Glacier National Park

Back cover photo credits: HighlineTrail © Becky Lomax (top); Moraine Lake © Andrew Hempstead (middle); Icefields Parkway © Andrew Hempstead (bottom)

Printed in China by RR Donnelley